Y0-CDA-527

IGNATIUS LOYOLA

IGNATIUS LOYOLA

THE FOUNDER OF THE JESUITS

BY

PAUL VAN DYKE

PYNE PROFESSOR IN HISTORY AT PRINCETON UNIVERSITY

KENNIKAT PRESS, INC./PORT WASHINGTON, N. Y.

CONTENTS

v

IGNATIUS LOYOLA

CHAPTER I

THE TASK

This chapter discusses three topics: first, the greatness of Ignatius Loyola; second, the difficulty of seeing him in the light of his own ideals; third, the materials for making a true picture of him.

The sixteenth century was an age of that "passion and strong desire" which young German writers toward the end of the eighteenth century wished to describe in poetry, romance and the drama. Their leader, the youthful Goethe, chose well when he took as the hero of his first play a robber baron of the sixteenth century. For during that century ideals, impulses, habits of thought, hopes, fears which their ancestors had ignored or suppressed became dominant in the lives of many people of western Europe. The whole mediæval conception of the universe faded like some grandiose dream as humanity awakened. Just as the prows of Columbus broke the bounds of the ocean which the Egyptians, Greeks, and Romans had not dared to pass; just as the telescope of Galileo finally proved in the teeth of theological authority that Joshua could not have made the sun stand still, so in the spiritual sphere large numbers of men broke through the scholastic tradition, not so much by a reasoned process, as because it restricted new beliefs, feelings and habits. The Renascence passed the Alps and during the sixteenth century flooded western Europe from Gibraltar to the shores of the Baltic.

Its influence appeared in the world of action. Two dynasties, each supported by the nascent pride of a great nation, fought for half a century over the spoils of weaker peoples and the hegemony of a new political world. Man lost interest in the ideals of chivalry and discussed the maxims of Machiavelli. One of the bitterest controversies in human history bred fear and hate. Roman Catholic and Lutheran, Anglican, Calvinist and Anabaptist solemnly put each other to death in fulfillment of what they thought to be their duty to God and man.

Out of strife and labour, out of growth and decay, out of effort to find new truths and struggle to defend old institutions, a great change in the attitude of humanity began to be accomplished. For many people the vision of man's place in the universe as Dante saw it, was changed into the vision of man's life as Shakespeare saw it.

The century which beheld these great and sometimes convulsive changes was a century of great personalities. New thoughts and feelings need mouthpieces, the defense of ancient institutions or of new ideals calls for captains who are braver and stronger and wiser than their followers.

Of all the results of this change and turmoil of that troubled century none is so outstanding as the breaking up of the Church. In 1500 Europe had left from the days when all the lands and peoples south of the Rhine and the Danube were united in the Roman Empire, only one universal institution; the Holy Roman Church Catholic and Apostolic. Into her membership all men were born, to her authority all men were subject. She spoke and prayed in all lands in the old universal language. In her the idea of the unity of Christendom was incorporate. The sixteenth century drew a line, so far as religion was concerned, across Europe from east to west. South of that line, according to the thought and phraseology of any previous generation, was orthodoxy and unity; north of it was heresy and schism. England, Scotland, the northern provinces of the Netherlands, most of the cantons of Switzerland, most of the secular states of the German

Empire, Sweden, Norway and Denmark, established their own national churches with their own creeds, their own prayers in their own tongue, their own system of government which owed no allegiance to any authority outside of their own borders, and tolerated no worship different from their own formularies. In France, Bohemia, Poland and Transylvania, although the bulk of the population remained faithful to the orthodox church, the fear of civil war brought about the toleration of one of the types of dissenting churches.

It was in connection with the change in the Universal Church that the power of the institution Ignatius Loyola founded became most evident. He did not plainly foresee from the beginning this mightiest of the labours of the Company of Jesus. But, soon after his death, his followers were quite certain that it was the will of God that they should be the leaders in saving the Church from what one of their modern writers calls "a whirlwind of passions let loose by hell against the spouse of Christ . . . the most fruitful heresy ever launched by the devil upon the earth." [1] This did become, therefore, the most conspicuous of four tasks undertaken with marked success by that Company of Jesus in which the spirit of Ignatius Loyola became incarnate.

In the eyes of those who believe that the changes of the sixteenth century opened to men's feet the paths of progress, Ignatius is therefore labelled as a reactionary and a conservative. Now a prevailing tendency of the modern world—one might almost say the prevalent temperament of the modern world—inclines it towards the assumption that no conservative can be a great personality, because conservatism is always the result of a weak intellect or a timorous character. The fundamental difficulty in showing to many people how highly developed and how rarely combined were the qualities of character which made

[1] Astrain L. LIII.

Ignatius Loyola a power among men, lies therefore just in this fact that he was an extreme conservative; in his main attitude a reactionary.

Certain other factors conditioning the way in which his character expressed itself—factors purely circumstantial, tend to obscure his greatness for many of us. The American of the twentieth century is a very different person from the Spaniard of the sixteenth, and Ignatius was born in those Basque provinces whose inhabitants still show the remnants of that trait of independent conservatism, shedding innovations as a duck sheds water, which became the most outstanding trait of the virile Spanish people, who in the sixteenth century threatened to dominate Europe and America and made in the realm of art and literature such magnificent contributions to the common treasure of humanity. The ideal of Ignatius was an international ideal. He thought and planned always in terms of Christendom, never in terms of Spain. He wished to look at humanity as God looks at it and to take toward the organized political world the attitude implied in the office of the visible Vicar of the Eternal Christ.

But, in spite of his extraordinary success in this effort, Ignatius remained in all the subconscious motives and forces of his personality, a Spaniard. Though he spent many laborious years in university study, Spanish and not Latin remained his natural medium of expression. He was very proud of the fact that his order could unite men of hostile nations in affectionate relations, but he found his most efficient lieutenants among Spaniards. So that while he lived, and for seventeen years after his death, Spanish influence was as dominant in the Company of Jesus as Italian influence has been for five hundred years dominant in the Papacy.

Then Ignatius was not only a Spaniard but in one respect a typical Spaniard of the sixteenth century. If any man ever made his faith his own, Ignatius did. It was strengthened by long converse with God in the silence of his soul, deepened by terrible self-denial, broadened by deeds of mercy. But, though his faith was his own, the extreme contented orthodoxy of Ignatius and his self-effacing obedience to the Church had its roots in his racial inheritance and the environment of his youth. A modern Spanish Jesuit, discussing the Spanish nation at the birth of Loyola, writes: "In the midst of such lamentable moral relaxations . . . whatever may be the reason . . . it is certain that, in the mind and heart of the Spanish people at that time, the faith of Jesus Christ reigned with a power which no passion, no sophism, no misery, no interest could dispute. How different appears the attitude of the Spanish people and the attitude of the German people in the presence of the Protestant heresy. Luther and some apostate priests preached rebellion against the Church and entire kingdoms and provinces gathered round the heresiarch. A few people preached in Valladolid the same errors and two hundred thousand Spaniards rushed to see those preachers burned and from two hundred thousand hearts burst a cry of anathema and execration against those who had tried to stain the purity of their faith."[2]

In noble Spanish families, during the youth of Ignatius, there was a tendency to regard heresy in any member as a stain on the honour of the family; a disgrace to be resented, like cowardice in a son or unchastity in a daughter of the house. That typical Spaniard, Philip II, said that if a son of his were condemned for heresy, he would carry a fagot himself to place at the stake.[3] He would not have said that, if his son were condemned for murder, he would sharpen the axe for the executioner to cut off his head.

A single incident preserves for us like a fly in amber this passionate horror of heresy. It is the celebrated

[2] Astrain—LXXXVI.   [3] Camb. Modern Hist. 409. The Reformation.

story (which was told all over Europe) of Juan Diaz.
Young Diaz, son of a well-to-do Spanish family, studied
for thirteen years in the University of Paris, specializing
in theology and Hebrew. Just before the middle of the
century he became a Protestant and went to Germany.
His older brother Alfonso, a lawyer occupying an important position in the courts at Rome, went to Germany as
soon as he heard of his brother's heresy and pleaded with
him to return to the faith of his fathers. Juan refused,
and finally the brother gave him a small present of money
and said a peaceful goodbye. But the disgrace to the
family weighed on Alfonso's mind. Early one morning
he came quietly back, with a trusted servant, to the small
town where Juan was seeing a book through the press.
Watching the door, he sent the servant in with a note.
As the half dressed Juan was reading it, the servant carried out his master's orders by killing him from behind
with a hatchet he had concealed beneath his clothes. The
murderous pair got to horse and rode as far as Innsbruck
before they were arrested. But the Pope claimed them at
Rome because they were both in minor clerical orders
and therefore must be tried by clerical courts. Neither
received any punishment and the historian Sepulveda said
that every Spaniard at the Court of the Emperor justified the deed as the necessary vindication by a Spanish
gentleman of the honour of his family.[4]

The intensity and the quality of an attachment to
orthodoxy which could produce the words of King Philip
and the deed of Alfonso Diaz, are strange to our land and
time—as strange to Roman Catholics as to Protestants.

Aside from any intensity which belonged to his age and
his people, the mere fact that Ignatius Loyola was a highly
orthodox Roman Catholic, will in itself, make it hard for
some readers to understand him. For many Protestants,
even with the best will in the world, find it hard to ap-

[4] Ranke IV, p. 287-279.

prehend certain types of Roman Catholic piety. When they read the lives of the saints, a sense of being in a strange atmosphere prevents them from feeling their power and beauty. This element of something unconnected with familiar motives and habits, must exist for them in any true life of Ignatius Loyola and only a strong effort of the sympathetic imagination can enable them to see the man as he was in the light of his own ideals and the power of his own faith.

Another bar to the understanding of Loyola for many readers is the fact that he was a monk. In 1500 the monk was a figure so common and conspicuous as to be inescapable and his picturesque presence constantly recalled to men's minds the ideals on which his life was based. Most Americans rarely see a monk and if called on to explain the fundamental principles and history of monasticism, would either confess they could not, or give an account distorted by ignorance or prejudice of an institution which in past centuries certainly did great service to mankind.

Perhaps the greatest barrier to the understanding of Loyola is something that has no direct relation to his life at all. In 1773 the Company of Jesus was entirely suppressed by a papal bull and the remnants of the once powerful society found refuge under the heretic governments of Russia and Prussia until 1814, when they were again restored to legal standing in the Church. The embittered discussions which preceded and followed this tragedy of the Company, suppressed by the Papacy it was founded to serve, have made the Jesuit one of the stock figures of historical fiction, dark, sinister and ambitious. The papal bull which apparently ended the history of the Order in complete ruin, accused them of certain distinct evils—whether justly or unjustly is entirely outside of the purpose of this book to discuss. If the Jesuits of the eighteenth century were guilty of the wrongs charged against them by the Pope, they had become so by forgetting the spirit of their founder and disobeying his distinct precepts. It would be as just to blame George Washington for the *crédit mobilier* or the oil scandal, as to blacken or obscure by the widespread bad reputation of the Jesuits of the eighteenth century, the figure of him whom his earliest followers called "the Father" of the Company of Jesus.

To these negative difficulties of the task of describing and understanding the story of the life of Ignatius Loyola, there must be added a profound positive difficulty. In one sense it is not a story at all. There are in it few incidents. This book cannot be anything but the description of the development of a soul and of a soul entirely absorbed, to a degree rare among men, by religion, and in religion concentrated absolutely upon one task, one affection, one hope: the formation of the Company of Jesus and the development of its service to the Church of God and the souls of men. Ignatius became, and the word is used in no depreciatory sense, self-hypnotized. This object alone roused his thought, stirred his heart, or fixed his attention; outside of this, life and the visible world in which we live it, ceased for him to exist.

For the description of the way in which his experience formed his soul and his character influenced his comrades and followers, the materials, though not extensive, are sufficient and trustworthy. They consist of four sorts of records.

I. The writings of Ignatius. Ignatius had none of the qualities of style which belong to great writers. Nevertheless his works, because of their influence on men, must be classed among the great writings of the world. "The Spiritual Exercises," a training of thought and emotion leading to complete devotion to the services of Christ, is a tremendous book wrought out of the struggles of Loyola's soul. In writing "The Constitutions," the charter of his foundation and the description of its ideals, he had the advice of others, but the dominant ideas and the spirit of the work are his. Of his letters we have over 6500, written by his own hand or under his orders by a secretary. But only twenty-seven were written before he was elected General of the Company and the rest are mainly concerned with the duties of that office.

II. Direct records of his words, deeds and traits by men who knew him.

a. His so-called "Autobiography," which would be more exactly entitled his "Confessions." This is a treatise about one-sixth as long as this book, into which most of it is incorporated, usually in direct translation.

Father Gonzalez de Camara writes that one day he was talking to Ignatius in the garden at Rome about his temptations and Ignatius, by telling his own experience gave him such comfort that he was moved to tears of joy. An hour or two later, speaking of this experience with some of the brethren at dinner, it appeared that Nadal (one of the most trusted helpers of Ignatius) had for several years been urging him to leave a record of the way in which God had led his soul. Ignatius thought he had too many more useful things to do. Now, however, his intimates succeeded in persuading him to dictate, as he found leisure, what God had done for him in his conversion. Ignatius kept postponing the dictation and it suffered long interruptions, but the gentle persistence of Gonzalez and Nadal finally got out of him a remarkable human document. Most of it is in his rough Spanish but lack of a scribe compelled Camara to dictate the last fifth of it in Italian. The only English translation the writer knows is from a Latin version made soon after Ignatius' death. It lacks the strength and naïve charm of the original. On the whole, it is as if a man had found a masterpiece of some rustic wood carver centuries old and sandpapered and varnished it to accord with modern taste.

b. A letter written eight years before Ignatius' death by Diego Lainez, one of his first followers "to set down in a few words faithfully and simply" what he remembers of the edifying sayings of Ignatius and the circumstances of the beginnings of the Company of Jesus as he took part in them or has heard them from others: a document about as long as two chapters of this book.

c. Collections of notes somewhat resembling the Table Talk of Luther or the notes on which Boswell based his Life of Johnson.

(1) One is by Father Gonzalez de Camara, and consists of notes of conversations or incidents; sometimes dated, sometimes not. There are four hundred and thirteen of these notes varying in length.

(2) A similar collection, made by Father Peter Ribadeneira, of one hundred and twelve items, entitled "Concerning the Acts of our Father Ignatius."

(3) Another collection by the same author, of ninety-eight items is called: "Words and Deeds of S. Ignatius." Ribadeneira had for eight years been quite intimate with Ignatius, had sometimes slept in his room and helped him in saying mass. Many of the sayings or stories are dated and, for most of them, he indicates by initials the source.

(4) A little collection of anecdotes and sayings made by Father Nadal, who was trusted by Ignatius.[5]

d. The Memorial of Father Faber, which after a brief account of his own experience, traces the foundation and progress of the Company to the year 1546. About two hundred pages.[6]

III. Legal or ecclesiastical documents concerning certain events in his life.[7]

---

[5] All the foregoing of Class II in Scripta I.   [6] Fabri Monumenta.
[7] Many of these are in Scripta I.

IV. The last class of material, much less important than the preceding three classes, consists of early lives. Of these two are by men who knew him well.

a. The life of Ribadeneira, a Spaniard thirty-six years younger than Loyola, was undertaken by the order of the General and published in Latin sixteen years after the death of Loyola. It is a small book—about one-half the size of this book—and was intended only for use in the Company. Strict orders were issued not to give it to outsiders. The purpose of the book is religious and not historical. The writer got much of his material from the sources already mentioned, and, as he was not endowed with a very strong critical sense, it must be used with caution when he goes beyond these. There were various editions of his work which were considerably enlarged. The one used here is usually the original edition of 1572.

b. Juan Alfonso de Polanco was a Spaniard about twenty-five years younger than Ignatius. For nine years under Loyola and fifteen years after Loyola's death, he was general secretary of the Company. Loyola suggested to him that he should prepare to write its history. This he finally did and it has been published in six volumes. The first seventy-three pages contain a life of Loyola previous to the foundation of the Company of Jesus. For it Polanco used the sources already mentioned, but also put in some things he had heard at Rome. It is therefore of more independent value than the lives of Ribadeneira. His account of the temper and labours of the Company during the life of Ignatius is based on letters and is trustworthy.

With the close of the century begins a style of biography of Loyola in which the legendary element grows stronger and stronger and the desire to make an edifying picture where the most sensitively hyper-orthodox could find no possibility of the slightest shock of offense, becomes more and more evident.

This type of writing, which runs down well into modern times, completely dehumanizes Loyola, who in spite of deserving the title of saint, was every inch a man. Frequently its style shows a kind of sugary sweetness which irresistibly reminds us of some of the overdecorated church interiors of the eighteenth century. It has been an absolute bar to the understanding of Loyola by Protestants and many Catholics find it unreadable.

Most Protestant treatment of the life of Loyola has been, at its best, without any strong effort to put itself in Loyola's place. At its worst, it shows a plain inclination to blacken everything connected with the name of Jesuit. Though this controversial temper has grown less intense, it still continues and in English the writer knows of but one life of Loyola by a Protestant, which makes an earnest and successful effort at sympathetic understanding: the recently published popular "Biography" of Mr. Henry D. Sedgwick.

Much light has been thrown, during the last twenty-five years, on the life and character of Ignatius Loyola. The publication by the Company of Jesus of its Monumenta has made accessible to everybody all existing important primary sources. Professor Pastor of the Catholic University of Innsbruck has in his great History of the Popes shown marked candour, and broad scholarship. He has given us a sure background for the life of Loyola, which has the advantage of being above the suspicion of any, even unconscious anti-Catholic bias.

Professor Boehmer of Marburg published in 1914 an account of the early life of Loyola based on profound study which shows a trained historical judgment, so fairly exercised that it is not always easy to tell whether the writer is Catholic or Protestant.

Finally, two Jesuit authors have given us large lives of

Loyola based on the best principles of modern historical science and using the utmost candour in stating all the evidence upon any disputable point, Father Astrain in Spanish and Father Tacchi-Venturi in Italian.

Both Venturi and Boehmer stop with the formation of the Company of Jesus. The narrative and the judgments of this book are based upon independent study of the original sources, but the discovery that a conclusion had been reached at variance with any of these three profound works has caused a restudy of the evidence. No judgment which all of these authorities reject has been stated as certain.

CHAPTER II

IGNATIUS AS A MAN OF THE WORLD

Ignatius Loyola was born among the Basques, who live at the western end and on both slopes of the Pyrenees, partly in Spain and partly in France. A resolute folk of tough fibre, they have always made hardy soldiers and daring seamen, who led in the dangerous hunt of the whale and were the first Europeans to form the habit of crossing the Atlantic in small boats to fish on the banks of Newfoundland. They are a self-respecting people, proud of their ancient liberties; and their independent conservatism has enabled them to keep, to a degree unusual in modern Europe, their strange language, their peculiar dress and their ancient customs.

Ignatius' father was Lord of Oñaz and Loyola and represented two of the most ancient lines of the nobility of the province of Guipúzcoa. The family, which possessed large estates, including a considerable income from a neighbouring iron works, was rendered illustrious by memories of bravery in battle. Seven sons of the house had fought for Church and king in the glorious victory of Beotibar won from the Moors in 1321.[1]

The Basque nobility shared to the full that desperate quarrelsomeness which in the first half of the fifteenth century filled so many of the provinces of Spain with bloodshed.[2] The twenty-four chief houses of Guipúzcoa were divided into two factions, fifteen of them related to the house of Oñaz and nine related to the house of Gamboa, and, in the time of Ignatius' grandfather, their

[1] Henao, Appendix, Pol. I, 523.   [2] Altamira II, 297.

14

destructive quarrels were incessant. Appeals to the King by their non-aristocratic neighbours brought a stern royal interference. Laws were imposed whose object, like that of the contemporary English acts of livery and maintenance, was to prevent the formation of factions of the nobility. The King of Castile destroyed twenty-five of their fortified manor houses, but spared the lower story of the Manor of Loyola, which was afterwards rebuilt. The King also banished, for four years, twenty heads of houses, including the grandfather of Ignatius.[3]

Ignatius was the last of thirteen children, with seven brothers and five sisters. A brother and a sister died in infancy and we do not know even their names. Another brother, Ochoa, died at home in boyhood, three of his sisters married nobles and four of his brothers became soldiers. Three fell in battle; two in the wars of Naples and the other in the conquest of America. The seventh brother died as rector of the church of Azpeitia—an office regarded as naturally belonging to the family.[4]

There is some doubt about the year when Ignatius was born. Polanco, the secretary, makes in his Life of Ignatius confused and contradictory statements about the age of Ignatius. Still more puzzling is the fact that Ignatius, in his Confessions, makes in passing two statements about his age, which cannot both be exact.[5] The simplest explanation of the contradiction is that offered by writers in two Catholic journals,[6] that Ignatius, or if you prefer it, his scribe, made a mistake. The attempts to avoid this obvious explanation would seem to any one unacquainted with the vagaries of the complicated explanations of textual difficulties common in literary or biblical controversies, like an exceedingly forced construction of very simple and plain language.

[3] Henao, Pol. App. I, 530.   [4] Pol. Vol. I, 516. Henao, and Genealogy Claire Rib. App. II.   [5] Scripta I, 37-55.   [6] Cited Astrain 3 Note 2.

There is no absolute demonstration that Ignatius was born in 1491, 1492 or 1495 and each of these dates has found advocates in modern times. After all the matter is not of fundamental importance for the understanding of the character and work of Loyola, who remains the same whether he was born three or four years earlier or later. No evidence compels us to refuse to accept the date fixed at his death by the friends who buried him at Rome. This is often called the nurse's date, because the General of the Company of Jesus second in succession from Loyola, had testimony taken at his birthplace, including that of his nurse, who must then have been over ninety years old. But there are better reasons than the memory of a very old woman for believing that 1491, the accepted date of his birth, is exact.

He was born at Azpeitia, the seat of his family, in their manor which (1)* stood something less than a mile outside the little city, back from the king's highway, in a park so planted that the house was not visible from the road. An ancient evergreen tree towered above the tiled roof of one corner.[7] The valley, through which flows a little river, is extremely picturesque, but there is nothing in the life or sayings of Ignatius to indicate that he was impressed by the beauties of nature. Although in his later life he loved solitude in the open air of a garden and found pleasure and consolation in the view of the starry heavens, there is no other trace in him of that poet's attitude toward the visible universe which is so prominent in St. Francis of Assisi.

We have no account of the life of Loyola up to the age of thirty. Gonzalez de Camara says: "Ignatius called me on a day in September in the year of 1553 and began to tell me his whole life and the *travesuras de mancebo* (pranks of youth) clearly and distinctly with all their

---

* Text numbers in parenthesis refer to numbers in the Appendix under the heading "Notes."   [7] Henao App. Polanco 531.

circumstances."[8]   The manuscript copies of the Confessions in existence give only a single sentence to his youth.   It is perfectly plain that the story which Loyola told of his own young manhood is gone and it is probable that we have here another instance of mistaken affection and a wrong application of the maxim that the whole truth is not always edifying.   Twenty-seven years after Ignatius' death, the General of the Company answered a request of the Castilian Jesuits that the Confessions should be printed, by saying there were things in it "not fit to be circulated in all hands."[9]   This attempt to replace the image of the real Loyola by an officially corrected image of him, went on for over a century and a half[10] when his Confessions were finally printed in 1731.   Certainly the picture which has been made of a pious Christian gentleman free from all the vices of the young nobles of his day, a perfect example for the lads who flocked by thousands to the Jesuit schools of the seventeenth century, is contrary not only to his own opinion but also to that of the men who knew him best.[11]   Ignatius of Oñaz and Loyola was like the other young men of his day of noble birth, given to gaming, fighting and women, proud of his orthodoxy, but not particularly interested in living like a Christian.   His education was limited to the ability to read and to write a beautiful hand.   Doubtless he composed bad poetry for the ladies like other young cavaliers, and knew how to dance, to ride and handle arms. His only literary culture, as he says himself, came from reading those popular romances of chivalry which would now slumber in deserved oblivion if the satire of Cervantes had not made them immortal.

The Confessions of Ignatius Loyola were dictated in the third person and so it is impossible to tell certainly

[8] Scripta I. p. 32.   [9] Cited, Astrain 17.   [10] Boehmer 316.
[11] Camara, Scripta, I, 32.   Lainez ib, p. 101; Polanco, p. 10; Nadal, Cited Astrain from mss, p. 14.

whether all that remains of his description of his youth
is his own words beginning the lost paragraphs, or the
summary of them made by some one else when they were
cut out.

"Up to twenty-six[12] years of age he was a man given
to the vanities of the world and his chief delight was in
martial exercises with a great and vain desire to gain
honour." (2)

From various trustworthy sources small pieces of information can be gathered, which supplement this vague
picture.

It was the custom for families of the lesser nobility to
send their sons to serve as pages in the houses of more
powerful nobles, where they might gain the manners of
society and have a larger experience of life than they could
get in the solitude of the ancestral manor.   The head of
the house of Oñaz and Loyola had accepted the hint
given by his father when the King half destroyed their
castle. After he inherited the estate and title, he did his
fighting on the side of the crown, and found strong friends
and patrons in great noble houses outside the bounds
of the province of Guipúzcoa.   With two of the most
distinguished of these his youngest son found honourable
service.

While still a small boy, Ignatius was sent as a page
to the household of Juan Velasquez de Cuéllar, Governor
of the fortress of Arévalo, not far from the manor of the
Loyolas, Chief Treasurer and trusted counselor of Queen
Isabella of Castile.   After the death of his royal patroness,
Cuéllar's wife renewed close relations to court by her
intimacy with the second wife of Ferdinand, Germaine
de Foix.   With his master and mistress, young Loyola
must often have gone to court, for it was the duty of pages

[12] According to the accepted date of his birth, this was a mistake and should
be thirty.

to serve their lord kneeling at table and to accompany him on all ceremonious occasions at home or abroad. Cuéllar and his wife had excellent reputations for justice, generosity and piety, and probably it would have been hard to find a better family for training the boy in the "exercises of a gentleman." More than thirty years later Ignatius had grateful memories of his first patron.[13]

But his visits to court could hardly have been conducive to the formation of a serious religious character; more especially after the pleasure loving Germaine had succeeded the pious Isabella as the centre of society. The feudal nobility once had two great pleasures, and only two, to relieve the monotony of their lives; hunting and fighting. In France, Spain and England, the heavy hand of the King was limiting the latter of these sports and they could no longer always relieve a sense of tedium by an attempt to surprise a neighbour's castle or vent their spleen by killing his vassals, driving off their cows or burning their ricks. They were changing from a feudal nobility to a court nobility. But they still felt that a gentleman must right his own wrongs and be quick to wipe out an insult with blood. The sword at their side, the dagger in their belt, were to them the symbol that they were a fighting caste and the romances of chivalry pouring from the Spanish presses showed in all their pages a passion for danger like a thirst for strong drink and a preposterous readiness to fight, as instinctive as that of young game cocks.

The atmosphere a page breathed when Ignatius must have been riding frequently up to court with his patrons, is shown by the following story of the experience of his future biographer, Ribadeneira.

Pope Paul III made his grandson, Alessandro Farnese, a cardinal at the age of fifteen and immediately en-

[13] Letts. I, 705.

riched him with a number of civil governorships and a long list of bishoprics and abbacies.[14] He spent his large income freely in generous patronage of letters and art and in maintaining an elaborate household. At the age of nineteen this splendid young prince of the Church came to Toledo and a palace was assigned to him opposite the house of the widowed mother of young Ribadeneira. The boy got admission to the palace as an extra page to help serve the Cardinal at table. He attracted the attention of his patron, who offered to take him to Rome as one of his household. The mother consented and the twelve-year old boy went. One day when Cardinal Farnese was being entertained by his grandfather, Paul III, the pages of the Cardinal's suite were waiting in an anteroom where there were also cardinals and other ecclesiastical personages. The lad took offense at some remark of one of his fellows, immediately boxed the other boy's ears and hit him over the back of the neck with the torch he carried to escort his master home. Nobody reproved him for this act. On the contrary the governor of the pages said that if he had not hit his insulter they would have had him punished.[15]

It is not surprising, therefore, to find that two incidents of Loyola's early ilfe of which we know, indicate that this young Basque noble shared the violent temperament of his fellows and was quick on the dagger; as most of them were.

When he was twenty-four years old he was in Azpeitia visiting his family and soon afterwards took the tonsure— that is, he had a spot on the back of his head shaved. This did not mean that he intended to become a priest like his brother Pedro Lopez. It was only the sign that he had entered into what were called minor orders, which might enable him to draw the income of some ecclesias-

---

[14] Pastor. V, p. 100, note.   [15] Ribad. Confessions. M. H. S. J. I, 7.

tical benefice without doing its duty, or possibly help him in case he got into any difficulty with the law. This he promptly proceeded to do. There was a family feud going on in the town, and Ignatius flung himself into it with the joyousness with which his comrades were accustomed to welcome trouble.

His brother Pedro Lopez, rector of the principal church, was not a very exemplary priest. In spite of his ordination vows, he had four illegitimate children.[16] This was not rare among the younger sons of Spanish nobles who took the family benefices as a matter of course, just as their brothers enlisted in the royal army as a means of livelihood befitting a man of noble blood.

It was just this "matter of course" feeling that the ecclesiastical patronage of Azpeitia belonged entirely to the house of Loyola, which made the trouble. The cantor, or choirmaster in the king's chapel, was regarded by all the Loyolas and their clients as an intruder hunting on their ecclesiastical preserves. So it was determined to teach him and his crowd a good lesson. Just what was done we do not know, but Ignatius and Pedro Lopez of Oñaz and Loyola found themselves facing a warrant of arrest issued by the royal judge of the jurisdiction in which they lived. The documents in the case show that they put themselves under the jurisdiction of the neighbouring bishop of Pamplona on the ground that they were clergymen. This could not be denied in the case of Pedro Lopez, and the royal official demanded simply that he should be arrested and given by the tribunal of the Church a punishment worthy of his crime. In the case of Ignatius, the corregidor asserted that in spite of his tonsure he had no legal right to the *benefit of clergy*, but was still a layman, because he had not kept the rules laid down in the bull of "the very holy Pope Alexander VI of glorious

[16] Venturi, II, 9 quoted Cros.

memory" for the conduct of clergymen without benefice.[17] The chief reasons given for regarding Ignatius as still a layman subject to the jurisdiction of civil courts, were that he had not been registered on the list of the vicar general at Pamplona, that he had "mingled in secular affairs not at all consistent with membership in the clerical order" and that he had appeared in public in a way "not decent" for a clergyman.[18] He had been in the habit of wearing "long hair covering his ears. His mantle was too short and was either blue or green or yellow (colours forbidden to clergymen). He also wore a coloured cap and hose in public and usually went about with a leather or iron cuirass, with sword and dagger and carrying a crossbow or some other weapon." Exactly what the "certain excess" committed by the young soldier and his brother the priest Shrove Tuesday 1515 was, we do not know. The judge wrote that it was "very enormous because it was committed at night with malice prepense and aforethought." It may be fairly assumed that it did not include bloodshed or great destruction of property; otherwise those details would have been mentioned. So far as we know the young rioter finally escaped without punishment.[19]

The second incident in the early life of Ignatius about which we have certain testimony, is very similar.

Four years after the death of Ignatius, Father Hernandez, rector of the college of the Company at Salamanca, took his final vow to Father Araoz, the head of the province of Spain. The bishop of Salamanca was present by invitation. In the middle of the ceremony he commenced to weep and the tears ran down his cheeks to the astonishment of all. Afterwards Father Araoz asked the bishop, at the dinner to which he had been invited, "Why. did your excellency weep so much in the church

[17] Church office.   [18] Scripta I, 591-2.   [19] Scripta I.

while the profession was going on?" "Don't ask me," he replied, "why I wept when I saw a man entering a religious order founded by a man like Ignatius whom I saw with my own eyes at Pamplona, when he met a line of men in the street and they bumped him and forced him to the wall, draw his sword and charge them so fiercely that if there had not been somebody to hold him back either he would have killed some of them or they would have killed him."[20]

Not long after Ignatius' encounter with the law, his patron the governor of Arévalo, got himself into very much more serious trouble by the same independent contempt of authority, more or less characteristic of the nobles of Spain. Charles I of the foreign house of Hapsburg became King of Spain by inheritance through his mother. Wishing to provide for the dowager queen Germaine, and knowing that Juan de Cuéllar was notoriously unfriendly to the Hapsburg succession, the Regent transferred his chief fiefs to Germaine. This piece of injustice Cuéllar rashly undertook to resist. A royal force was sent against him and after a defense of the castle of Arévalo which cost the life of his eldest son, Cuéllar was obliged to surrender and go to Madrid to make his peace with the Regent. Broken in spirit, the old man soon after died, heavily in debt, and his wife was obliged to become a court lady of the crazy queen Júana.[21]

It seems evident that Ignatius stood by his old patron in the days of trouble and probably fought with him to defend the castle of Arévalo against the royal troops, for the widow, closing up the estate and leaving the scenes of her ancient grandeur, gave Ignatius as a parting gift two horses from the stable and a purse of five hundred ducats.

Whether Ignatius had become a *mesnadero,* some-

[20] Scripta I, 566.   [21] Boletin 17, p. 502-504, 498, ib. 19, 6. 1-18.

thing like a member of the *gens d'armes* in France, receiving a small income from the king on condition of constant readiness for active service, is not certain. At all events the moment was not propitious for royal service and he turned to another old friend of his father's, the Duke of Najera; one of the richest and most powerful grandees of Spain, able to put into the field an army of some four thousand men from the vassals of his own estates. Ignatius with his two horses, his arms and his gay clothing, betook himself to Pamplona, fifty miles away and became an officer in the bodyguard of the Duke. This was in effect the royal service, for the Duke was the Viceroy of the province of Navarre; conquered five years before from its French King and constantly threatened with attack from the French side of the Pyrenees and revolt from within. It was three years, however, before he saw any military service under his new patron. Then the city of Najera revolted against its Duke and Loyola marched with the army to reduce it to obedience.[22] When the city was stormed, he was one of the first to enter and on this occasion showed a generosity which makes plain that he was more avid of honour than greedy for money. The city, as a punishment for its rebellion, had been given over to the soldiers for plunder. But Ignatius refused to take this chance to enrich himself on the ground that it was unworthy of a hidalgo who was serving for honour and not for wages. This idea probably came to him from the romances of chivalry which were his only reading; but it was an idea which most of the readers of such books were not apt to apply to actual war. About a year later, when he was a wounded prisoner in the hands of French captors who finally released him without ransom, Ignatius refused to be outdone in chivalry by a kindly enemy and gave away to those who courteously

---

[22] Pol. 13.

came to call on him, all his personal possessions: to one a dagger, to another his shield, to another his corselet, as pledges of gratitude and friendship.

He had already gained the reputation of not bearing malice against those with whom he had quarrels or duels on points of honour.[23] This generous and conciliatory temper, together with that native ability for handling men which he afterwards developed in so extraordinary a degree, had already been remarked by his patron, the Duke of Najera. So when the old factious quarrel of the nobility of Guipúzcoa, in which his ancestors had played a leading part, threatened to break out again, Loyola was sent on a diplomatic mission of reconciliation and obtained the triumph of bringing them to an accord which gave satisfaction to both parties.

Ignatius, who had made his way with courage, fidelity and wisdom among civil brawls and petty faction fights, was now to have the first and last experience of "la grande guerre."

The Kings of France and Spain had long hated each other and each watched for a good chance to take the other at a disadvantage; "which," as the chronicler dryly remarks, "is generally the justice that precipitates princes into war." Francis I made a league with the Pope which enabled him to attack Charles in Naples and the insurrection of Castile gave an excellent occasion to attack Navarre in the name of its young dispossessed King. An army made up of French and French Basques suddenly attacked St. Jean Pied de Port, the outpost of the Spanish conquest covering the pass into Navarre. After a brief bombardment it surrendered rather than stand an assault and the forces holding the mountains retreated from their strong positions. The fort built to defend the road on the southern slope of the Pyrenees surrendered at the second cannon shot and the army was across the moun-

[23] Polanco 13.

tains and on the way to the important city of Pamplona. The Viceroy, the Duke of Najera, unable to make head against the superior force of the invader, hurried to ask more troops of the Regent, leaving in Pamplona a garrison with orders to stand out until help came. No sooner was he gone, than the people who hated their Spanish conquerors, rose, and sent representatives to carry the keys of the city to the invaders. The advance guard of the French entered the gates and the garrison of the city withdrew leaving, however, a garrison in the citadel, which mounted seventeen great guns and many small pieces of artillery. Ignatius went into the citadel, apparently as a volunteer. At the council of war the senior officers were against fighting. But Ignatius insisted that it was better to be killed than to continue the surrenders and retreats which had already brought the invaders into the heart of the country at the cost of a few cannon shots. When the siege was formed, the Commandant took Ignatius and two other officers to a conference with the French General. The terms offered gave so little of the honours of war to the garrison that the indignant Ignatius again persuaded his comrades to stand to it on the point of military honour and the bombardment began as soon as the French could plant their batteries.[24] Here also begins the invaluable information of the Confessions of Loyola.

Realizing that the fight would be desperate and because there was no priest at hand to help him make his peace with God, "he confessed his sins to one of his comrades in arms." This detail, which might be found unedifying or even shocking to extreme Catholic orthodoxy, was, like some other details, suppressed in the early lives of Ignatius, even though they were based on the Confessions. The garrison stood the bombardment a good while until the wall was breached and the storming

[24] Polanco 12; Bordenave 6-8; Boissonade 548.

column was being formed. At this critical moment a cannon ball smashed Loyola's right leg, and made a flesh wound in the left. The Commandant showed the white flag and after conference agreed to surrender on better terms than those first offered: for the garrison were to march out with arms and baggage, leaving behind all munitions of war. The French entering the fortress, found the wounded Loyola, treated him with kindness and courtesy and after twelve or fifteen days sent him (fifty miles) in a litter to the family castle at Azpeitia.

He arrived at home in very bad condition. His brother called all the doctors of the neighbourhood to a conference and they decided that his smashed leg must be reset; because, either the journey or lack of skill in the doctors at Pamplona, had left the bones in a condition which made knitting impossible "and so they began once more that butchery" (*carneceria*). More than forty years later enough of his soldierly pride had survived in the subconscious self of the monk Ignatius to make him recall with pleasure how "in all those operations which he suffered before and after this, he never spoke a word, nor showed any sign of pain except clenching his fists hard." He sank after the operation and on the day before the festival of St. Peter, Loyola was told that if he were not better by midnight he would die. But "the sick man had always been devoted to St. Peter and so it pleased God that by midnight he was better" and in a few days out of danger.

But not out of pain. The new doctors had set his leg badly. As it began to knit, it was evident that it threatened to be shorter than the other and a piece of bone stuck out below the knee. As he was determined to follow a career in the world, he judged that this would be too disfiguring and asked the surgeons if they could not cure it. They said yes, but that the pain would be terrific. His older brother protested that he could never himself bear such terrible pain, but the wounded man bore it with his usual patience. An instrument was then applied day and night to keep his leg from shortening, which "martyrized" him. His general health improved, but he was obliged to stay in bed because he could not bear his weight on his leg.[25]

[25] Confessions Scripta. 1, 39.

CHAPTER III

LOYOLA'S OWN STORY: HIS CONVERSION AND HOW GOD TAUGHT HIM

To relieve the tedium of lying in bed, the convalescing soldier asked for a romance of chivalry such as he had been used to reading. But none could be found in the house. So they brought him two books, a Life of Christ and the Lives of the Saints. They were big folios; the first in four volumes. But, in spite of their heavy appearance, the wounded man found them very interesting. The author of the Lives of the Saints is not known. But the Life of Christ was the work of a Carthusian Prior of Coblenz, known as Ludolf the Saxon. It had been written some hundred and fifty years and had gained great popularity. Manuscripts of it are very numerous and during the fifty years before Ignatius was wounded there had been twenty-six editions of it printed in Latin, besides translations into French, Portuguese, Dutch, German and Spanish.[1]

"When he laid aside these books, he did not always think of what he had read, but, sometimes, of the worldly things about which he used to think before. And out of many vain things which offered themselves to his mind, one took such possession of his heart that he was buried in thought about it two or three and even four hours without noticing it; imagining what he had to do in the service of a lady: the means he must use to go where she was, his motto, the words he would say to her, the deeds of arms he would do in her service. And he be-

[1] Boehmer 304.

came so filled with pride in this that he did not consider how impossible it was for him to put it into action because the lady was no ordinary noble woman, neither was she countess or duchess, but of a much higher station than either of these."[2]

This sort of hopeless but not unhappy day dreaming passion for an unattainable woman was quite in the style of the time and its prototype could be found in the poems of Dante and Petrarch. Ignatius had never read these poets, but the things they sang were in the air as a sort of aftermath of chivalry. Who the woman of Ignatius' dreams was, no one knows. It is a good guess that it may have been the Queen of Spain, Ferdinand's second wife.

"However, Our Lady helped him, bringing it about that to these thoughts there succeeded others which were born of what he read. Because reading the Life of our Lord and of the Saints, he thought, talking with himself, 'How would it be if I did what St. Thomas did, or what St. Dominic did? . . .' These thoughts lasted a good while and when other things came in between, there succeeded the worldly thoughts spoken of above and they lasted also a long time and this succession of different thoughts continued many days, he being always fixed on the thought which occupied him; whether it was of those worldly exploits which he desired to do, or of those others of God which offered themselves to his imagination, until, tired out, he left them and attended to other things. There was, however, this difference. When he was dwelling on the worldly day dream he found much pleasure, but, when tired out, he ceased to think of that, he found himself arid and discontented; and when he imagined going barefooted to Jerusalem and eating only herbs and doing all the other penances which he saw the saints had done,

[2] Confessions.

he was contented and joyful not only in such thoughts
but after, wearied, he had ceased to dwell upon them. At
first, however, he did not really weigh that difference,
until one time his eyes were a little opened and he commenced to wonder at that difference and to reflect on it,
catching hold by experience of the fact that after one sort
of thoughts he remained sad and after the others joyful,
and so, little by little, coming to know the diversity of
spirits which moved him; the one of God, the other of the
devil. This was his first reasoning about the things of
God."[3]

This conception, wrought out of his experience, that
the world was divided between God and the devil, who
stirred impulses in the soul for good or evil which he
might resist or foster, was the beginning of his conversion and it always remained in his mind the starting point
of personal religion, either for himself or for others. The
proof of this is plain in the opening of his great book, the
Spiritual Exercises.

He continues in the Confessions to describe the awakening of his soul. . . . "And having gained no little light
from that reading, he commenced to think more truly
about his past life and the great necessity he was under to
do penance for it. And here there arose again in his mind
a desire to imitate the saints and to promise to do by the
grace of God what they had done. But all that he definitely desired to do, as soon as he was well, was to go to
Jerusalem with such self-discipline and abstinence as a
generous soul inflamed with God is wont to desire to carry
out. So he was gradually forgetting those past thoughts
because of these holy desires which were taking possession of him; which were strengthened by a visitation of
this sort: lying awake one night, he saw clearly the
image of Our Lady with the Holy Child Jesus; in which

[3] Confessions 40-41.

sight he had for a considerable time very great comfort and it left him with such loathing for all his past life, especially for his carnal indulgences, that he seemed to be entirely freed from all evil pictures which had before been in his soul. And so, from that hour (1521) until August 1555, when this is written, he never again felt the least assenting to any lustful impulse. And by that result it may be concluded that the thing was of God: although he did not dare to so decide and does not now desire to do more than affirm the above facts. But his brother also, and the whole household, recognized in his conduct the change which had taken place in his heart. He persevered in his reading and in his good intentions, and whenever he talked with those of the household, he spent the whole time on things of God by which he might do good to their souls. And taking much pleasure in those books, the thought came to him of setting down briefly the things most essential in the life of Christ and the saints. So he set himself to write a book with great diligence (for he was now able to move about the house), putting the words of Christ in red ink, those of Our Lady in blue, and the paper was glazed and ruled, and the letters were well formed because he was a very good writer. (3) Part of his time he spent in writing and part in prayer. And the greatest consolation he had was in looking at the heavens and the stars, which he did very often for a long time, because when he did that he felt in himself a very great power to serve Our Lord."[4]

He then tells us how he was undecided about what he should do when he got back from his pilgrimage to Jerusalem, whether it would be better to enter the Carthusian monastery at Seville, "never eating anything but herbs" or wander about the world as a free penitent. He ordered a servant of the house who went to Burgos to

[4] Confessions.

get information about the rule of life of the Carthusians and found it good.

The impression is given in many brief accounts of the life of Loyola that his wound left him unfit to go back to the life of a soldier or aid to some great royal officer. This is a mistake. His lameness was very slight. He had no difficulty in riding and he walked from Gaeta to Rome and then to Venice, a tramp which took him across Italy and nearly its whole length. It was natural, therefore, when he was strong enough to start and did not wish to confide his plans to his brother, the head of the house, that he should say to him, " 'Señor, the Duke of Najera, as you know, is well aware that I am recovered. It would be well for me to go to Navarette.' (The Duke was then at that city). His brother and some of the household suspected that he wanted to make a great change in his life. And so his brother took him first into one room and then into another and began to beg him with great feeling not to throw himself away but to look at the great hopes he had from people of importance and how much he could amount to in his life, and similar words; all with the intention of turning him from his good desire. But the answer was of such a sort that without departing from the truth, because he had great scruples about that, he avoided by artifice the difficulty of his brother.

"He set out riding on a mule, accompanied by another brother, whom he left on the way at the house of a sister at Oñate while he went on to Navarette. . . . And remembering that the Duke owed him a few ducats, he presented a claim for them to the treasurer and when the treasurer replied that he had no money and the Duke heard of it, he said he might fail to pay everybody else but not Loyola; to whom the Duke wanted to give, because of past services, a good lieutenancy if he was willing to accept it. And he got the money, sent part to certain

persons to whom he was under obligation and spent part
of it on a picture of Our Lady in a shrine which was in
bad condition, to restore it and to adorn it very well. And
so dismissing the two servants who had travelled with
him, he started alone on his mule from Navarette to go
to Montserrat."

Montserrat was a shrine which had great attraction
for pious pilgrims. It was a Benedictine monastery,
dating back to the beginning of the eighth century, and
its church sheltered an image of the Virgin which was
said to have been carved by St. Luke and brought to
Spain by St. Peter.

"On that journey something happened to him which
it will be well to write down because it shows how God
dealt with that soul, which, although blind, had such
strong desire to serve Him in all that it understood. . . .
It seemed to him then that holiness was entirely measured by exterior asperity of life and that he who did the
most severe penances would be held in the divine regard
for the most holy, which idea made him determine to lead
a very harsh life.[5]   In such thoughts he found all his
consolation, not considering anything interior, nor knowing what humility nor charity, nor patience, nor discretion, in ruling and measuring those virtues, were; but all
his purpose was to do those great outward works, because
the saints had done them for the glory of God."[6]

"Then, going on his way, he overtook a Moorish cavalier on a mule, and the two, falling into conversation, began to talk of Our Lady and the Moor said that he
believed that the Virgin had conceived superhumanly, but
he could not believe that she had remained a virgin after
the birth of Christ: which opinion the pilgrim could not
shake in spite of many reasons he gave. Then the Moor

[5] This is Lainez' summary of what Ignatius had said before he dictated the
Confessions. Scripta I, p. 101.   [6] Confessions, 45.

rode on and was lost to view, leaving him in doubt in regard to what had passed between them, for he began to be discontented with himself because it seemed that he had not done his duty and this aroused indignation against the Moor because it seemed to him that he had done evil in consenting that a Moor should say such things about Our Lady and that he was obliged to defend her honour. And so the desire came to him to go seek the Moor and give him the dagger for what he had said and he had a long struggle over this desire which left him in doubt what he ought to do. The Moor before riding on, had said that he was bound to a place which was a little ahead on the same road very close to the king's highroad, but that the highroad did not pass the place. And so, after having thought what would be right to do without being able to come to a decision, he decided to let his mule go with loose reins to the point where the roads divided and if the mule took the road to the town, he would seek out the Moor and give him the dagger and if the mule did not go to the city, but followed the king's highroad, he would let him be. And doing this it pleased God that although the town stood little more than thirty or forty yards from the highroad and the way to it was very broad and good, the mule took the king's highroad and not the way to the town." (4)

"And arriving at a big town before he got to Montserrat, he wanted to buy there the clothing which he had determined to wear to Jerusalem, and so he bought cloth of the sort they used in making sacks, of a kind which is very prickly and ordered a garment made of it reaching to his feet. And he bought a staff and a gourd for water and tied them to the bow of the mule's saddle. And he bought also some straw sandals, of which he only used one and that not for appearance but because one leg was still bandaged and in somewhat bad condition, so much so that although he rode, he found it swollen every night. So he thought it necessary to wear a shoe on that foot. And he took up his journey for Montserrat thinking, as was his wont, about the deeds he had to do for the love of God. And as his mind was filled with ideas from Amadis of Gaul and other books of chivalry, things came into his head like them. And so he made up his mind to watch over his arms all one night without sitting or lying down, but now standing and now kneeling before the altar of Our Lady of Montserrat, where he decided to leave his garments and clothe himself with the arms of Christ. . . . Arrived at Montserrat, after praying and arranging with the confessor, he made a general confession in writing. And the confession lasted three days and he agreed with the confessor that he should order the mule to be taken away and that he should hang up his sword and dagger in the church by the altar of Our Lady. And that was the first man to whom he made known his determination; because up to then he had disclosed it to none of his confessors.

"The 24th of March, 1522, the eve of Our Lady, as secretly as possible he gave to a poor man all his clothes and put on the clothes he longed for and went to kneel before the altar of Our Lady, and now there and now on foot, staff in hand, passed the whole night, and left for Barcelona at daybreak. In order not to be recognized he went, not by the direct road where he would find many people who would know him and show him honour, but by a roundabout way to a town called Manresa; where he determined to stay in a hospital some days and note down some things in his book which he took with him very carefully and in which he found much consolation. And when he was about a league from Montserrat, a man who came rapidly behind him caught up and asked him if he had given clothes to a poor man as the poor man said. And when he answered yes, tears filled his eyes out of compassion for the poor man to whom he had given the clothes because he was told that they had arrested him on suspicion of being a thief. But although his desire to escape all public notice was very strong, he could not be very long in Manresa before people began to talk much about him, getting the gossip from Montserrat, and soon rumors about his worldly position made it greater than it really was—saying that he had abandoned the income of great estates, etc.

"And he sought alms in Manresa every day. He ate no meat and drank no wine, although they were given to him. On Sundays he did not fast and if a little wine was given he drank it. And because he had been very particular in the care of his hair, as was the custom in those days, he determined to let it grow naturally without combing or cutting. And for the same reason he allowed his finger nails to grow, because he had been very nice in taking care of them. While he was in that hospital it often happened to him to see, in the clear light of day, something in the air not far from him which gave him much consolation because it was very beautiful. He could not clearly make out exactly what it was, but it seemed to him, in a general way, to have the form of a serpent with many things that shone like eyes although they were not eyes. He found much delight and consolation in the sight of that thing and the more often he saw it, the greater consolation he found in it and when it disappeared he was displeased." [7]

"Up to that time he had always remained in a certain invariable inner condition of great joyfulness, without, however, having any understanding of inner spiritual things. On the days when that vision continued or a little before it began (for it lasted many days) there came a thought which troubled him, bringing before him the

[7] Confessions, 49.

difficulty of his life as if some one had said to him within his soul, 'And how can you endure such a life for the seventy years you have to live?' But to that he answered, also in the inner places of his soul, with great force (because he felt the question came from the enemy), 'Oh, wretch, can you assure me of even one hour of life?' And so he conquered the temptation and was at peace. And that was the first temptation he had after the one mentioned above.[8] And this happened when he was entering a church in which he heard every day high mass, vespers and compline all chanted. He had found in them great consolation and ordinarily he read during mass the passion of our Lord; always in his unchanging inner joy. But after the above mentioned temptation, there began in his soul a time of changing feelings; sometimes he was so insipid that he had no taste for prayer, nor in hearing mass nor in any other prayer which he made. And other times quite the contrary feelings arose within him, and that so suddenly that it seemed to him that he was freed from sadness and desolation as if some one should lift a cloak from a man's shoulders. And here he began to drive away these inner changes which he had never experienced before and to say to himself, 'What new life is this which we are commencing?' At that time he conversed sometimes with spiritual persons who believed in him and wanted to talk with him because, although he did not yet understand spiritual things, nevertheless in his talk he showed much zeal and a strong will to go forward in the service of God. There was in Manresa at that time a holy woman of many days and an ancient servant of God, known as such in many parts of Spain; so much so that the King had once summoned her to talk with him about certain matters. This woman, talking one day with the new soldier of Christ, said to him, 'Oh! would that my Lord Jesus Christ might appear to you some day!' But

[8] Apparently the temptation to kill the Moor.

he was frightened by this, taking it materially and saying to himself, 'How could Christ appear to me?' He persevered in his habitual confessions and in taking communion every Sunday.

"But he began to be much troubled by scruples. Because, even though the general confession which he had made in Montserrat had been made very carefully and all in writing, nevertheless it seemed to him sometimes that he had not confessed some things, and that idea afflicted him very much because, though he confessed this idea itself, he found no inward satisfaction. And so he began to seek out spiritual men who might aid these scruples of conscience but nothing helped him, and at last a doctor of theology, who was preaching in the church of Manresa, a very spiritual man, told him one day in confession to write everything he could recollect. He did it and after confession his scruples of conscience came back, so that he was in great tribulation and although he knew that these things caused him great loss and that it would be well for him to free himself from them, he could not. He thought sometimes that there might be a cure in having his confessor order him in the name of Jesus Christ not to confess again any things in his past life and he wanted to have his confessor so order him, but he had not the boldness to say it to his confessor. But the confessor, without being told, ordered him not to confess anything in his past life unless it was a very clear, distinct sin in his memory. He did not profit at all by that order and remained troubled. At that time he lived in a room which the Dominican monks had given him in their convent and kept up his daily seven hours of prayer on his knees, rising always at midnight, and all other exercises of the spirit, but in all these he found no cure for the scruples of his conscience and many months passed in torment. And once, when he was in great tribulation because of them, he took to prayer and in his fervour called aloud on God, saying, 'Help me, Oh Lord, for I find no help in man nor in any other creature; though if I thought I could find help no work would seem too great for me. Show me, Lord, where to find help, because, even though it should be necessary to follow a little dog in order that he might lead me to the remedy, I would do it.'

"Possessed by these thoughts there came to him many times with great force, the temptation to throw himself into a large opening there was in his room close to the place where he prayed. But realizing that it was a sin to kill himself, he began to say aloud, 'Lord, I will not do anything which is an offense to Thee,' repeating those words many times. And there came to his memory the story of a saint who, to obtain from God something he much desired, went many days without food until he obtained it. And thinking of that a good while, at last he made up his mind to do it, saying to himself, that he would neither eat nor drink until God provided for him or he saw himself near to death: because if he saw himself so far in extremis that if he did not eat he must die, he determined that then he would beg bread and eat it. (This was a foolish plan, for in truth how could he in the very article of death either beg or eat bread?) That happened on a Sunday after he had communed and the whole week he persevered without putting anything in his mouth and without giving up his accustomed exercises, even going to divine services and praying on his knees at midnight, etc. But when the next Sunday arrived when it was necessary to go to make his confession, as he was wont to tell his confessor very much in detail what he had done, he told him also how in that week he had eaten nothing. The confessor told him to break his fast: and although he found himself still with force, nevertheless he obeyed his confessor and found himself that day free from his scruples of conscience. But the third day, which was a Tuesday, while he was praying he commenced to remember his sins and as if he were threading beads, he kept on passing in thought from sin to sin of his past life and it seemed to him that he was obliged to confess them again. But at the end of these thoughts there came to him disgust with the life he led and impulses to leave it. And with that, it pleased God that he awoke as if out of sleep. And as he already had some experience in the diversity of spirits by the lessons which God had given him, he began to regard the way in which that spirit had come and so determined very clearly not to confess any more anything of his past life,[9] and so from that day on he remained free from those torments of conscience; holding it for certain that our Lord had freed him by His mercy.

"Aside from his seven hours of prayer he occupied himself in aiding the souls of some who came to him seeking help in spiritual things and all the rest of the day not occupied in these two things, he gave to meditation on the things of God and what he had read and heard. But when he came to go to bed, often great spiritual consolation came to him and intimations of divine things which made him lose a large share of the time destined for sleep— which was not much. And considering this, he thought that he had a certain time set aside for communion with God and in addition the rest of the day. And by this road he came to doubt if those intimations came from the good spirit, and he came to the conclusion that it was better to neglect them and sleep the hours allotted to sleep. And he did so. He still persevered in his determination to eat no meat and was so firm in it that he had no thought of changing it in any way. One day when he got up in the morning there appeared to him meat ready to be eaten; as if he saw it with his bodily eyes without any wish to eat meat preceding the appearance of it. And there came to him, at the same moment, a strong assent of his will to eat meat for the future. And though he recalled his for-

[9] I. e., he concluded the devil was tempting him to despair.

mer determination, he could not doubt that he ought to eat meat. Afterwards his confessor said he wondered if it was not a temptation, but he (Ignatius) examining the whole matter carefully, could not doubt that it was a sign. (5)

"In those days God was treating him like a boy in school, teaching him and that because of his rudeness and gross mind either because there was no one to teach him or because of the firm will which had been given him by God Himself for His service. At all events he clearly judged and has always judged that God was so teaching him. First if he doubted it he would think he was sinning against the divine majesty and then it can be seen by the five following points.

"He was very much devoted to the Holy Trinity and offered prayer every day to the three persons separately. And offering prayer to the most Holy Trinity the thought came to him 'How would it be to offer four prayers to the Trinity?' But the thought gave him little or no trouble as a thing of small importance. And standing one day praying the hours of Our Lady on the steps of the monastery, his understanding began to be raised as if he saw the most Holy Trinity as the three keys of an organ and that with so many tears and sobs that he could not restrain them. And, taking part that morning in a procession, he could not until dinner time keep back the tears, nor, after dinner, cease to talk about the Trinity: and that with much joy and consolation, so that all his life the impression remained with him to feel great devotion in offering prayer to the most Holy Trinity.

"Once he saw in his understanding with great spiritual joy the way in which God had created the world, because he seemed to see a white thing from which issued rays and from that God made light. But he would not know how to explain these things, nor does he remember entirely well everything about that information which at that time God was impressing on his soul.

"Also at Manresa, where he stayed almost a year after he began to be consoled by God and saw the fruit of his efforts to help souls, he gave up those extremes which he had before practiced and cut his nails and hair. One day when he was in the church of the monastery hearing mass and the body of Our Lord was raised, he saw, with the inner eyes, so to speak, rays of light which came from above. And although he cannot after so long a lapse of time explain it well, nevertheless what he saw clearly with the understanding was how Our Lord Jesus Christ was in that most Holy Sacrament.[10]

"On many occasions and for a long time when in prayer he saw with the interior eyes the humanity of Christ and the figure which appeared to him was like a white body, neither very big nor very small, but he could not see any distinction of members. He saw that in Manresa many times. If he should say twenty or forty he would not dare to judge that it was a falsehood. Another time he saw it when he was in Jerusalem and again when he was journeying near Padua. He also saw Our Lady in a similar form without distinguishing the parts of her body. Those things which he has seen gave so much confirmation to his faith that he has often thought within himself that if he had not read the scriptures which teach us those things of the faith, he would determine to die for them solely because of what he has seen.

"Once he went to a church which stood a little more than a mile from Manresa which was called, I think, St. Paul, and the road runs next to the river. And walking and saying his prayers, he sat down for a little with his face toward the river. And thus sitting, the eyes of his understanding began to open and, without seeing any vision, he understood and knew many things—as well spiritual things as things of the faith and things in the realm of letters and that with a brightness of illustration so great

---

[10] The mystery of transubstantiation.

that they seemed to him entirely new things. And the details of what he then understood cannot be explained though they were many. All that can be said is that he received a clarity in his understanding of such a sort that in all the reasoning of his life up to the age of more than sixty-two years, collecting all the help he had received from God and all he has known and joining them into one, it does not seem to him that he has gained as much from all these advantages as from that single illumination when he sat by the river.[11]

"And that left him with an understanding so enlightened that it seemed to him he was another man and that he had an intellect different from the one he had before. And after this had lasted for some time, he went on his knees before a roadside cross which stood nearby to give thanks to God and there appeared to him the vision which had appeared to him many times but which he had never understood; the thing of which it has been said before that it appeared very beautiful with many eyes. But he saw plainly, being before the cross, that the thing had not as beautiful a colour as usual. And he recognized very clearly, with a powerful assent of the will, that it was the devil and since, although for a long time the devil continued to appear to him often, he, as a sign of contempt, drove him away with a pilgrim staff he always carried in his hand.[12]

"Once at Manresa when he was ill and a very high fever brought him to the point of death, so that he judged clearly his soul was about to take flight, there came to him the thought that he was a righteous man; at which he was so troubled that he did nothing but put forward his sins and that thought troubled him more than the fever, but he could not conquer that thought in spite of all the effort he made to conquer it. But, relieved a little from the fever, he began to call fervently to some ladies who had

[11] Ignatius studied letters and theology thirteen years. [12] Confessions.

come to visit him, that, for the love of God, if they saw him again at the point of death, they should cry out with loud voices saying to him 'Sinner! Remember the offenses you have committed before God.' "

Ignatius now tells two other instances of his experience in the face of death which occurred years later. And then resumes his story in regular order.

"When winter came he fell seriously ill and to cure him the city put him in the house of the father of a certain Ferrera who has since become servant of Baltasar de Faria and there he was very well cared for. And because of the interest which many of the chief ladies took in him, they came to act as nurses at night and when he recovered from this illness he was left very weak and with frequent pains in his stomach. And for these reasons and because the winter was very cold, they made him wear more clothes and put on shoes and cover his head and so they made him two robes of gray cloth very thick and a head covering of the same colour. And at that time there were many days when he was very anxious to talk about spiritual things and to find people who were capable of doing it. Meanwhile the time was drawing near when he had decided to start for Jerusalem."[13]

[13] Confessions.

CHAPTER IV

"And so at the beginning of the year 1523 he left Manresa for Barcelona to take ship. And though some companions offered themselves, he wished to go alone, because all his intent was to have God only as his refuge. And so one day, to some people who insisted strongly that, because he spoke neither Italian nor Latin, he had better take a companion, and saying how helpful a companion would be, he replied that, even if the son or brother of the Duke of Cardona wanted to go, he would not go in his company. Because he desired to cling to three virtues, charity, and faith and hope, and, if he had a companion, when he was hungry he would expect aid from him and when he fell down the companion would help him get up, and so he would trust in and love his companion and he wished to put all his trust and affection and hope in God alone. . . . And he desired to embark not only alone but without any provisions. And beginning to arrange for his passage, he persuaded the master of the ship to take him for nothing because he had no money, but on the condition that he brought some ship's bread: otherwise he would by no means let him come on board. And when he started to arrange for the ship's bread, he began to have great scruples, 'Is that the hope and faith you put in God,' etc. and he was much troubled and finally, not knowing what to do, . . . he determined to leave it to his confessor . . . The confessor told him to ask what was necessary and take it with him: and asking it of a lady, she asked him where he was going. He hesitated for awhile if

he should tell her and at last did not dare to say more than
that he was going to Italy and to Rome. And she, as if
smitten with astonishment, said, 'You want to go to
Rome?' Because of those who go there no one knows
how they return. (For she wished to say they gain little
profit at Rome in the things of the spirit). And the reason he did not dare to say he was going to Jerusalem was
for fear of vainglory; which fear beset him so much that
he never dared say where he came from nor what his
family was. At last, having gotten his ship's biscuit, he
embarked. But going down to the shore with five or six
small pieces of silver money in his pocket, which had been
given him at the doors of houses, for he lived by begging
from house to house, he left them on a bench near the
shore. And so he took ship after having spent a little over
twenty days in Barcelona. While he was in Barcelona, he
sought out, according to his habit, all spiritual persons,
even though they were in hermitages far from the city, in
order to talk with them. But neither in Barcelona nor in
Manresa during all the time he was there, could he find
persons who could help him as much as he desired: except
in Manresa that woman of whom he has spoken who
said she had asked God to let him see Christ. She alone
seemed to him to enter deeply into spiritual things. And
so after he had left Barcelona, he lost entirely that anxiety to seek out spiritual persons.

"They had so strong a following wind that they crossed
to Gaeta in five days and nights, though all the ship's
company were much afraid because it was tempestuous.
And in all that country they were afraid of the pestilence.
But when he disembarked he commenced to walk towards Rome. Of those who came in the ship, there joined
company with him a mother, with a daughter dressed as a
young man, and a little boy. They followed him; for they
also were begging their way. Arriving at a village, they
found a big fire and many soldiers around it, who gave

them food, and much wine inviting them in such a way
that it seemed they intended to warm them. Then
they separated them, the mother and daughter eating above in a room and the pilgrim and the boy in a
stable. But at midnight, he heard loud screams coming
from upstairs and rising he found the mother and daughter down in the courtyard weeping bitterly and com-
plaining that they had tried to do them violence. There
came to him with that an impulse so great that he commenced to cry out, 'Is this tolerable?' and similar complaints, which he uttered so effectively that all in the house
were afraid and no one did them any harm. The boy had
already run away and all three took up their journey in
the night. And arriving at a city which was near by, they
found the gates shut, and all three, wet through with the
rain, passed the night in a church. In the morning they
would not let them through the gates, and because they
could not ask alms outside, they went to a castle which
they could see near by. Meanwhile the pilgrim found
himself used up and, as he could not walk any farther, the
mother and daughter went on towards Rome. That day
there came out of the city much people, and knowing that
the lady of the place would come there, he presented himself before her, saying that his illness was only weariness
and beseeching her to let him enter to seek help. She
granted it easily, and beginning to beg, he got many pen-
nies and after he had recovered his strength there for two
days he continued his journey and got to Rome on Palm
Sunday.

"Everybody who talked to him at Rome, when they
knew that he had no money for the journey to Jerusalem,
commenced to persuade him not to go to the Holy Land,
affirming, with many particulars, that it was impossible to
find passage without money. But he had a great certainty
in his soul, so that he could not doubt that he would find a
way to go to Jerusalem. And having received the benedic-

tion of Pope Adrian the Sixth, he left eight or nine days
after Easter to walk to Venice.[1] He had six or seven gold
ducats which they had given him for the passage from
Venice to Jerusalem. And he had taken them, conquered
somewhat by the fears they had put into his heart that
he could not get across the sea without money. But two
days after he left Rome, he began to see clearly that this
had been a lack of confidence in God. So he was much
weighed down by the thought that he had taken the ducats
and he began to question whether it would not be better
to get rid of them. At last he determined to use them
freely on those he met who were poor. And he did it in
such a fashion that he arrived at Venice with no more
than a few small coins which he needed for that night.

"During all that road to Venice on account of the guards
against the plague, he slept in doorways and porticos. . . .
Once when he was all alone just at dusk in a great plain,
Christ appeared to him in the way he was accustomed to
appear, as we have said above, and comforted him much.
. . . When he arrived at Venice the guards came to the
boat to examine the passengers one by one, but they stopped before they came to him. He sustained life in Venice
by begging and he slept in the square of St. Mark, but he
never wanted to go to the house of the Ambassador of the
Emperor;[2] nor took any special pains to get money for
his voyage, and he had great confidence in his soul that
God would show him a way to go to Jerusalem and that
strengthened him so much that no reasons and fears suggested to him could make him doubt. One day he ran
across a rich Spaniard who asked him what he was doing
and where he wanted to go, and, learning his intention, the
Spaniard took him to dinner at his house and looked after
him until the time came to sail. The pilgrim was accustomed since he was in Manresa, when he dined with other

[1] 375 miles away.   [2] Also King of Spain.

people, never to talk much at table except to answer briefly, but to listen to what was said and so to find some thing which gave him an opening to speak of God and when the meal was over he did it. And that was the reason why the good man with all his family became so much attached to him that they wanted him to stay with them and his host also took him to the Doge: that is to say, he got entrance and audience for him. The Doge when he had heard the pilgrim, gave orders to give him a passage in the government ship for Cyprus.

"Although many pilgrims to Jerusalem had come that year, the greater part of them had gone home because of the new situation caused by the capture of Rhodes.[3] However, there were thirteen pilgrims in the ship which sailed first, and eight or nine were left for the ship of the governors. When this was about to start, the pilgrim was attacked by a high fever which, after he had been extremely ill for some days, left him the day the ship sailed. The people of the house asked the doctor if he could embark for Jerusalem and the doctor said he could embark to be buried, but he took ship and started that very day because he found himself very easy and commencing to get well. In that ship were committed openly certain obscene and filthy deeds which he reproved with severity. The Spaniards who were of the pilgrimage advised him not to do this, because the sailors were talking of leaving him on an island. But it pleased our Lord that they arrived quickly at Cyprus from whence they went by land to another port called Las Salinas, which was ten leagues away. There they went on board the pilgrim ship, on which, however, he embarked nothing for his sustenance except the hope he placed in God, as he had done in the other ship. During all this time Our Lord appeared to him very often, which gave him great consolation and

[3] Taken by the Turks, 1522.

force: generally it seemed to him he saw a large round thing as it were made of gold and that presented itself to him. After leaving Cyprus they reached Jaffa, and, taking up their journey to Jerusalem on donkeys as was the custom, two miles before they would arrive at Jerusalem, a Spaniard, apparently a nobleman, by name Diego Manes, with much feeling, said to all the pilgrims that in a short time they would arrive where they could see the holy city and that it would be well for all to make preparation in their conscience and to do it in silence. And this seeming good to all, each began to collect his thoughts and, a little before arriving at the place where the city is seen, they dismounted because they saw the friars with the cross who were waiting for them. And at sight of the city the pilgrims received great consolation and judging by what the others said it was universal in all, with a joy which seemed supernatural and he has always felt the same feeling in visiting holy places.

"His firm intention was to stay in Jerusalem visiting always the sacred places and also he intended, besides these acts of devotion, to help souls: and for this reason he carried letters of recommendation to the guardian which he presented, and told the guardian his intention of remaining there for acts of devotion, but not the second part of his intent—to be of service to souls; because that he told no one, but about the first he had often talked. The guardian answered that he did not see how his staying could be arranged because the house was in such necessity that it could not provide for its own friars and he had determined for that reason to send some back with the pilgrims. And the pilgrim answered that he would ask for nothing from the house except that sometimes they would hear his confession. And with that the guardian said it could be arranged that way, but he must wait until the provincial came (I believe he was the head of the Order in that country). He was at Bethlehem. With this promise

the pilgrim felt secure and began to write letters to spiritual persons in Barcelona. When one was written and he
was writing the other, the eve of the departure of the pilgrim company, they came to summon him in the name of
the guardian and the provincial who had gotten back. And
the provincial said to him in a very kind way that he knew
of his good intention to stay among those sacred places
and he had carefully thought about the affair and out of
his experience he had concluded that it was not best. Because many had shared that desire and some of them had
been taken by bandits and some killed and the Order was
obliged to ransom the captives. And, for all those reasons, it seemed that he must be ready to go the next day.
He answered that he was very fixed in his intention and
decided not to fail to carry it out for anything; making
it plain that he would still do it in spite of the provincial's
disapproval and any fear that was suggested: unless it
became sinful to stay. To that the provincial answered
they had authority from the Pope to send people away
or let them remain according to their judgment and to shut
out from communion those who would not obey and that
in this case their judgment was that he ought not to stay,
etc.

"And when they wanted to show the papal bulls giving them authority to excommunicate, he said it was not
necessary to see them, that he believed their reverences,
and since they had so decided with the authority they had,
he would obey. And when this was settled, there came
to him a great desire to go back to visit the Mount of
Olives before he left; since it was the will of Our Lord
that he should not stay among those holy places. In the
Mount of Olives there is a stone from which Our Lord
went up to heaven and one can see now the footprints
left in the stone. And that was what he wanted to go
back to see. And so, without saying anything or taking
a guide (those who go without a Turk as a guide run great

danger) he cleverly got rid of the others and went alone
to the Mount of Olives. And the guards would not let
him go in. He gave them a little knife from his writing
case and after praying with much consolation there came
to him the desire to go to Bethpage and when he arrived
there he remembered that he had not well examined on
the Mount of Olives on which side the imprint of the right
foot was and on which side the left foot, and going back
he believes he gave his scissors to the guards to let him
go in. When they knew in the monastery that he had left
without a guide the friars hastened to find him, and as he
was coming down the Mount of Olives he met a Christian
convert who worked in the monastery, who, with every
sign of great anger, made motions as if he were about to
give it to him with a big stick, and coming up he grab-
bed him by the arm: but he went along easily. Going
that road thus along side of the Christian convert, he received from Our Lord great consolation, for it seemed that
he saw Christ all the way in the air above him. And that
lasted until he arrived at the monastery.

"They left the next day and arrived at Cyprus, where
the pilgrims were separated among different ships. There
were in port three or four ships for Venice: one was Turkish, another was very small and a third was a heavily
laden ship belonging to a rich Venetian. Some of the pilgrims begged the captain of this ship to take the pilgrim,
but the captain, when he learned the pilgrim had no
money, was not willing, in spite of all their asking and
praising him, etc. And the captain answered that if he
was a saint, he might cross as Santiago crossed and that
sort of reply. The same petitioners got permission very
easily from the captain of the little ship. They left with
a prosperous wind during the morning and ran into a great
storm at evening, which scattered the ships and the big
ship was lost near Cyprus and only the people saved, and
the Turkish ship was lost with all on board in that storm.

The little ship had a hard struggle, but finally reached a harbour in Apulia. And that was in the midst of winter, very cold and snowy, and the pilgrim had no other clothes but breeches of coarse cloth down to the knees, leaving his legs bare, and shoes and a jacket of black cloth much torn at the shoulders and a short cloak of cloth worn very thin. He arrived at Venice in the middle of January of the year 1524, having been at sea after leaving Cyprus all the months of November and December and half of January. At Venice he found one of the two friends who had given him lodging before he started for Jerusalem, who gave him alms: fifteen silver julios and a piece of cloth which he doubled many times and wore over his stomach because of the great cold.

"Since the said pilgrim had learned that it was not the will of God for him to stay in Jerusalem, he was always thinking what he ought to do and, in the end, he inclined on the whole to study some time in order to be able to help souls and he decided to go to Barcelona and so left Venice for Genoa. And one day when in the chief church of Ferrara for his devotions, a poor man asked alms and he gave him a marquete, a piece of money worth five or six quatrini. And after the first beggar came another, and he gave him a piece of money a little larger. And when the third came, the pilgrim had no coins but his silver julios, so he gave him one. And when the poor saw that he was giving alms they did nothing else but come, and so he finished all the money he had and finally a whole crowd of poor came together to ask alms. He answered that they must excuse him for he had nothing more.

"And so he left Ferrara for Genoa. On the road he fell in with some Spanish soldiers who treated him well that night and they expressed astonishment at his taking that road because it would lead him through the middle of both armies, French and Imperial, and they asked him to leave the high road and to follow another safe road they would

show him. But he did not take their advice,[4] but going
along the direct road he came across a village burnt and
destroyed and so he found no one all day who could give
him something to eat. But at sunset he arrived at an enclosed village and the guards seized him, thinking he was a
spy, and taking him to a little house near the gate, they
commenced to examine him as they are wont to do with
suspected persons: and he answered to all questions that
he knew nothing. And they stripped and searched him
down to his shoes to see if he carried any letter. And
when they were unable to learn anything from him in
any way, they ordered him to come to the captain who
would make him talk. And when he asked for his clothes
they were not willing to give them back and took him as
he was with only the breeches and jacket mentioned above.
And the pilgrim looked on that as an image of the way
in which they took Christ; although this was not a vision
like the others. And they led him through three long
streets and he went with no sadness but rather with contentment and joy. It was his custom to address everybody without distinction with 'thou' as an act of pious devotion, because Christ and the apostles talked thus, etc.
While on his way through those streets it came into his
mind that it would be well to address the captain as 'Señor'
and the thought was accompanied by some fears of the torture they might put him to, etc. But when he recognized
that it was a temptation, 'since it is so', he said to himself,
'I will not call him Señor nor bow to him, neither will I
take off my hat.'

"They came to the house of the captain and left him in
a room below and after a while the captain talked with
him. And he, without showing any sign of courtesy, answered in a few words and very slowly. And the captain took him for a crazy man and said to those who had
brought him, 'This man has no sense. Give him what be-

[4] Evidently because he thought it would be a sign of lack of trust in God.

longs to him and put him out.' On leaving the house immediately he found a Spaniard, who lived there, who took him to his house and gave him wherewith to break his fast and what he needed for the night And leaving in the morning, he walked until evening, when two soldiers in a tower saw him and came down to stop him. And when they had taken him to their captain, who was a Frenchman, the captain asked him among other things where he came from. And on hearing he was from Guipúzcoa said, 'I come from near there, for it seems it is near Bayonne': and then he said, 'take him and give him supper and treat him well.' On that road from Ferrara to Genoa nothing else happened of importance and finally he came to Genoa, where he recognized a Biscayan called Portundo who had talked with him when he served in the court of the Catholic King. This man let him embark in a ship which was sailing to Barcelona in which he ran great danger of being taken prisoner by Andrea Doria, who gave chase to the ship. Doria was then a partisan of the French.

"Arrived at Barcelona, he talked of his wish to study to Isabel Roser and with a teacher by the name of Ardébalo who taught grammar. Both thoroughly approved and he offered to teach him for nothing, while she promised to give him enough to live on. The pilgrim knew in Manresa a friar, if I remember right, of St. Bernard, a very spiritual man, and he wanted to go and stay with him in order to study and to be able to give himself more easily to spiritual things and also to help souls. And so he answered Isabel Roser and Ardébalo that he would accept their offer if he did not find in Manresa the advantages he hoped to find. But when he went there he found the friar was dead and, returning to Barcelona, he commenced to study with great diligence.

"But one thing was a great hindrance to his progress. Whenever he commenced to commit to memory, as it is

necessary to do in beginning the study of grammar, there
came to him new understanding of spiritual things and
new delight in them, so that he could not commit anything
to memory nor drive away these importunate thoughts because he was so reluctant to do so.   And thinking this over
many times, he said to himself; 'when I am praying and
when I am hearing mass these vivid understandings do not
come to my mind' and so little by little he recognized that
this experience was a temptation.   And after having
prayed he went to the church of Holy Mary of the Sea
near the master's house, having asked the master to be
good enough to listen a little in that church to what he
had to say.   And so, both being seated, he explained
frankly to the master all that had happened in his soul
and how little, for that reason, he had yet gained.   He gave
a solemn promise to the master saying 'I promise you
never to fail to listen to you for two years if I can find in
Barcelona bread and water to sustain life.'   And after he
had made that promise he was never troubled any more
by those temptations.   The pain in his stomach which had
before attacked him in Manresa, because of which he had
ceased to go bare-footed, had left him and he had no trouble with his stomach after he started for Jerusalem.   And
for that reason now that he was studying in Barcelona, he
wanted to go back to his old penances and so he commenced to cut holes in the soles of his shoes.   He went
on widening the holes little by little in such a way that
when the cold of winter came he was wearing only the
uppers.

"When two years of study were finished in which they
said he had made great progress, the master told him he
was ready to begin the study of the liberal arts and that
he should go to the University of Alcalá.   However, he had
himself examined by a doctor of theology who gave him
the same advice, and so he parted for Alcalá alone, although, if I remember rightly, he had already some com-

rades. Arrived at Alcalá he began to beg and to live by alms. And after he had been living thus for ten or twelve days, a clergyman and others who were standing with him in a group began to laugh and to give him some insults as is the custom to do to able bodied people who beg. And just at that moment the superintendent in charge of the new hospital of Taraçana happened to pass and seeming to be sorry for Ignatius, called him and took him to the hospital; in which he gave him a room and all that was necessary.

"He studied in Alcalá about a year and a half and since he had arrived in lent of the year 1524 at Barcelona, where he studied two years, the year 1526 he arrived at Alcalá and studied dialectics in Soto, physics in Albertus and theology in the Master of the Sentences. And while he was at Alcalá he gave spiritual exercises and explained Christian doctrine and from this he gathered fruit for God. And there were many persons who grew in understanding of spiritual things and in liking for them. And others underwent various temptations, for example, one woman who, wishing to inflict discipline on herself by scourging could not do it because her hand was, at it were, held by force; and other similar things. These· things aroused notice in the city, especially, because of the large assembly which gathered whenever he wished to explain Christion doctrine. Immediately on arriving at Alcalá he made the acquaintance of Don Diego de Equia, who lived in the house of his brother, who had a printing press in Alcalá, and they did not suffer him to want for anything. And also they helped him by their alms to maintain poor people and kept three companions of the pilgrim also in their house. Once coming to ask alms for some people in need, Don Diego said he had no money; but he opened a chest in which were various things and gave him bed spreads of various colours, candelabra, and other things of the sort; all of which, wrapped in a piece of linen, the

pilgrim put on his shoulder and went to sell them to help
the poor.

"As has been said above, there was much talk in that
country about what was happening in Alcalá and some
said one thing, others another. And the matter came to
the ears of the Inquisition at Toledo, who came to Alcalá.
The pilgrim was informed by his host, who told him that
they were 'Alumbrados,'[5] and that the Inquisition was
commissioned to inflict capital punishment. And so they
began to make inquiry and Inquiry into his life and
finally they went back to Toledo and left the process in the hands of the Vicar Figueroa, who is now with
the Emperor. Some days later he called them and said
he had made inquest for the Inquisition into their life, and
had found no error in their teaching or morals, and, so far
as that was concerned, they might continue to do what
they were doing without any hindrance. But, as they
were not members of a monastic order, it did not seem to
him advisable for them to go around all dressed in the
same way. It would be well, and he so ordered, for the
pilgrim and Arteaga to wear black clothes and for the
other two, Calixto and Cáceres, to wear tawny and Juanico, who was a French lad, could remain as he was. The
pilgrim said he would do what he was ordered, but he said,
'I don't know what good these Inquisitors are, because the
sacrament was refused the other day to so and so because
he communicated every eight days and they made difficulty about giving it to me. We would like to know
whether they have found any heresy in us.' 'No,' said
Figueroa, 'if they had found any they would have burnt
you.' 'Yes,' said the pilgrim, 'and they would burn you too
if they found heresy in you.' They dyed their garments as
they had been ordered and, fifteen or twenty days later,
Figueroa sent word to the pilgrim not to go barefoot but to

[5] Heretics who claimed special light from the Holy Ghost.

wear shoes, and he did it quietly as he did everything of the sort he was ordered to do.

"Four months later the same Figueroa began again inquiry about them. And beyond the usual causes I believe it was occasioned by the fact that a lady, married and of high rank, who had a special reverence for the pilgrim, in order not to be seen, came in the morning to the hospital veiled, as is the custom in Alcalá, and when she was in the hospital took off her veil and went to the room of the pilgrim. But the inquisitors did nothing this time nor after the inquiry did they summon him or say anything to him.

"Four months from that time when he was in a little house outside the hospital, a constable came to his door and said, 'Come along with me a bit.' And leaving him in the jail the constable said, 'You do not go out from here until further orders.' That was in the summertime and he was not strictly kept and many came to visit him. And among them was his confessor, and he had the same chance as when he was free to teach doctrine and give spiritual exercises. He was never willing to take an advocate, although many were offered. He remembers especially Doña Teresa de Cárdenas, who sent to visit him and many times offered to get him out of prison. But he accepted nothing, saying always; 'He for love of whom I came in here will take me out, if it seems best to Him.' He remained in prison seventeen days without examination and without knowing the reason for his arrest. At the end of that time, Figueroa came to the jail and examined him about many things; even to asking him if he kept the sabbath, and he asked if he knew two women, mother and daughter, and he said 'yes,' and asked if he had known about their leaving before they left, he said, 'No, under his oath.' And then the vicar, putting his hand on his shoulder with signs of joy, said to him, 'That was the reason why you are come here.'

Among the many people who were following the pilgrim, there were a mother and daughter, both widows, and the daughter very young and very beautiful, who were much interested in spiritual things; especially the daughter. So much so that, although noble women, they had started for the shrine of Saint Veronica at Jaén on foot, without attendants, and I don't know whether begging their way or not. And this made a great stir in Alcalá, and Doctor Ciruelo, who was their guardian, thought the prisoner had induced them to go and for that he had been made a prisoner. Then when the prisoner heard what the vicar had said, he said to him, 'Do you want me to talk more fully about this affair?' The vicar said 'Yes.' Then you must know,' said the prisoner, 'that these two women urged upon me many times that they wanted to go all through the world to care for the poor; now in one hospital and now in another. And I always dissuaded them from this intention because the daughter was so young and beautiful and I said to them that, if they wanted to visit the poor, they could do it in Alcalá and go with the most holy sacrament when it was carried to the sick.' And when the conversation was finished, Figueroa went away with the notary who had taken it all down in writing.

"At that time Calixto was in Segovia, and when he heard of the imprisonment of the pilgrim, although he was just recovering from a severe illness, he came to join him in jail. But the pilgrim said it would be better to go and see the vicar, who treated him well and said he would send him to the jail because it was necessary for him to remain there until those women came back to see if they confirmed what had been said. Calixto was in the jail some days, but the pilgrim, seeing that confinement was bad for his health because he was not yet entirely well, got him released by the help of a doctor who was a great friend. From the day he entered the jail until they released him forty two days passed; at the end of which the two devotees having returned, the notary came to the jail to read the sentence that he was free and that they should dress like the other students and that they should not talk about things of the faith for four years,[6] when they should have studied more; because they did not know the liberal arts; because of a truth the pilgrim knew most and his knowledge was not well-grounded and that was the first thing he said when he was examined.

"He was left a little in doubt after this sentence what he should do, because it seemed as if they had closed the door to helping souls and that without giving him any reason except that he had not studied. And at last he determined to go to the Archbishop of Toledo, Fonseca, and put the thing into his hands. He left Alcalá and found the archbishop in Valladolid, and, recounting frankly what had happened, said to the archbishop that although he was not under his jurisdiction and not obliged to obey his sentence, nevertheless he would do what he ordered (he addressed the archbishop as *thou*, as he was accustomed to do to all). The archbishop received him very well and, understanding that the pilgrim wanted to go to Salamanca, said that in Salamanca he had friends and a college. He offered to do everything and ordered four pieces of gold to be given to him."[7]

[6] This is a mistake. The sentence reads three years. Scripta p. 621.
[7] Confessions.

CHAPTER V

AT THE SPANISH UNIVERSITIES AND IN THE HANDS
OF THE INQUISITION

Up to this point in the life of Ignatius Loyola it has
seemed best to let him tell his own story, not only because
of fear of marring his naïve recital, but also because we
have no other important information about what happened to him during this crisis of his life. That he himself knew this was the crisis of his life is shown by the fact
that he devoted more than half his confessions to the
three years which passed between his wound at Pamplona and his beginning to study at Barcelona, and
crowded fourteen years into the rest of it.

From the time of his return to Barcelona as a student
after his pilgrimage to Jerusalem, we begin to get pieces
of important and trustworthy information from other
sources, and it seems wise to combine these into a narrative with citations and paraphrases from his Confessions. There are indeed two documents which throw some
small light on his pilgrimage to Jerusalem. These are
the accounts of the journey given by Peter Füssli of
Zurich and Philipps von Hagen of Strassbourg; two of
the twenty-one pilgrims of five different nationalities who
went to Palestine when Loyola went. Their accounts
give many picturesque details of pilgrim experience, but do
not mention Loyola. He spoke no language but Spanish
and Basque, and they could therefore have no intercourse with him. Nor could these German burgher
patricians, men of the ordinary type of piety who loved
the sights of Venice, a chance to see more of the world,

and a good glass of wine, have any particular sympathy
for one absolutely absorbed as Ignatius was in the things
of the soul and therefore scornful of the pleasures of this
life. He saw the wonders of God, to use the phrase of
Kant, in the starry heavens above him and the moral
world within him; beyond that he saw only his fellow-men and the great battle going on between God and
the devil. When the disciples came to show Christ the
buildings of the temple, he saw no architectural splendour
but only the judgment of God on sin and he said, "See
ye not all these things? Verily I say unto you, there shall
not be left here one stone upon another." The visions
God showed continually to the "inner eyes"[1] of Ignatius,
filled him with an ecstasy which paled the glories of Rome
and Venice until he did not see them.

The arrival of Ignatius at Venice on his way back to
Jerusalem marks a stage in the development of his soul
related in his Confessions. His conversion began with the
wish to rival the saints in self-denial and in penance for
his sins. Then he wished to practice these austerities to
please God. His ideal in all this was a solitary one and
the Christian life seemed to him to lie entirely between
himself and God. Whether he should enter a very strict
monastery or wander about the world as a mendicant,
human companionship did not at first appeal to him. He
was never disappointed in God when he sought help from
Him, but he was much disappointed with what he got from
people supposedly very wise and holy and he finally
ceased to consult them. He refused to accept a companion for his pilgrimage.

On the contrary, before he left Manresa, people had
begun to come to him for help and in giving it he evidently found strength and comfort. Reflecting on this
during the long journey to Jerusalem, he formed the
secret purpose of devoting his life to helping souls in

[1] His own phrase. Confessions, p. 54.

Jerusalem; as we should say of being a missionary to the Mahommedans. When that door was closed he decided during the voyage back to Venice to devote his life to trying to spread to others the joy and peace in his own soul. To do this, he realized that he needed more knowledge and the beginning of getting knowledge in those days was the ability to understand Latin; for none but the most elementary instruction was anywhere given in any other language. We see, therefore, the penitent and mystic suddenly turning into a student, and, although over thirty years old, poring over his Latin grammar with children. This man who once let his hair and nails grow wild like a hermit, was not only caring for them in order to be less impeded in helping his fellows, but he had changed his hermit's heart and now eagerly sought not only persons whom he might help in religion, but companions who might aid him in Christian life and work.

Of these last he found in the two years of his stay in Barcelona three: Calixtus de Sa and Lope de Cáceres, both from Segovia, and Juan de Arteaga. To them there joined himself in Alcalà a young Frenchman, Juan Reinalde, a wounded page of the Viceroy of Navarre, found by Ignatius in the hospital. Ignatius found during these school days in Barcelona not only comrades but also pupils who wished to learn the things God had taught him: some eight or ten ladies, wealthy and of high social position.

When he went to the University of Alcalá, his three friends followed him, and all began to wear very simple clothes: a long narrow robe of coarse gray cloth and a gray cap. Ignatius went barefooted. In the intervals of their studies they began to gather around them followers who wished their help. These were mainly women, as in Barcelona. But, unlike the learners of Barcelona, they were mainly from the poorer, many from the poorest, classes of the people. We have already heard from the lips of Ignatius himself how this brought him and his companions under the suspicion of heresy. We know more about these three inquiries at Alcalá than Ignatius did, because we have what he was never allowed to see, the depositions of the witnesses examined. In all the depositions some thirty people are named as among the visitors or disciples of Ignatius and his friends, and, in addition, one of the deponents said, "Some students came to the hospital asking for Loyola," and another, after mentioning a number of names added, "and other women and girls came." All those who regularly engaged in spiritual exercises under Loyola and his comrades at Alcalá were women and women of the humbler classes, wives of a baker, a saddler, a wine-seller, a weaver, etc. Their depositions suggest very simple and even ignorant people. The more intelligent depositions show that he "taught them the commandments and the articles of the faith, and explained the mortal sins and the use of the five senses and the powers of the soul in religious experience and other good thoughts about the service of God. He taught these very well and explained them by St. Paul and the other saints and bade them examine their consciences twice every day and confess and take communion at the beginning of every week." [2] He warned them that in the service of God they must meet temptations of the enemy and showed them how to examine their conscience beginning on their knees with this prayer: "My God, my Father, my creator, thanks and praise I give Thee for the great gifts Thou has given me, and I hope will give me. I pray Thee by the merits of thy passion, grant me the grace to examine my conscience well." [3]

On the third inquest, after Loyola and his companions had been in Alcalá about nine months, some new facts were brought out before the vicar in regard to the effects of their teaching on many of their followers. Some of

[2] Scripta p. 609.　　　　[3] Scripta p. 612.

these women, while listening to Ignatius, fell suddenly from joy into deep depression of spirits and then into fainting fits, where they either lost consciousness or fell down and rolled upon the ground in convulsions mixed with nausea. The vicar, when he went to see Ignatius in the episcopal jail, asked him not only about the noble ladies who had gone on pilgrimage, but about these seizures of his penitents. The vicar has recorded that Loyola said he had seen these fainting fits in five or six women and he suggested that "the cause of them is that, because of the amelioration of their lives and the giving up of their sins, they are attacked by great temptations, now from the devil, now from their kin and that these cause the fainting fits because of the repugnance they feel within themselves. He had consoled them, bidding them stand firm in these temptations and torments and saying that if they did, within two months they would not feel any of these temptations. He said this because in the matter of temptations it seemed to him that he knew about it from his own personal experience; though he had never had these fainting fits."[4]

Such results of religious stimulation are of course in no sense peculiar to Loyola and his disciples. If we pass over more than three hundred years to the middle of the eighteenth century, we find similar effects from the preaching of a man who was the very opposite in every respect to Loyola—John Wesley. He records in his journal a number of instances of such results of his own ministrations and those of his followers; only the nervous reactions were more violent and more widespread because the audiences were larger.

Here is a written account from an eye witness of one of these scenes.[5] "I believe there were present three times more men than women. The greatest number of those who cried or fell down were men, but some women.

[4] Scripta, I, 619.   [5] Journal IV 318.

. . . I stood up on a pew seat, as did a young able bodied,
fresh, healthy country man. But in a moment when he
seemed to think of nothing less, down he dropped with
a violence inconceivable. I heard afterwards the stamp-
ing of his feet ready to break the boards as he lay in
strong convulsions at the bottom of the pew. Among
several that were struck down in the next pew was a man
who was as violently seized as he. . . . Almost all in
whom God laid his hand turned very red or almost
black."[6]

Many of Wesley's friends disliked these things very
much and wrote to him protesting about them, but he held
they were of God, and in one meeting led his followers
in praying "for forgiveness for blaspheming God's work
among us, imputing it either to nature, the force of imagination and animal spirits or even to the delusions of
the devil." In one case at least he did not attribute these
physical reactions to religious ideas to the power of God
convicting of sin. He agreed with Loyola in attributing
them to the efforts of the devil to maintain his hold over
the soul. He was preaching in a crowded chapel and
"a vehement noise arose, none could tell why, and shot
like lightning through the congregation. The people
rushed upon each other with the utmost violence. The
benches were broken in pieces. In about six minutes, all
being calm, I went on with my preaching. . . . None can
account for it without supposing some preternatural influence. Satan fought that his kingdom should not be
taken away from him."[7]

It is noticeable that these faintings on the part of the
women at Alcalá are the only instances of such violent
convulsive nervous reactions to preaching, recorded in
the ministrations of Loyola or of the Jesuit missioners
who during his life incorporated his spirit and followed
his instructions. (6) It seems as if we might divine

[6] Everton, 1759.   [7] Tyerman III 531.

here another of the many instances in which Ignatius learned by experience what to do and what not to do in the care of souls.

One physical reaction indeed, the Jesuit preachers who were the voices of Ignatius did produce very frequently. His missioners who fifteen years or so after this, stirred profoundly Venice, Parma, Florence, Palermo, Messina, Oporto, Salamanca, Saragossa, Valladolid, Valencia, Madrid and scores of smaller places, very often moved their hearers to tears and mention it in their reports as a normal result of preaching which was blessed of God.[8] When towards the end of the life of Ignatius, his missioners began to preach in Germany, they were quick to note the temperamental difference of their new audiences as compared with the thousands who crowded to hear them in Italy, Spain and Portugal. "The first preachers sent to the Viennese College of the Order used the tones of voice they had been wont to use in Italy. Later they wrote to Rome that these tones were not acceptable in Germany because that people like the preacher to preach quietly without great changes of voice and gesture."[9]

When Ignatius withdrew from the University of Alcalá, to follow his comrades to the University of Salamanca, the little band had put away one of the things which gave offense to public opinion: the wearing of a common dress which suggested that they were members of a monastic order. We know from other sources that there was a great deal of feeling among orthodox people about correct monastic costume. In one of the colloquies of Erasmus, published about this time, we find the following passage. "The Butcher. If anybody sees a Carthusian in a dress not of the order . . . how he trembles and falls into a fright lest the earth should open and swallow them both up, one for wearing, the other for looking, at the

---

[8] Pol. Passim. [9] Pol. III 279.

wrong dress. The Fishmonger. So if any one sees a
Franciscan with a girdle without knots, or an Augustinian
girt with a woolen one instead of a leather one, or a Car-
melite without one, or a Rhodian with one, or a Franciscan
with whole shoes on his feet, or a Cruciferian with half
shoes on: will he not set the whole town in an uproar?"[10]

This cause of suspicion and scandal had now been removed with the help of the episcopal vicar, for Loyola
tells us "When they gave sentence in Alcalá that they
must be dressed like students the pilgrim said: 'When
you bade us dye our clothing we did it, but now we cannot do what you bid us because we have not the where-
withal to buy.' And so the vicar himself provided them
with garments and hats and the rest of a student's costume and they left Alcalá dressed in that manner."[11]

As he had passed beyond the jurisdiction of the bishop's
court, Ignatius intended to begin again "to help souls."
But he had no chance to carry out the intention, to forget
the bishop's advice. Although he had changed his dress
and his residence, he had not changed the atmosphere of
suspicion around him and soon after his arrival at his
new university he met a persecution much more hostile
and deadly than that of Alcalá.

There was at Salamanca a convent of Dominicans.
Many of the Dominicans were always ready to give warning against heresy, and inclined to be proud of the popular pun on their name which made them Domini Canes,
dogs of the Lord. It may be suspected that they had
perhaps a little feeling that they would show the right
way of handling heretics to the blundering inquisitors of
the secular clergy in the vicar's court at Alcalá, who had
let these dangerous people off so easily. So they laid a
snare for Ignatius in which, if he had been as much of a
heretic or as much of a simpleton as they thought, his
small knowledge of technical theology might have fatally

[10] Icthyophagia. Bailey's Trans. II, 291.   [11] Confessions.

entangled him. His native boldness, simplicity and shrewd knowledge of men, saved him from the dungeons of the Inquisition. These were then in Spain easy to get into and their hinges were stiff in turning outward. All we know of this affair comes from him, so we will let him tell the story in his own words:

"He made his confession in Salamanca to a friar of St. Dominic and, ten or twelve days after his arrival, his confessor said, 'The fathers of the house want to talk with you,' and he said, 'In the name of God.' 'Then,' said the confessor, 'it will be well for you to come there to dinner Sunday, but I must tell you they want to know from you many things.' And so on Sunday he went with Calixto and after dinner the subprior, in the absence of the prior, with the confessor, and, if I remember rightly, with another friar, went with them into a chapel and the subprior with great affability began to say what good news he had of their life and habits, that they were preaching like the apostles and that he would be glad to know these things more particularly. And so he began to ask what they had studied. And the pilgrim replied, 'I am the one amongst us who has studied the most,' and he gave a plain account of the little he had studied and how small a foundation of general learning was beneath it. 'Well, then, what do you preach?' 'We do not preach,' said the pilgrim. 'We talk familiarly with some people about the things of God, as, for instance, at dinner with people who invite us.' 'But,' said the friar, 'about what things of God do you talk? That is what we want to know.' 'We talk,' said the pilgrim, 'now of one virtue and again of another, praising them, and now of one vice and again of another, blaming them.' 'You are not educated men,' said the friar, 'and yet you talk of virtues and of vices and nobody can talk on this subject except in one of two ways, either by education or by the Holy Spirit. You do not talk by education, therefore you do it by the Holy Spirit,

and we want to know what you get from the Holy Spirit?'
Just at this point the pilgrim ceased to reply, that way
of arguing not seeming to him very good, and, after keeping silence for awhile, he said it was not necessary to
talk any more about the subject. When the friar, insist-
ing, said 'Nowadays when there are so many errors of
Erasmus and of many others in the air which have led
astray the world, are you not willing to declare what you
say?' The pilgrim replied, 'Father, I will not say more
than I have said, except before my superiors who have the
right to demand it of me.'

"Before that, the friar had asked why Calixto came
dressed as he was. He wore a short loose coat and a big
sombrero on his head and a staff in his hand and boots
halfway up his legs and, because he was very big, he
looked very clumsy. The pilgrim told how they had been
arrested in Alcalá and ordered to dress like students and
his comrade because it was very warm weather had given
his mantle to a poor clergyman. Here the friar mut-
tered between his teeth, giving signs that he was not
pleased. 'Charity begins at home.' The subprior not
being able to get another word out of the pilgrim, said,
'Well, then, you stay here and we'll make you talk about
everything.' And so all the friars hurried away. At
first, when the pilgrim asked if they wanted them to stay
in the chapel or where they wanted them to stay, the subprior answered that they should stay in the chapel. Then
the friars had all the gates closed and sent word, as it
seems, to the judges. However, the two remained in the
monastery three days without any one from the courts
of justice speaking to them. They ate in the refectory
with the friars. And nearly always their room was filled
with friars who came to visit them and the pilgrim talked
always as he was wont to talk, so that there was a sort
of division among them and there were many who favoured
the prisoners.

"At the end of three days a notary came and took them to jail. And they did not put them with the criminals below, but in a room higher up where, because the room was old and unused, there was much dirt. And they fastened both with the same chain, each by a foot, and the chain was fastened to a post in the middle of the house. And all that night they kept vigil. The next day, when it was known in the city that they were in prison, something to sleep on was sent to them and necessary food in abundance. And many came to visit them, and the pilgrim continued his spiritual exercises by talking of God, etc. The bachelor of Theology, Frias, came to examine them each separately and the pilgrim gave him all his manuscripts, which were "The Exercises," to examine. And when the bachelor asked the pilgrim if he had companions, the pilgrim said yes, and they were at Salamanca and then men went by the order of the bachelor and brought to the jail Cáceres and Arteaga, but they left Juanico, who afterwards became a friar. But they did not put them on the upper floor with the two, but below where the ordinary prisoners were. In this situation also the pilgrim was not willing to have an advocate to defend them.

"And some days afterwards he was called before the judges, four in number, the three doctors Sanctisidoro, Paravinhas and Frias and the Bachelor Frias, all of whom had seen 'The Exercises.' And they asked him many things; not only about The Exercises, but about theology, about the Trinity and the sacrament, how he understood those articles of the faith. And, ordered by the judges, he made his first response and he spoke in such a way that they found nothing to blame in him. The Bachelor Frias who showed himself more zealous in the matter than the others, put to him a case of canon law and he was obliged to reply to all asked, saying always first that he did not know what the authorities said about these things. Then they ordered him to explain the first commandment in the way he was used to explain it. He set himself to do it and did it at such length and said so much that they had no desire to ask him any more. Before that, when they were talking of "The Exercises," the judges insisted a great deal on a single point which was at the beginning of The Exercises; to wit, when an evil thought is a venial sin and when it is a mortal sin. And the trouble was because, without being educated, he tried to define that difference. He answered, 'Make up youɪ minds whether it is true or not, and if it is not true condemn it.' At last they went away without condemning anything.

"Among the many people who came to the jail to talk to him there came once Don Francisco de Mendoça, who now is called Cardinal of Burgos, and he came with the Bachelor Frias. Asking him familiarly how he got on in prison and if he found it hard to be a prisoner, the pilgrim answered, 'I will answer as I answered today to a lady who uttered words of compassion on seeing me in prison; I said to her: 'You show that you have no wish to be put in prison for the love of God. Does prison then seem to you so terrible? I tell you there are not in Salamanca so many fetters and chains as I desire to bear for the love of God!' It happened at that time that the prisoners in the jail had a chance to escape and all fled; but the two comrades who were with them did not flee and when in the morning they were found with the doors unlocked, it gave great edification to all and made much talk in the city and so they immediately gave them for prison a house which stood near the jail.

"After they had been shut up twenty-two days, they were called to hear the sentence; which was that no error had been found in their doctrine and no evil in their life and so they could do as they had done, teaching doctrine and talking about the things of God without, however, defining at any time this is a mortal sin or that is a venial sin, until they had studied for four years more. When the sentence had been read the judges took a very friendly attitude as if they were very anxious to have it accepted. The pilgrim said he would do all the sentence commanded, but that he could not accept it because without condemning him in anything, they closed his lips so that he could not help his neighbours so far as he was able. And in spite of the insistence of Doctor Frias, who made a great show of friendliness, the pilgrim said nothing except that, so long as he was in the jurisdiction of Salamanca, he would do what he was ordered to do. Then they were taken out of prison and he began to put himself in the hands of God and to think what he ought to do. And he concluded it was very difficult to stay in Salamanca because it seemed that the door to helping souls was closed by that order forbidding him to distinguish between a venial sin and a mortal sin. And so he made up his mind to go to Paris to study."[12]

In spite of his experience in two prisons, Loyola "remained fixed in his desire to help souls and for that purpose first to study and then to add to his company some who shared this purpose besides keeping those comrades he had gained already. Determined to go to Paris, he arranged with his comrades to wait where they were while he went to Paris to see if he could find means for them to join him and study there."[13]

No one of them came to join him. The French lad Juanico became a monk, Calixto was sent by one of Loyola's noble patronesses to the court of Portugal to see if he could get one of the fellowships given for Paris by the King. He did not get it, and returning into Spain went twice to India, from whence he returned very rich to lead a life of luxury and display in Salamanca. Cáceres

[12] Confessions.   [13] Confessions.

went back to his native city of Segovia and lived in a way which did not suggest any serious religious purpose. Arteaga, twelve years after Loyola left him in Salamanca, was given a bishopric in the Indies and wrote to Loyola offering to give it to one of the Company of Jesus recently formed. Loyola refused, because he wished none of the Company to take church appointments. Arteaga therefore took the bishopric and died in his diocese.

This disappointment over his comrades was repeated at Paris, where soon after his arrival, he gained three other comrades, Spaniards, who for one reason or another did not continue with him. One finally became a Carthusian monk, another starting on a pilgrimage to Jerusalem was ordered to Spain by the Pope through family influence, and became a canon of Toledo. We do not know the fate of the third. Apparently up to the time of going to Paris Ignatius had not yet learned completely the art of binding men fast to common purpose under his leadership, in which he finally became such a master of souls.

CHAPTER VI

SEVEN YEARS AT PARIS AND THE COMRADES HE GAINED THERE

"Many leading citizens made a great effort to persuade him not to go, but they never could succeed in it and so fifteen or twenty days after he was set free, he started to walk to Barcelona driving before him a donkey on whose back he had tied the bundle of his books. At Barcelona all who knew him tried to dissuade him from going to France because of the danger of war." [1] They even told him, as he recalled years afterwards [2] that Frenchmen were putting Spaniards on spits to roast them. But he met none of these prophesied dangers on his solitary walk of about a month to Paris, and on the third of March wrote this letter to Agnes Pascual of Barcelona, "May the true peace of Jesus Christ our Lord visit and protect our souls.

"Considering the great good will and love which you have always had for me in God Our Lord, and which you have shown in deed, I have thought to write you this letter to let you know about my journey since I left you. With favourable weather and in entire health I arrived by the grace and goodness of God Our Lord, in this city of Paris the second of February; where I shall stay studying until the Lord orders me to do something else.

"I send my best remembrances to Juan and tell him always to obey his parents and keep the festivals of the

[1] Confessions. [2] Probably he smiled.

Church and he will live long upon the land and also in heaven.

"Give my best remembrances to your neighbour. May her good will and love through God Our Lord never leave me. May the Lord of the world repay her and may He always be in our souls through His infinite goodness in order that His will and wish may accomplish itself in us. From Paris March 3rd, 1528.

"Poor in goodness,

"Ignigo."

When he arrived at Paris, Ignatius had a bill of exchange on Barcelona for twenty-five escudos. This was enough to live simply for a year without the need of begging; which he had found at Barcelona and Alcalá was a great interruption to his studies. He cashed his bill of exchange and gave the money to another Spaniard at the inn where he stopped, to keep safe for him. The motive for this was probably the desire by confidence to win the confidence of the other Spaniard whom he evidently hoped to gain as a companion in his work.

There were forty-nine colleges in the University of Paris, of which three were frequented by Spaniards and Portuguese; Montaigu, Sainte Barbe, Coquerel. He inscribed for Montaigu. Why we do not know, for Ignatius devoted only half as much space in his Confessions to his seven years' experience at Paris as he devotes to half that time spent at Barcelona, Alcalá and Salamanca. He tells us that he studied in Montaigu the humanities, because he found that his two years' work at Barcelona had not given him a well-grounded knowledge of Latin.

Montaigu was an ancient college dating from the beginning of the fourteenth century. There were two sorts of students, *the poor* and *the rich*. *The poor* were an organized community of students for the priesthood who were supported by the College and what they could beg to supplement it. *The rich* were ordinary pensioners who paid their board and fees. The two sets of scholars were kept entirely apart. The discipline inflicted on *the poor* was terribly severe and their food reduced to the lowest terms. Erasmus had been a *poor* and he wrote, two years before Ignatius entered, a bitter account of what he had to undergo thirty-seven years before. "But what with hard beds, by bad and spare diet, late and hard studies, within one year's space, of many young men full of hope, some are killed, others are blinded, others are driven crazy. . . . Some of whom I know very well." Apparently this severity and asceticism extended from *the poor* to *the rich,* for Erasmus adds: "Neither did this cruelty only destroy mean persons but many gentlemen's sons too and spoiled many a hopeful genius. . . . In the very depth of winter a morsel of bread was given them for breakfast, and as for their drink, they must draw out of a well of bad water. I have known many that were brought to such a state of ill health that they have never got over it to this day. There were chambers on the ground floor in which none ever slept but he either got his death or some grievous distemper. I shall say nothing of the unmerciful whippings even of innocent persons. . . . Nor shall I take notice how many rotten eggs were eaten nor how much sour wine was drunk. Perhaps these things may be mended now, but 'tis too late for those that are dead already or carry about an infected body."[3]

This situation, harsh enough even with all allowance for the exaggeration of a chronic grumbler, was slightly amended when Loyola entered Montaigu, but the best modern authority says: "During all the sixteenth century life there remained terrible."[4]

Loyola learned (as he says himself) much at Paris and

[3] Erasmus, Colloquies, Bailey Trans. II, p. 304, 306. [4] Godet, VII.

probably he learned partly from what he saw at Montaigu, the tender paternal care for the health of all his spiritual children from the professed to the youngest novice, which was so marked in his later life.

He joined the college of Montaigu as an externe and continued to live at the lodging house or inn where he had first put up. But misfortune came to him. Soon after Lent, he found he was penniless because his Spanish friend had industriously spent in a few weeks, the money which would have lasted Ignatius for a year. He had to leave his lodging house for the poorhouse of St. Jacques which was so far from Montaigu that he was obliged to miss some of his classes. The first scholastic exercise began at five in the morning, work ended at eight in the evening and the gates of the hospital closed on the stroke of Ave Maria. In addition his begging took up so much time that he made little progress in his studies. He tried without success to get a place as servant to some professor. One day when he was about hopeless a Spanish friar said it would be better for him to go to Flanders to get alms from the rich Spanish merchants there. Thus by losing two months, he would have the rest of the year free for study. After praying over it, he took this advice, went twice to Flanders and once to England where he found most generous alms.

It must have been after the first of these trips that the Spaniard who had stolen his money started for Spain and while waiting for a passage fell ill at Rouen. "And being thus ill the pilgrim learned it from a letter of his and had the desire to go to see him and take care of him, thinking that under such circumstances he could win him to leave worldliness and devote himself entirely to the service of God. And to be able to carry out this intention there came to him the desire to travel the twenty-eight leagues between Paris and Rouen on foot, without shoes and without eating or drinking and, praying over this desire, he found himself very fearful about it. Finally he went to the church of St. Dominic and there he made up his mind to go that way and he escaped from the great fear he had of tempting God. The morning of the next day when he ought to start, he got up early and when he commenced to get dressed there fell upon him such a fear that it almost seemed to him he could not get dressed. Nevertheless in spite of that shrinking he went out of the house and of the city before it was fully light. But the fear lasted and remained with him as far as Argenteuil, which is a castle two leagues from Paris on the road to Rouen, where they say is the garment of Our Lord. While he was passing the castle, in much travail of his soul, while he was going up a hill, something began to change within him and there came to him a great consolation and spiritual force with so great a feeling of happiness that he commenced to cry aloud and to talk with God, etc. And he passed that night with a poor beggar in a hospice having walked that day fourteen leagues. The next day he slept in the house of a merchant of straw; the third day he arrived at Rouen: all that time without eating or drinking and barefoot as he had resolved. In Rouen he consoled the sick man and helped to get him on a ship to go to Spain and gave him letters recommending him to the comrades who were in Salamanca, that is to say, Calixto, and Cáceres and Arteaga.[5]

When he came back from this trip, he found himself in trouble because of three Spaniards whom he was training for companions of his work. Their new zeal suggested to them the need of doing something extraordinary to mark their readiness for the service of God, so after Ignatius had started for Rouen, they sold their books with all they had, left their colleges for the poorhouse where Ignatius used to dwell, and began to beg their bread. This roused great excitement among the Spanish

[5] Confessions, 84.

students who finally went in arms to the poorhouse, dragged the three mendicants out and would not release them except under promise to resume their studies and their ordinary life. Loyola was denounced to the inquisitors of the faith. When he heard of this, he did not wait to be summoned, but went at once to the Inquisitor, who dismissed him without any blame.

It may be conjectured that the three Spaniards gave up begging their food and returned to their ordinary way of living, at least with the consent, more probably with the advice, of Ignatius. He continued, indeed, to regard begging as sometimes a necessary adjunct to evangelic poverty, willing to distribute all its own goods to the poor and trust that God would always give us this day our daily bread, or a useful discipline for pride, or a proof to the soul and the souls of neighbours of a genuine humility.[6] To the end of his life he called it "holy mendicity." It is therefore evident that his discouragement, and final practical prohibition, for the students under his care of that mendicity he had practiced in his early days at Paris, was not based on moral grounds, for he thought begging might be good for the soul of him who did it in the name of God.

Neither was it based on social grounds. He was later the author of a law to prevent the abuse of begging in his native town, but there is nothing in what he wrote or said to suggest that he came to think that begging by students was an imposition on the public. It was an old custom in many European countries for poor students to beg. Some forty-five years after this time it was prevalent enough to cause an English Parliament in its "Acte for the Punishment of Vagabondes and for the Relief of the Poore and Impotent," to provide for the punishment of all scholars of the Universities of Oxford and Cambridge "that go about begging, not being authorized under

[6] Letts. IV, 494, 565.

the seal of the said Universities by the Commissary, Chancellor or vice-Chancellor of the same."[7] Ignatius came to abandon the common practice and finally practically to prohibit it for all students under his care, entirely for practical reasons drawn from his own experience.

These reasons are clearly explained in a letter written by his orders twenty years after this time to Father Araoz about founding new colleges. "It seems to Father Ignatius, generally speaking, that no students of the Company ought anywheres to beg their bread, because, just as in those who devote themselves to helping souls mendicity is all right, so it seems to him that in students, who ought to be devoted to themselves, it is not very edifying and in addition it does not help their studies for them to be distracted either by the need of the necessaries of life or the need of begging for them. And it seems to him that if, before a college is opened, provision is made of an income sufficient for a certain number of students, it is better to take one or two less rather than more."[8]

During his first year at Paris, Loyola found other distractions. These were not the ordinary pleasures which keep students from studying. They were the pleasures of the soul.

"Not long after came the feast of St. Remigius with the beginning of October, and he began to hear the course in arts under a master called Juan Pegna, and he joined the class with the intention of preserving those comrades who had already determined to serve the Lord but not for the present to try to gain others, in order that he might be better able to study. When he commenced to hear the lectures of the course, the same temptations began to come to him which came when he studied Latin grammar at Barcelona, and every time he began to listen to the lecture, he could not keep his attention fixed on it because

[7] 14 Eliz. C 5-1572.   [8] Letts. I, 623. Compare Pol. III 78, e. g.

of the many spiritual thoughts which came into his mind. And seeing that he made little progress in letters, he went to his master and made him the promise never to fail to attend the course as long as he was able to find bread and water to sustain life. And when he had made that promise, all those devotional impulses which came to him so inopportunely left him and he went on quietly making progress with his studies. At this time he had converse with Mtro. Pierre Lefevre and Mtro. Alfonso Salmeron, whom he won to the service of God by means of the Spiritual Exercises. In addition he made an agreement with his roommate not to talk in study hours about spiritual things."[9]

He succeeded in so arranging his money affairs that they made him little trouble. The Spanish merchants in the Netherlands and England sent him their alms and his old friends in Barcelona continued to help him. He writes to thank Isabel Roser for three letters and twenty ducats and hopes that God will put them to her account on the day of judgment and "pay them for him in very good money." Another letter delicately suggests to Agnes Pascual that he needs more help. He wrote that "some of the sisters in Christ" have "excused themselves" for not being able to send more at present and asks advice about writing to others for help, adding, "I should prefer to decide this by your judgment rather than by my own."

So far as the Flemish and English alms were concerned, he became a sort of student relief agent for rich merchants who liked that form of good works and trusted him. In organizing this small business Ignatius showed the beginnings of his later marked executive ability. No money passed through his hands. Wherever he was or had been, the gifts were paid to some well known person who gave or sent him a bill of exchange on Paris. He gave that letter to a banker to cash and when he found a

[9] Confessions, 85. Compare Ribad. de Actis. Scripta I, 385.

poor student needing help he drew a draft on the banker, so that his accounts kept themselves and were always in order.[10]

In spite of all his diligence, Ignatius did not become a man of great learning, nor did he learn to write with facility and eloquence. This was recognized by his most intimate followers.[11] He said once "he believed no one had ever studied in spite of such great difficulties and obstacles as he. He named: (1) poverty; (2) great ill-health; (3) because he had no hope of gaining power or rising, nor any of the human impulses which are a solace in effort; (4) because he was not drawn to study by any liking but rather found it a very uphill effort. He studied twelve years only because he thought it would fit him for God's service."[12] This was a reminiscence of the long effort of will it cost the soldier beginning at the age of thirty-three to fight his way from the declensions of the Latin grammar to the degree of Master of Arts of the University of Paris.

If Loyola would not permit the pleasure of religious thought to interfere with his studies; neither, on the other hand, would he let academic rules interfere with religious duties. Soon after he changed from the College of Montaigu to the College of Sainte Barbe, probably in the summer of 1529, this faithfulness to religious duties brought him into trouble with the principal, Dr. Gouvea, who, it was reported to Loyola, had before threatened him with condign punishment if he caught him in Sainte Barbe because of the affair of the three Spaniards already related.[13] The Doctor had probably forgotten about this, or at least his wrath had cooled, when Loyola entered the College of Sainte Barbe. But he was soon to be brought again into a whipping mood towards this trouble-

[10] Araoz, Scripta I, 735. Pol. 49. [11] Lainez, Scripta, I, 394.
[12] Pol. quoted Ribad. Scripta I, 394. [13] Confessions p. 83.

some Spanish student. We do not get the story from
Loyola himself, but from his earliest biographer, Ribadeneira. He says: "I heard this in Paris in 1542," that is,
about ten or twelve years after it happened, and it is probable that he wrote down his report of what he heard in
1542, about another ten years after he heard it.[14]

It was the custom in Sainte Barbe for the students in
arts to hold disputations on the feast days of the church.
Loyola began to counsel students to go to confession
and communion on feast days and, employing these days
in devotions, they ceased to go to the disputations. The
master of Ignatius told him not to divert students from
their academic exercises. He explained what he was
advising but paid no attention to the words of the master
and the number of those who went to the holy sacrament instead of the disputations, increased. The master
complained to the principal, who sent a warning to Loyola
to stop. Loyola went on and, after three or four warnings the principal one day ordered the gates to be closed
and the bell rung for assembly in the great Hall. All
the masters being assembled there with bundles of rods,
Loyola heard that it was certain the assembly was for
the purpose of giving him a whipping. For this was done
at Paris even to adult scholars. It was called giving a
man "A hall." Loyola went to the room of Dr. Gouvea,
who had not yet come down. "He explained what he
had done and said he was ready to be whipped for it,
but pointed out that it would be a great scandal for the
small boys if he were publicly whipped. In short, our
Father talked in such a way that finally Dr. Gouvea led
him by the hand into the great hall where all the masters
were armed with rods and especially the master of Ignatius. All the students were gaping to see the end of the
spectacle which was that, before all that assembly, Doctor

[14] Boehmer 324.

Gouvea kneeled down and with tears begged pardon of our Father for what he had intended to do, saying to all that he was a St. Jerome, etc. And so Our Lord brought greater good out of what the devil had arranged to break up the good work already begun, because from then on others commenced to follow the first in paying attention to the counsels and Spiritual Exercises of Our Father."[15]

The end of this story is highly improbable, and sounds like "college gossip." [16] If a Parisian college of the beginning of the sixteenth century was anything like as gossiping a place as an American campus at the beginning of the twentieth century, ten or twelve years was quite long enough to form a plain story into a pious legend. (7) Surely Ignatius himself would have deprecated such an outcome. For if, in talking to the principal, he justly and persuasively insisted that it would be an injury for the little boys if a man of his age were publicly whipped for advising students to go to church, he would have judged it far worse for the small boys to see their principal kneeling in tears at his feet to ask pardon.

But underlying this story, whose dramatic, edifying and improbable end so naturally excites suspicion, there was a solid fact: the memory of the persuasiveness of Ignatius in handling men, and his forgetfulness of self in the care of souls.

Later Ignatius said that "as the devil showed great skill in tempting men into perdition, equal skill ought to be shown in saving them. The devil studied the nature of each man, seized upon the traits of his soul, adjusted himself to them and insinuated himself gradually into the victim's confidence, suggesting splendours to the ambitious, gain to the covetous, delight to the sensuous and a false appearance of piety to the pious, and a master in saving souls ought to act in the same cautious and skilful

[15] Scripta, 383. Ribad. de Actis.　　[16] Boehmer, 136.

way."[17]   The memory of his tact, already remarkable, and afterwards developed to so high a pitch, found expression in two other stories of his life at Paris which are not alluded to by his three modern biographers; though they are less highly improbable than Dr. Gouvea's repentance and have the same degree of authentication.

Ignatius knew a man who was involved in an illicit love affair from which he could not be withdrawn by any argument.   The woman lived in the suburbs and the road to her house passed over a bridge.   Ignatius waylaid the lover and "plunged himself into the freezing cold water up to his neck.   Then he called out as his man was passing over the bridge 'Go on, wretched one, go on to your disgusting pleasures.   Do you not see ruin hanging over your head?   Are you not horrified by the curse which is close upon you?   Here will I afflict myself for you until the just anger of God appears to be turned aside.'   The man was very much alarmed and struck by so extreme a proof of charity.   He stopped, turned back and immediately broke off his wicked relation."[18]

"There was a certain distinguished doctor of philosophy at Paris whom Ignatius desired to win for Christ.   After he had tried many things in vain, he went to see him one day accompanied by a friend from whom we have this story.   He found the Doctor taking a little honest recreation in a certain game.   That was a game of balls thrown upon a table according to certain rules and the Doctor said, 'Ignatius, you have come in the nick of time to play with me.'   Ignatius said he had no practise in the game and no skill at it.   But the Doctor insisted that he should play with him.   When he practically forced him to play, Ignatius said, 'I will play with you but not for fun and for this stake: if I am beaten, I will do something for your sake; if I win, you will do something for me.'   The

---

[17] Ribad. 1st Life fol. 204.   [18] Ribad. 1st Life fol. 174.

other accepted the bet and it was agreed between them that the loser should obey the honest commands of the winner. Ignatius, new at the game, without any practise (because he had never had the balls in his hand) beat the Doctor head over heels so that the friend said, 'Domine Doctor, this is the hand of God.' He was beaten and gave his hand on it that he would do all that Ignatius said. Ignatius bade him give thirty days to meditation and, all other cares being put aside, to apply himself heartily to the Spiritual Exercises, which he did with a great reform of his life and to the wonder of men." [19]

Whatever may be the truth about these anecdotes there is unquestionable proof of his skill as a fisher of men in the band of six steadfast and faithful comrades he won to replace the six whom he had persuaded to share his ideals only to see them drift away from him. Three of them were, like Ignatius, younger sons of noble families. Most of them were poor. After Ignatius left Paris three more decided to join them. One of these men caused Ignatius later a great deal of trouble and was of a temperament which adjusted itself with difficulty to his ideal. But the rest gave every sign of a deep and steadfast affection, undimmed by labours or hardships and willing to accept, without murmuring, any severity of discipline. Ignatius would himself gladly have admitted that the loyal aid of these friends was one of the chief means God gave him to carry on his work.

The first to cast in his lot with Ignatius was Pierre Lefèvre, the son of a pious Savoyard peasant farmer. When he became a roommate of Ignatius at the College of Sainte Barbe, he was drifting, dreaming vaguely of all sorts of futures from practising medicine to becoming a monk; troubled from time to time by the fear that he had not fully confessed his sins and beset by fierce temptations. Ignatius helped him four years, before he

[19] Rib. 631. Not in 1st Life.

would consent to give him the Spiritual Exercises. He was not distinguished for intellectual ability but for a certain beauty of character. He was as gentle as he was loyal and insisted that the worst heretics ought to be loved. He notes in his sketches of his own life that he prayed even for Henry VIII and Martin Luther.[20] Ignatius shortly before his death ordered masses to be said and prayers offered for Germany and England,[21] but this anxiety for the personal fate of men so plainly given over to the counsels of the devil, seems to have been peculiar to the gentle Lefèvre.

Another roommate of Ignatius was Francesco Javier (Xavier), youngest son of a Basque noble whose father had been president of the council of the French kings of Navarre. Faithfulness to the fallen dynasty had reduced the family almost to poverty. Young Xavier was an athlete, the best jumper in the university, able, ambitious, a lover of ease and pleasure; kept from debauchery only by a certain fine-fibred dislike for the grossness with which so many of his fellow students practised it. His strongest desire, apparently, was to get a fat canonry near home in the city of Pamplona. He shared the room of Lefèvre and Loyola and for some time was rather inclined to laugh at this elderly Spanish student of mediocre abilities and peculiar fanatical ideas about religion. The two were, however, kept more or less together by their common liking for Lefèvre and once when Xavier was telling both of them about the great ecclesiastical career he planned to make, Loyola suddenly asked him, "And what shall it profit a man if he gain the whole world and lose his own soul?" It was one of those sudden unforgettable impressions which so often has brought about such complete changes in men.[22] Though Xavier

[20] Memoriale, Fabri Monumenta.   [21] Letts. V, 221, 229. VIII, 226.   [22] See William James, Varieties of Religious Experience. Beggs, Twice Born Men.

and Loyola were shortly afterward separated for life by oceans, they remained bound together in heart like David and Jonathan with a love "passing the love of women."[23]

Diego Lainez was perhaps the ablest intellectually of all the early fathers. His great grandfather had been a Jew, which in the eyes of many Spaniards left a mark of inferiority on all his descendants, even the most Christian. Loyola as a soldier had evidently shared this prejudice, but since his conversion he had escaped from it and finally chose Lainez to succeed him as general of the Company. They took to each other from the start, when Lainez, already a Master of Arts of Alcalá, came up to Paris and Loyola gave him the Spiritual Exercises almost immediately. He was a man of an extremely ardent temperament, capable when heated in argument of attacking his opponents with the verbal ferocity Luther showed against the Papacy. When Lainez was attending the Council of Trent some fifteen years after he left Paris, he and Salmeron went to call on Melchior Cano, a celebrated Spanish Dominican theologian who had expressed very unfavourable opinions of the Company of Jesus. The conversation lasted about two hours and grew steadily warmer. Lainez finally insinuated that Cano after all was nothing but a simple Dominican friar, and was setting himself up to be chief shepherd in the Church of God in place of the Pope. To which Cano replied with a sour sweet smile, "Ah, Señor, then your wisdom does not think that the dogs ought to bark when the shepherds are asleep?" "Yes," said Lainez, "They ought to bark but at the wolves, not at other dogs." Cano went further and charged the Company with "novelties in religion." This so stirred up "the good father Lainez" that he dropped into vernacular Spanish and said—the word Victor Hugo glorifies so rhetorically in Les Miserables as Cambronnes' answer to the demand for surrender at Waterloo. But

[23] II Samuel I, 26.

Lainez, who had rushed from the room with this last shot at his distinguished opponent "had not gone out of the house before he repented of that liberty of his tongue. So coming back he knelt at Cano's feet and begged pardon."[24] When Lainez had succeeded Ignatius as general, he went to France with the papal legate, visited the conference with the Huguenot theologians held at Poissy in 1560 and "spoke with vehemence." He addressed to the Queen Mother (Catherine de Médicis) reproaches which brought tears to her eyes and threatened her with the ruin of the kingdom if she did not drive from it "these evil minded people, these adversaries of the faith and of religion, these wolves, foxes, serpents, assassins."[25] (8) Lainez was manifestly of a strong and excitable temperament. But Ignatius was aware that some of the best horses are extremely hard to break. He knew how to handle this fiery descendant of Spanish Jews who had become a Christian. The temperament of Lainez bowed completely in reverence and affection to the person and ideals of Loyola.[26]

Alfonso Salmeron was a friend of Lainez, of marked ability, well trained in Latin and the new study of Greek.

Nicolas Alfonso surnamed from his birthplace Bobadilla, came to Paris in order to study Latin, Greek and Hebrew: the three languages whose study marked a man as an adherent of the methods of the New Learning. At first he gave some anxiety to his comrades and superiors by a probably unconscious impulse to put himself forward. He had at one time a tendency to express his opinion on important matters which were not his business. He talked too much, often interrupting other people. He had a very regrettable habit of expressing his opinions on matters of state, even writing ill-advised letters to princes and cardinals. He became at times extremely excited in disputation—so much so on one occasion that

<hr />

[24] Nadal II, 45.   [25] Bouillé II, p. 159, cited mss. de l'Abbaye St. Germain.
[26] See his extraordinary letter quoted later.

bystanders thought he had drunk too much.[27] He toned down, however, and became a useful member of the order.

Simon Rodriguez was a noble Portuguese who came to Paris on one of the scholarships maintained there by the King of Portugal. He seems the one marked mistake of Loyola in picking men. His unwise and headstrong and disloyal conduct, which will be discussed later, certainly did very great harm for a time to the Company in Portugal. Ignatius, against the advice of the court of his peers which tried Rodriguez, treated him with an indulgence unusual and rather puzzling, and it seems to an outsider that some historians of the Company have been inclined to follow Loyola's example.

Of the three comrades gained after Ignatius left Paris not much need be said. Codure died five years later. He was tenderly remembered by his comrades. Claude Jay served faithfully as preacher and professor of theology of the University of Ingolstadt. Broet was a faithful servant of the Company for twenty-seven years, as preacher, as nuncio to Scotland, as rector of the College at Bologna, as provincial of Italy, and, for the last ten years of his life, in the difficult office of provincial of his native country, France.

These ten men, whose age ranged from the early twenties to the early forties, five Spaniards and one Portuguese, two Savoyards and two Frenchmen, were filled with newly won joy and zeal for religion which they all wished to express in the same way. However much it may have seemed to any one of them that he had spontaneously and separately chosen this way of service for himself, it was undoubtedly, psychologically speaking, imposed upon their hearts and wills by the persuasion and the dominant personality of Ignatius. Otherwise it would have been either less unanimous or less vague. The first seven of them determined to have some sort of a religious

[27] Salmeron, I 20.

ceremony to express their common expectation: for it
could hardly be called a plan. In the month of August,
1534, when the university was in vacation, Ignatius and
his six comrades went outside the gates on the slopes of
Montmartre where, about six hundred yards from the
summit, stood a little church called Notre Dame de Montmartre. It was not used for public worship and doubtless
was not in the best repair. This remote and venerable
little building was controlled by the abbess of the neighbouring convent of the sisters of St. Benedict, who gave
permission to the pious students to use it and they got
the keys from the woman who kept them.

They kneeled around the altar while Lefèvre, the only
priest amongst them, said mass. Then, each in turn, they
took oath and communed. The exact words of the vow
have not been preserved, but they promised before God
to go to Jerusalem, giving up their family and all worldly
goods except fare for the journey, in order to devote themselves at the holy city to helping their neighbours. If,
however, war with the Turks stopped shipping for a year,
or if they were sent back by the guardian of the holy
sepulchre (as Ignatius had been) they would go to Rome
to ask the Vicar of Christ when and how they could best
serve the souls of their neighbours. (9)

When the simple ceremony was finished the little group
of friends crossed over the hill to eat their frugal meal
together by the fountain of St. Denis and to spend the
rest of the day in converse about the things of the soul.

CHAPTER VII

THE POOR PILGRIM PRIESTS: WORKING AND WAITING

This vow was taken for the first time in August, 1534, and repeated on the same date in 1535 and 1536. But Ignatius was not with his friends on the last two anniversaries. He had passed his examinations as a licentiate and a master of arts and made progress in the special study of theology; but he was unable to finish his course. At the beginning of the year 1535 he became very ill and suffered agonies whose seat seemed to be in his stomach. These pains returned intermittently during the rest of his life and it was not until near the end that the doctors discovered that the cause of the trouble was gallstones.[1] Naturally they were unable to help him and finally as a last resort ordered him to try to return to his native air: a remedy much in fashion with puzzled doctors of the time. "His comrades also gave him the same advice and urged him strongly to follow it. . . . At last the pilgrim let himself be persuaded by the comrades because in addition to other reasons those who were Spaniards had arrangements to make at home in which he could be useful. And the agreement was that when he was better he should go to attend to their affairs and then travel to Venice where he should await their arrival. . . . So he mounted a little horse the comrades had bought for him and started off home alone."[2] His health became very much better during the journey. Just before he started Loyola heard that he had been charged with heresy for the fourth time

[1] Pol. VI, 35. [2] Confessions 88.

during his student days. The moment was a very dangerous one for a charge of heresy. Four or five months before some heretics had made a rash move which had aroused an excited desire for vengeance among the people and shaken Francis I out of a half-tolerant attitude; partly a liking for the New Learning and partly a shrewd sense of the political advantage of being on good terms with the German Protestant princes. In October, 1534, the walls of Paris were covered in the night with placards attacking the sacrament of the mass, and denouncing "the Pope and all his vermin of cardinals, bishops, priests and monks and all others who say mass and consent to it" as "false prophets, damnable deceivers, apostates, wolves, false shepherds, idolaters, seducers, liars and execrable blasphemers, murderers of souls, renouncers of Jesus Christ, false witnesses, traitors, thieves, insulters of God's honour and more detestable than devils." The King, on whose bedroom door in the Château of Amboise a copy of this document was posted by one of his choir (afterwards burnt for it), ordered the courts to leave no stone unturned to punish the insult to God and to him. A great expiatory ceremony was ordered and a huge crowd watched the procession as it passed from the Church of St. Germain l'Auxerrois to the cathedral of Notre Dame. The four princes of the blood royal carried the canopy over the host which was borne by the Bishop of Paris. Behind it, alone, his head bare and a candle in his hand, walked the King. After mass all the dignitaries went to dine with the bishop and after dinner the King called into the great hall the bishop and clergy, the rector of the University and the leading professors, the city magistrates, and chief merchants, and, sitting in his chair, surrounded by the princes, cardinals, his counsellors and all the ambassadors, made a solemn speech, which ended by the declaration that "if his arm were infected with heresy he would cut it off." The day's solemnities were finished by burning six heretics; three near the beginning and three near the end of the line of march of the procession. "Many other heretics were burnt in great number on different days following, so that in Paris one saw nothing but stakes set up in different places; which frightened the people of Paris very much."[3]

It was not strange that, in such an atmosphere of excitement, where everyone might be inclined to suspect his neighbour of secret heresy, Loyola and his little band of Iñiguistas should arouse suspicion. We have a record of this more personal than an anonymous denunciation before an inquisitor. Nadal was a student at Paris, who some ten years later joined the Company of Jesus, but now he met all Loyola's advances with a suspicious eye. They had the same confessor, who urged Nadal to talk with Ignatius. "Since you are not an Igniguista yourself," Nadal replied, "why do you want me to become one?" When visits from the comrades, three of whom Nadal had known at Alcalá, failed, Ignatius tried himself. He had written a long letter to a nephew to persuade him to leave the world and begin a more perfect life. He read this to Nadal in a little church where they both went to say their prayers. "Then," writes Nadal, "the devil recognized the power of Ignatius and turned me aside from the spirit which was drawing me towards good. I said to him: 'I wish to follow this book (I had the New Testament in my hand). Don't talk to me any more of these things.' What I was saying to myself was, 'I do not want to join these people. Who knows whether they will not fall into the hands of the inquisitors?' After that I did not see again at Paris either Ignatius or any of his friends."[4]

It was the habit of Ignatius always to meet boldly this danger of charges of heresy which beset his whole early

[3] Guiffrey, 125, 129.　　　　[4] Nadal, Vol. I, p. 1-3.

life. Without waiting for a summons, he went at once to the inquisitor, said he had heard of an accusation, that he must go at once to Spain and would like an immediate sentence. The inquisitor said the accusation was not important enough to need any trial but he would like to see the manuscript of the "Spiritual Exercises." Ignatius gave it to him and pressed for a trial. When he could not induce the inquisitor to hold one, he brought a notary to make a legal record that the accusation had been dismissed without trial.[5]

Ignatius, when he left Paris, steered straight for home, which he had not seen during fourteen years. We have only five of his letters previous to his departure from Paris. Three of them are to Agnes Pascual, another to Isabel Roser. These were two of his wealthy friends at Barcelona. The fifth letter was written, two years before Ignatius left Paris, to his brother Martin Garcia, the Lord of Oñaz and Loyola. It is in answer to a letter asking about the advisability of sending a nephew of Ignatius' to study in Paris. Ignatius approves, but advises that he should study theology rather than canon law because theology is better adapted to gaining "the riches which do not pass away and to give rest in old age. . . . For his expenses, tuition fees and other necessities, I believe fifty ducats a year will suffice. I think that in a strange land with a cold climate, you should not wish your son to lack any of the necessaries of life because, in my judgment, this impedes study." He promises, if the lad comes, to do what his father wants him to do—guard him against evil associations and extravagance.

"You say you are very glad to see reason to think I have given up my habit of never writing to you." To this brotherly sentiment Ignatius makes a long reply filled with Latin phrases and quotations from St. Paul. The substance is that for the first years after leaving home

[5] Confessions 88.

it was not for his good to write; that for the last five or six years he would have written oftener but for two reasons, first, his studies and many conversations—but not about temporal things; second, because it did not seem probable that his letters would do service to God or increase His praise. He adds, no one loves God with the whole heart who loves anything for itself and not because of God. He hopes that his family will show love and zeal in the service and praise of God that he may love and serve them more and exhorts his brother to think less of the world and more of God; "setting a good example and teaching holy doctrine to his children, servants and relatives, ruling his household without anger and doing much for poor orphans and those in need."[6]

The long journey was entirely uneventful until Ignatius got on the border of Guipúzcoa and near home. "He turned aside from the high road and was following a solitary road among the hills which led through a region noted for murders. He had not gone far when he saw two armed men coming towards him who passed him and then turned around to come galloping after him. He had a touch of fear, but speaking to them, found they were servitors of his brother who had heard from Bayonne, where the pilgrim was known, that he was on the road and had sent these men to escort him through the dangerous region. When he got almost to the city he was met by the priests come out to escort him to his brother's house. He refused to go there and resisted the pressing efforts by which they almost tried to force him to go. So he went to the house of refuge for the poor and when the fitting hour came went out to beg his bread. And in the hospital he commenced talking of the things of God with many who came to see him, and by God's grace he did some good. He determined to teach Christian doctrine every day to children. His brother opposed this very

⁶ Letts. I, 77.

much and said that no one would come to hear him. The pilgrim replied that one would be enough. But as soon as he began to do it, many came regularly—his brother among them. Beside this he preached every Sunday with profit to souls; so that they came from many miles to hear him." [7]

He was not content with preaching and teaching. He tells us how he brought about certain reforms through the government of the little city. By his influence with the officers of the courts, gambling was effectively prohibited. He also arranged an ordinance that the church bells should ring for Ave Maria three times a day, "in order that all the people might pray as is done in Rome." The most striking thing he did during his three months' stay in his birthplace, was to introduce a poor law based on the best recent models as he had seen them at work in the Netherlands. No reform was more obvious; for begging was admitted to be one of the curses of Spain, and the Cortez of the previous year had asked Charles V to take some means to repress it. One of Ignatius' patrons in the Netherlands had been a Spaniard, Louis Vives, a man of international reputation as a scholar, who had written a celebrated pamphlet, translated into three languages, on the care of the poor. Ignatius had probably seen this plan in actual operation at Ypres and other cities of the Netherlands. At all events, the main ideas of "The Ordinance for the Care of the Poor in Azpeitia" are very like those of the plan of Vives. Ignatius did not invent anything in this matter of poor laws. He only took ideas which were in the air and applied them for the first time to a Spanish city.

These ideas were entirely opposed to the whole mediæval and monastic practice in regard to almsgiving. They were opposed to the whole earlier practice of Ignatius as he described it: e.g., his giving away all his

[7] Confessions, 89.

money to a swarm of beggars at Ferrara when he was on his way back from Jerusalem eleven years before.[8] This is only one of many instances in which this extreme conservative in the realm of thought showed himself, in the realm of action, a friend of new ideas and skilful in adapting them to the needs of a given situation.

The new regulation appointed officers called major-domos of the poor, who, on Sundays and festivals, were to make regular collections and justly distribute the money to the poor, native or strangers. Other collections by agents of charitable or religious institutions (with two named exceptions) were forbidden under pain of prison: those who gave to them were punished by fine. Ordinary begging, or giving alms to beggars, was forbidden under pain of prison; persistent begging by sturdy beggars was punished by a whipping.[9] Shortly after he suggested this law, Ignatius tells us, he begged at Bologna. The inconsistency of his subsequent practice with the principles of this Ordinance for the Care of the Poor, is not explained by him. Probably he would have said that, where no good laws existed, he who was poor for Christ's sake must do the best he could under the old system. Begging from door to door became on the whole less and less prominent in the practice of the Company of Jesus as time went on; though it was never formally abandoned in the lifetime of Ignatius.

"When Ignatius' health was restored he made up his mind to leave and do the errands confided to him by his comrades and go without a cent. His brother was very much put out at this, and felt bitterly ashamed of having a member of the family go on foot.[10] Finally the pilgrim yielded so far as to agree to ride to the boundary of the province of Guipúzcoa in company with his brother and his relatives. At the border he dismounted and continued

---

[8] See page 54. [9] Scripta, 536 ff. [10] This was very undignified for a Spanish cavalier.

on foot after refusing to accept any money." He then visited the families of his four Spanish comrades, "always refusing to accept from them any money though it was most pressingly urged upon him. At Valencia he had a talk with Castro,[11] who had become a monk." [12]

From Valencia he sailed to Genoa and there took the road for Bologna. In the mountains he lost his way and following a footpath which led him high up on the rocks along a torrent, the path grew narrower and narrower until finally he felt he could go neither forward nor backward. Finally he ᴛ on his hands and knees and made a very long distance this way, "in great terror because he feared he would fall into the river at every moment and that was the greatest fatigue and bodily effort he ever went through."[13]

At Bologna he begged but did not get a penny. Somebody must have been charitable, however, for he was ill in bed with fever, chills and pain for seven days;[14] probably in the hospital. Then he walked to Venice begging his way, and arrived in the last days of December, 1535. He immediately set himself to the study of theology; expecting to finish in about fifteen months his studies interrupted at Paris. His living was taken care of by his his friends in Barcelona; especially Isabel Roser, who sent him twelve escudos and offered to send him more.[15] Jacob Cazador also sent him money and promised more. We have seen that Ignatius when he was a pilgrim on the road would not take money even from his brother or the families of his friends. He thought that was to doubt the care of God. But this money he did not scruple to take gratefully because he had learned by experience that a student could not beg his living and study well.

Loyola spent eighteen months in Venice but he de-

---

[11] One of his first comrades at Paris. [12] Confessions, 90.
[13] Confessions, 91. [14] Letts. I, 94. [15] Letts. I, 93.

votes to his stay there only a few lines of his Confessions. He became acquainted with a number of influential and important people and it was perhaps during this Venetian stay that he completely got out of his early habit of a rustic, almost a rude, simplicity of address to which (like the early Quakers) he had once felt himself impelled by conscience.[16] At least, if we can judge by a letter he addressed to "The Magnificent Lord Pietro Contarini, my most dear friend in Christ," he had now or before given this up. This was one of the many instances where Ignatius learned by experience what was useful to his great purpose of helping souls. As time went on he evidently became conscientiously careful to give every one his due of outward respect. Five years before his death, when he sent a deputation to Florence to open a college, their carefully written instructions told them to kiss the hand of the Duke and kneel and kiss the hand of the Duchess and not to cover their heads unless ordered to do so.[17]

Of these friends he made in Venice by "spiritual conversations" many remained his steadfast well-wishers. Some took the Spiritual Exercises, and became closely bound to him in spiritual friendship. We have nine letters of Ignatius dated at Venice; extracts from two of them written to an old Barcelona friend, Theresa Rejadella, give us an idea of these spiritual conversations.

He tells her that "the enemy (the devil) is weakening her usefulness and disturbing the peace of her soul in two ways. The first is by persuading her to a false humility; the second by persuading her to a great fear of God. . . . Your own words prove this wile of the devil has succeeded with you, for you write that you are a poor religious person who wishes 'as it seems to me' to serve God, and you do not dare to say, 'I want to serve God'. . . .

[16] Confessions, 67.   [17] Letts. III, 719.

You see how the martyrs brought before idolatrous judges, said they were servants of Christ. So you, facing the enemy of all mankind . . . ought to confess that you are Christ's servant and that you would rather die than leave His service. . . . When the devil suggests to me justice, I think of mercy. If he brings up mercy, I, on the contrary, say justice. So it is necessary for us to proceed in order not to be disturbed in heart and to leave the tricksters tricked." Ignatius describes two lessons of God: "He gives one and permits the other. The one He gives, is inward consolation, which casts out all perturbation and draws us to a complete love of God. To some in this state, He shows a great light, to others He discloses many secret things. . . . Finally, with that divine consolation, all difficulties become pleasures and all fatigue rest. He who walks with that glow, warmth and comfort in his heart, cannot bear any burden which does not seem to him light. Nor is any penance, nor any toil so great that it does not seem very sweet." The second lesson (which God permits) is when "our ancient enemy fills us with sadness and we do not know why we are sad and we can neither pray with any devotion, nor even talk, nor hear about God Our Lord with any zest or savour in the heart. And not only that . . . but He fills our mind with the thought that we are forgotten of God and separated from our Lord." Ignatius goes on to say we must resist our enemy and wait patiently for the consolation God will surely send us.

In another letter he warns Theresa not to let the religious pleasures of prayer and meditation make her forget to take necessary food and natural sleep. . . . "Above all think that God loves you—which I do not doubt—and respond with love to Him; paying no attention to evil thoughts or cowardly impulses when they are against your will. . . . For just as I do not hope to be saved by

the good works of the good angels, so I do not expect
to be lost because of the evil and weak thoughts which
bad angels, the world and the flesh, suggest to my mind
against my will."[18]

This letter makes evident a stage in that slow change
of attitude towards ascetic austerities in which the new
soldier of Christ had once hoped to rival the lives of the
saints.[19] He had now come to be afraid lest, in some
cases at least, they might interfere with God's service.
Three years later, he put into the first sketch of the
Constitutions of the Company of Jesus the prohibition
against imposing general ascetic practices by rule that
was such a contrast with the law and custom of most of
the older orders. He thought however that these ascetic
practices might be useful to individual souls as a means
of keeping the body under or expressing contrition for
sin.

While Ignatius was thus engaged in studying theology
and helping souls in Venice, his comrades were doing the
same thing in Paris. Lainez wrote a few years afterward,
"We frequently ate together, bringing out food to the
room now of one and then of another, which, together with
frequent visits, enflamed our spirits and, I believe, added
much to our steadfastness. God helped us in our studies
and also in helping our neighbours. We had great love
among us and we aided each other, even in natural things,
so far as we could. That was the word Father Ignatius
had left with us, with the good Master Lefèvre as a sort
of older brother to all of us."

It had been agreed when Ignatius left Paris, that his
comrades should start to join him at the feast of the conversion of St. Paul (Jan. 25th) in 1537, that is to say,
in about two years. As the year 1536 drew to its close,
he began to be much worried about them. So he wrote

[18] Letts. I, 107.　　　　[19] Confessions, 41, 45.

the following letter: "To my spiritual Father—The Confessor of the Queen of France: May the grace and love of Christ Our Lord be always in our favour to help us.

"Remembering the good will which for the love and service of God Our Lord you have shown me, without my being worthy of it, I have concluded to write this letter, not to repay you in any way, but to ask new kindness and gifts in the service and praise of His Divine Majesty. Magister Pedro Fabro with some companions intends to make a troublesome journey. I think, considering the disturbances and wars grown so great in Christendom because of our sins, that he and his company will find themselves in extreme necessity. For the service and reverence of God Our Lord, I beg you to be willing to turn your attention to and favour them so far as God inclines you, and it may be possible for you to do it."[20]

When Ignatius wrote on their behalf, his comrades were already on their way to join him. In face of the renewed war between Francis I and Charles V, it seemed better to forestall the date agreed upon for leaving Paris, and they set out about the middle of October, taking a circuitous route through Germany and Switzerland. The little band of nine marched with their sacks on their backs carrying clothes and their precious books. On the road they sang psalms or repeated in chorus the prayers of the Church or talked of the things of God. One of the three priests among them said mass every day and the others confessed and communed. When they arrived at an inn, or left it, they kneeled down in prayer. It rained all the time they were walking in France and snowed all the time in Germany. In France they had a few disturbing hours with soldiers or magistrates who suspected them of being spies. In Germany, where they were for a long time in Protestant territory, they were once threatened with jail by an angry minister they had refused to allow

[20] Letts. I, 109.

to eat at the same table with them in the inn. But they met with no serious misadventure and arrived in Venice January 1537, safe and sound after their eight weeks' tramp. Two of them who some years later wrote little accounts of the journey, seemed to look back on it with pleasure.[21]

Ignatius was full of joy at seeing them and filled with an innocent pride in so goodly and faithful a company of friends; as appears very plainly between the lines of the letter he wrote when Isabel Roser sent word that his old friend, Juan de Verdolay, would be glad to hear from him.

"I expect to stay here about a year, a little more or less. I do not know after that what God Our Lord will ordain for me. There arrived here from Paris, about the middle of January, nine of my friends in the Lord, all masters of arts and well versed in theology, four of them Spaniards, two Frenchmen, two from Savoy and one from Portugal. They entered here into two hospitals to serve the sick poor in the humblest, most repugnant services. After they had gone through this exercise for two months, they went to Rome to keep holy week there and, as they were in poverty, without money and without favour of lettered persons, in short had nothing to back them, they put their trust and hope solely in God for whom they went. They found, and without any trouble, much more than they sought; that is to say, they talked with the Pope, and many cardinals, bishops and doctors of theology discussed with them. . . . The Pope and all who heard them were so content that they commenced to show them all possible favour. In the first place, the Pope gave them permission to go to Jerusalem and bestowed on them once or twice his benediction, exhorting them to persevere in their intention. Secondly, he gave them sixty

[21] Rodriguez, Lainez.

ducats in alms and from cardinals and other persons they received one hundred and fifty ducats more, so that they brought here in bills of exchange two hundred and sixty ducats. Thirdly, to those who were priests he gave power to hear confession and absolve in all cases of episcopal jurisdiction. Fourthly, to those who were not priests, he gave letters empowering any bishop to ordain them without benefice. So when they got back here to Venice, we took all the orders, including the priesthood, and we voluntarily gave a vow of perpetual poverty into the hands of the Legate of the Pope who was here. . . . So far as the ordination was concerned, two bishops wanted to do it. Neither in Rome nor in Venice did we have to pay any fees. All was done gratuitously. The Legate also gave us complete authority to preach, interpret the scriptures and teach publicly and privately in all Venetian territory, together with power to confess and absolve all episcopal, archepiscopal and patriarchal cases.

"I have explained all this not only to carry out what I said but also to show our great blameworthiness and confusion of face if we do not help ourselves after God has so much helped us; because without our knowledge nor asking, it seems that all the means to carry out our designs come to our hands. . . . Hence I beg you, for the service and reverence of His Divine Majesty, be instant in prayer for us, asking your devout friends to do the same; for you see how we need prayer, because he who has received much is indebted for more.

"This year, in spite of our hope to go to Jerusalem, there has been no ship, nor will there be any because of the great fleet the Turk is forming. So we have agreed to send back to Rome the bills of exchange for two hundred and sixty ducats . . . because we do not want any one to think that we hunger and thirst for the things about which worldlings are now preparing to die. All of us are going, divided up two by two, through Italy, until next year, when we will cross to Jerusalem if we can."[22]

The same suspicions which had beset Ignatius in Alcalá, Salamanca and Paris, attacked him in Venice. It was said that he was a fugitive from justice who had been burnt in effigy in Spain and France. These constantly recurring accusations of heresy brought against a future saint of the Church, are not so surprising as at first sight appears. One of the results of the tremendous breaking up of old ecclesiastical institutions which was rapidly going on, was to strengthen in many minds the tendency to regard everything strange as dangerous. In the case of people to whom religion is in effect little more than an inherited prejudice in favor of certain ideas and customs, this tendency breeds a zest in the pursuit of heresy which they find in no other expression of their belief. For it combines a sense of importance in being an assistant district attorney of God to prepare indictments for the last judgment, with the excitement of playing the amateur detective in uncovering mysterious evildoers.

The outcome of the accusation at Venice suggests that it was probably brought by this sort of people. Loyola, according to his custom, did not wait to be summomed but boldly presented himself before the tribunal. Their sentence, given the 13th of October, 1537, says that after hearing Ignatius himself and considering all possible testimony, written and oral, given and insinuated to this court, they find the charges "frivolous, vain and false" and they impose silence on all who would repeat them. They declare that Father Ignatius "has been and is a priest of good and religious life and of holy doctrine, of the highest character and reputation, who up to now has taught doctrine and given a good example in Venice. And thus we say, pronounce, give judgment, absolve, and declare in every way we can and ought. Praise be to God." [23]

[22] Letts. I, 118.   [23] Scripta, I, 624.

The service of the comrades at Venice in the care of the sick poor which became a regular part of the good works done by all Jesuit missionaries, caused the erection later of a statue in a niche of the chapel of a cloister which bore this inscription. "S. Franciscus Xaverius ulcera lambendo aegrotum sanavit." "St. Francis Xavier cured a sick man by licking his ulcers." [24]

There is no doubt that Xavier did what the first part of this inscription said he did, for Lainez recorded it only ten years later in words even more realistic. He does not say whether the sick man recovered or not, but records it as an example of a "notable proof of charity and victory over self." [25] By it Xavier overcame, once and for all, his disgust and shrinking from people afflicted with loathsome and dangerous diseases. Ignatius records during his Paris life a somewhat similar victory over himself. A sick man was in a house ill with what was suspected to be the pest. Ignatius went to comfort and help him. When he came out, his hand with which he had touched the sore of the patient "commenced to give him pain so that he thought he had the pest and that imagination was so strong that he could not conquer it, until, with a strong impulse, he thrust his hand into his mouth saying, 'If you have got the pest in your hand you will have to have it in your mouth.' And when he had done that the imagination left him and also the ache in his hand." [26]

These two men had never heard of germs, but we must remember that what they did seemed just as dangerous to them as it does to us—and just as disgusting; for they were both Basque nobles, a class of people noted for cleanliness. As patriots in time of war steel themselves to face dirt, hardship and death through months or years for the sake of their country, so these men of delicate conscience and iron will were fixed on dying daily for all the years of

²⁴ Venturi, II, p. 90, n. 2.   ²⁵ Scripta, I, p. 114.   ²⁶ Confessions, 86.

their life in the great war between God and evil. No discipline seemed too hard if it fitted them for this service. They asked for no relief except from sin and any human shrinking which might weaken them for this duty. In their ideal of living there was no room for ordinary pleasures or natural disgusts. They were determined to strip their life absolutely bare of all motives except obedience to the Church, the wish to help the sins and sorrows of men, joy in God and the fellowship of those like minded with themselves.

CHAPTER VIII

A POWERFUL ENEMY. BEGGING AND FINANCE
THE INQUISITION AGAIN

Ignatius did not go to Rome with his nine comrades. He tells us why in a line of his Confessions, "The pilgrim did not go because of Dr. Ortiz and also because of the new Cardinal Theatine." [1]

Ortiz was a doctor of theology, influential with the Emperor; who had shown himself very critical of the conduct of Ignatius at Paris.[2] The Cardinal Theatine had been called to Rome from Venice and made a cardinal in December 1536. Giovanni Pietro Caraffa was then a man of sixty. A descendant of one of the oldest families of the Neapolitan nobility, he showed from childhood an inclination for the Church. One of his uncles was a cardinal and obtained for him at the age of twenty-eight a promotion to the bishopric of Chieti. He wrought great reforms in his diocese and was sent two years later as papal nuncio to Naples. At the age of thirty-seven he was sent as legate to Henry VIII. In England he met Erasmus who praised his knowledge of Latin, Greek, Hebrew and Theology.[3] Two years later, he was sent as nuncio to Spain where he became one of Ferdinand's council and a royal chaplain. In 1524 he resigned both his bishoprics, distributed his property to needy relatives and the poor and founded a new order of priests who could own no property and were forbidden to beg. They must live on unasked gifts and their special object was the reform of the clergy.

[1] Confessions, p. 93.   [2] Ortiz's change in favour of Ignatius is not explained, Astrain 86. Venturi, II, 91.   [3] Pastor IV (2) 596.

He became the director of this order,[4] and, after the sack of Rome by the army of the Emperor settled in Venice. In two outbreaks of the pest his Theatines, as they were called, won great love and admiration by their courage and kindness to the ill and dying, and Caraffa obtained very strong influence both with the council of Venice and with the Pope. The reason why Ignatius, during the year when he was waiting at Venice for his comrades, excited the disapproval of Caraffa might have remained unknown; for Ignatius never gave any reason why he feared Caraffa's opposition. But it is explained by a letter, without signature or address, unquestionably written by Ignatius Loyola to Pietro Caraffa during the year 1536.

The paragraphs essential to the full understanding of this long and sometimes obscure document are given because it seems to the writer Loyola's only serious mistake in handling men.

"Considering that the blessed life we so long for consists in an intimate and true love of God Our Creator and Lord, which binds and obliges us all to a sincere love . . . in the same Lord, who hopes to save us if we do not falter through our weakness, fault and misery, I have concluded to write this letter, without the ceremony so many use (which does no harm if it is done in the Lord). . . . So, laying aside all things which might incite or move us to leave true peace, internal and eternal, I beg you by the love and reverence for Christ our Creator, Redeemer and Lord, to read this with the same love and good will with which it is written. . . .

"So with that will prompt and prepared to serve all those whom I perceive to be servants of my Lord, I will speak of three things with simplicity and love as if I were speaking to my own soul; I do this not in order to give counsel —which it is always better for us to take, and with humility, than to give without humility—but rather to sug-

[4] Pastor 357. Not the ostensible head.

gest that we should dispose ourselves to ask it of the
Lord; from whom comes all good judgment and all sane
counsel.

"The first is this. I think I have enough arguments . . .
to believe, speaking in true peace, love and charity, that
you ought not to separate in any way the company God
has given you; so that, remaining better accompanied,
you will be better able to offer greater service and praise
to God: and certainly I do not express all my understanding on this point. . . .

"The second is this. For a person like yourself, advanced in years and of a family so noble, so dignified and of
such estate, to be a little better clad, and to have a room
somewhat larger and somewhat better furnished than the
others of your company chiefly because of those who come
and go—so far as this is concerned I see no scandal or lack
of edification in it. Nevertheless it appears great and grave
wisdom, remembering how the blessed saints like St.
Francis and St. Dominic and many others bore themselves
when they founded their institutions, to have recourse to
the true and highest wisdom, to ask and obtain more light
in order to arrange all things to His greater service and
honor. Many things are permitted which are not expe-
dient, as St. Paul says of himself, in order that others may
find no occasion for weakness but rather an example to
go forward. . . .

"The third is this. As I hold it a maxim that God Our
Lord has created all things in this life for the use and pres-
ervation of man, a fortiori for those who are better, and,
as your holy and pious profession is a road toward growing
better . . . I believe, that all those who are obedient to
your rule and of stainless life, even although they do not
preach nor exercise themselves so much in visible works
of bodily mercy in order to devote themselves to other
good works spiritual and of greater importance, ought to

have food and clothing, according to the rule of Christ-
tian charity; . . . For those who are more infirm or
under greater care about the necessities of life have some
apparent foundation for saying that it is most difficult
to maintain themselves in the profession for these three
very apparent reasons. In the first place they do not ask
alms even though they have nothing to live on; secondly,
they do not beg: thirdly, they do not exercise themselves
so much in works of bodily pity like burying the dead,
saying mass for them, etc. So far as the others are concerned: although they do not seek alms either, they do
good works which are visible to the public: preaching,
helping parish priests, etc. . . . and it is evident that the
people would always be moved to support them and with
much greater charity. . . . But so far as concerns those
who live righteously more for the increase of inner piety,
I can say that, not seeking alms but serving God Our Lord
and confiding in His great goodness, it is enough to entitle
them to be kept and sustained.

"Besides the more infirm or more solicitous can answer
. . . that St. Francis and the other blessed saints put their
hope and trust in God Our Lord, but, for all that they did
not neglect to use the most convenient means to preserve
their convents for the greater service of the Divine Majesty. They can say further that to do otherwise seems
more like tempting the Lord they serve than taking the
way most fitting for His Service.

"There are other things of more moment which I will
leave in order not to discuss them in a letter—not things
said or thought by me, but suggested and raised by others.
All these things thus weighed and thought over, it is
enough to suggest them as I would to my own soul. . . .
always recommending ourselves to God Our Lord, ...
as I do in my own affairs, that He may be pleased by His
lofty grace to put His own most holy hand to all things so

that all may turn out for His greater service and glory.

"He who desires to be the servant of all the servants of God Our Lord."

It was rather strange that Ignatius, who was to become the greatest servant of the Papacy of his times, should at the first meeting with Caraffa have offended him. For the greatest historian of the Papacy has written of Caraffa's election twenty years later: "For sixty years the new Pope had directed all his gifts of mind with the strength of an iron will and the fixity of a character which suffered no contradiction, towards one object—-the restoration of the position and the might, the purity and the dignity of the Church, beset within and without by foes."

It is true that Caraffa at sixty, when Ignatius met him at Venice, probably had some of the characteristics which marked the Pope of seventy-nine "who suffered no contradiction and was very easily angered," "who liked better to talk than to listen" and "took sudden likes and dislikes." It is also probably true that the dislike of Spaniards for which he was so noted as Pope, may have been fixed on him twenty years before.[5]

It may also perhaps be conceded, as two of the most scholarly modern biographers of Ignatius say, that this letter is written "with every delicacy" of phrase and thought by one who "did his best to express himself as politely and carefully as possible."[6]

Making all these allowances, it seems difficult to avoid the conclusion that the fault in this break between two mighty servants of the same great ideal was with Ignatius. If we say that Caraffa might have pardoned the letter, we can also say that Ignatius, even if he had written it, might have torn it up. Caraffa was a man of varied experience in the most difficult services of the Church. He had

---

[5] All this on Caraffa is based on Pastor V, 364 ff. [6] Venturi, II, 88; Boehmer, 188.

founded an order of reforming priests and directed it for
some years. He was a scholar who had won the praise of
the king of letters, Erasmus. Why should this bran-new
master of arts from Paris, the mediocrity of whose scholarly attainments [7] was suggested in the vague and clumsy
style of his letter, undertake to give any advice on such
intimate questions as the proper distribution among the
members of Caraffa's order of the alms which came to it.
The suggestion that Caraffa lived in too luxurious a way
was superfluous for the man who, when he was forced
against his will to obey the Pope's command to become a
cardinal, had so simple a room in Rome that he had to
drive a nail in the wall to hang up his red hat because there
was no table where he could lay it. [8] The suggestion that
the members of the Order should be kept together and not
dispersed, was not adopted by Ignatius himself; for he
sent his comrades two by two throughout Italy. Ten or
fifteen years later Ignatius might reasonably have assumed that he had valuable advice on such subjects to give
to any man. But then ten years later Ignatius would not
have written this letter. There is no other like it among
the 6800 printed in his correspondence and it seems so
lacking in that knowledge of human nature and skill in
handling men which later characterized Ignatius, that it
would be hard to find anywhere a better example of the
exception which makes plain the rule.

When the comrades got back from Rome to Venice they
found it impossible to start for Jerusalem because of the
war between the Venetians and the Turks. So they made
their disposition to complete the year of waiting defined
in their vow at Montmartre. Those who were not already
ordained took the usual vows of a poor priest, i.e., a priest
without benefice binding to certain duties and bringing
in a certain income. It was decided that it would be

[7] Lainez thought Ignatius had slight gifts, either for style or scholarship.
Scripta, I, 394. [8] Pastor, V, 357.

better to separate and visit various cities of the Venetian
territory, so Loyola, Lainez and Lefèvre went to Vicenza,
Xavier and Salmeron to Mont Celasius (Montelas), Hoces
(a new recruit gained by Ignatius at Venice) and Codure
to Treviso, Le Jay and Rodriguez to Bassano, Broet and
Bobadilla to Verona. Loyola and his two comrades lodged
in a ruined house outside the walls of Vicenza which had
neither door nor windows, where they slept on a little straw
they had brought with them. Twice a day two of the three
went to beg in the city, getting only bread without meat or
wine; but sometimes they were given a little vinegar.
The one who remained in the house softened the crusts
of bread by steeping them in hot water; but even of this
rough fare they had barely enough to sustain life. In this
way they passed forty days in prayer. At the end of that
time, Codure joined them and the four began to preach;
each going to a different public square. There he began
his sermon by calling loudly to the people and waving
his cap. Few came to listen but some good was done.
People began to talk about them and gained enough
confidence to give them plenty of food. The other comrades had similar experiences before they all met at
Vicenza, where they remained for a while together before
separating to seek alms through the cities of the neighbourhood. They still hoped to go to Jerusalem, but, as
there was no chance of a ship sailing at once, they agreed
to divide among the university cities of Italy "to see if the
Lord wished to call some students to join us." So in
couples they visited Rome, Siena, Bologna, Ferrara,
Padua, "in all of which cities by the grace of Our Lord
they gathered fruit." They still were in danger of persecution from oversuspicious zealots, for at Padua the missioners were arrested and put in chains. Over this imprisonment for Christ's sake Hoces "was so joyful that he
did nothing but laugh all night. However in the morning

the suffragan who had caused their arrest, when he learned
what they were and what they wanted, set them free and
treated them like his own sons, showing them all necessary
spiritual favors so that by their ministrations many began
to lead a new life and from morning until night they were
busied in exhorting and hearing confessions." [9]

At Ferrara, the Duke himself came to some sermons,
confessed to the missioners, took communion and offered
to give them all the alms necessary to get them to
Jerusalem. At Bologna they had the same success and also
in Siena, where they undertook another task, that of
"teaching Christian doctrine to children with great satisfaction to the parents." In Rome two of them lectured
in the College of the Sapienza: one expounding the scriptures and the other scholastic philosophy. At the end of
the year, since it was plainly impossible to go to Jerusalem,
they decided to go to Rome and this time "the pilgrim
also was to go because, the first time, when the comrades
went, those two whose opposition he feared had shown
themselves very kind." [10] So they all united in Rome about
April 1538.

During this time of the first missionary work and spiritual preparation for offering their first mass, Ignatius, tells
us he went through a new stage of his inner spiritual life;
or rather he returned to an older stage of spiritual experiences.

He says: "During the time when he (the pilgrim) was
at Vicenza and quite contrary to what happened to him at
Paris, he had many spiritual visions besides many, so to
speak, ordinary consolations from God—especially when
he was in Venice getting ready for ordination to the priesthood and also when he was preparing to say his first mass
and during all his journeys of this time he had great supernatural visitations like those he used to have when he was

[9] Lainez, Scripta I, 118.   [10] Confessions 94.

at Manresa. Also when he was in Venice he knew (in his soul) that one of his comrades at Bassano was lying ill at the point of death. He himself was at that very moment ill of fever. Nevertheless he started on the journey and walked so fast that Lefèvre who went along could not keep up with him and on that journey he received from God the assurance that his comrade would not die of that illness and he told Lefèvre, and, when they arrived at Bassano the ill man was much consoled and quickly got well." [11]

On the journey to Rome, Ignatius had the most celebrated of his visions. He relates it in a few lines in his Confessions and Consalvez de Camara to whom he was dictating adds this note to the passage, "I who write these things said to the pilgrim when he narrated this, that Lainez told about it with some particulars. And he said to me that all Lainez said was true, because he himself did not remember with such particularity. But at the time when he told Lainez about it he knows certainly that he said nothing which was not accurate." [12]

Lainez's account is as follows: "When we were going to Rome by the road through Siena, the Father had many spiritual sentiments; especially in relation to the eucharist. Lefèvre and I said mass every day. He did not, but he communicated. Then he said to me that it seemed to him that God impressed on his heart these words: 'I will be propitious to you at Rome,' and our Father, not knowing what these words might mean, said: 'I do not know what will become of us at Rome, perhaps we shall be crucified.' Then another time he said that he seemed to see Christ with the cross on his shoulder and the Eternal Father near by, who said: 'I wish you to take this man for your servant' and so Jesus took him and said: 'I will that thou shouldst serve me.' And gaining from that vision great devotion

[11] Confessions 94.   [12] Confessions 95.

to the name of Jesus he wanted his congregation called
The Company of Jesus." [13]

This vision of assurance was needed, for evidently
Loyola was depressed on entering Rome. He said to his
companions that: "he saw the windows closed; meaning
that they were to meet much opposition. He said also we
must keep to ourselves and not enter into relations with
women unless they are women of distinguished position." [14]

These forebodings were not at first fulfilled. The comrades lived in a vineyard house near the monastery of the
Holy Trinity given to them as a lodging place by a Roman
"for the love of God." This they afterwards abandoned
for a rented house nearer the centre of the city. It was not
necessary for them very long to beg their bread, for the
gifts of their friends soon sufficed for their support. Not
long after their arrival at Rome, the comrades were joined
by Pietro Codacio, a Lombard priest who gave up rich
benefices to join them. He was an amicable and godly
man, with a gift for practical affairs, and became their
procurator or financial agent; not only for the Roman
house but for the larger affairs of the company. He man-
aged these for some ten years and showed himself so
capable that the fathers were able to leave to him all care
for collecting alms and to devote themselves to their
spiritual duties toward their neighbours. He finally
obtained the piece of ground chosen by Loyola and built
on it the house of the Company. It was also due to him
that they obtained their own church. [15]

These poor pilgrim priests, as they called themselves,
who gathered around Ignatius were extremely fearful of
seeming to make a business of their services to their neighbours. It was against their custom to receive money from
anyone with whom they had talked about religion or whose

[13] Venturi, I, 586, printed. Essortations, etc. [x] Confessions, 95. [15] Pol. I,
66-81-362.

confession they had heard, or for whom they had said mass; nor did they allow collections to be made when they preached.

When Simon Rodriguez went to Lisbon on his way to the Indies by the request of the King of Portugal, he was received in the most intimate and friendly fashion by the King and Queen. But he would not accept their hospitality and insisted so firmly on begging his bread from door to door, that they were obliged to permit him to do it. Of course the guest of the King did not really need to beg from door to door and it was manifestly an act of piety and self-humiliation rather than a means of supplying want. Begging from door to door, "sancta mendicitas," [16] continued to be used as a means of livelihood and still more as a means of grace, but it is evident that Ignatius learned by experience in regard to his comrades in the Company what he had learned by experience about students at Paris: that the need of begging their living often interfered very much with their work.

Apparently the support of the labourers in the vineyard of the Lord, in all places where they were permanently established, drifted in the direction of money given by what might almost be called subscribers; regular or occasional. For example, two years after the assembly of the comrades at Rome when Lainez was on mission to Piacenza: "At length toward the end of the year he began by the order of Father Ignatius to accept what he needed from alms spontaneously offered. Before this, because of his love of poverty, and in order that he might freely give what he had freely received from God, he had lived by begging from door to door and with his comrade Lefèvre had suffered great need of the bare necessities of life." [17]

Codacio organized the expenses of the Roman establish-

[16] Letts. IV, 494, 565, e.g.   [17] Polanco, I, 83.

ment as best he could on the sort of irregular volunteer income which finally came to him; much of it from friendly cardinals He raised special building funds when they were needed Ignatius must at times have been rather difficult to serve for a man like Codacio in whom the busi- ness sense was highly developed. For Ignatius would never consent to let financial considerations interfere too much with his decisions on spiritual matters. One of the comrades at Rome wrote "Even in the days of the most extreme narrowness of our resources he would never refuse to accept anyone who seemed fit for the society and called of God to it." [18]

On the other hand, in dark days when there was no money and disaster hung like a black cloud overhead, his calm trust in God cheered all hearts. When they were building their new house and creditors came to seize the furniture, Ignatius was not at all disturbed. "Well," he said, "if they take the beds we will sleep on the ground. We are paupers and we can lead the life of paupers." [19] A totally unexpected gift of two hundred gold pieces paid the threatening note of hand. Another time, near the end of Ignatius' life, his secretary Polanco could not beg or raise in any way the money to continue the German College at Rome. Ignatius shut himself in his room for prayer. Then calling Polanco and two of the old fathers, he said he had commended the situation to God. "I am," he continued "neither a prophet nor the son of a prophet but I am certain God will provide. You" he said, turning to Polanco "will see it within six months." When the six months drew near its end Ribadeneira, who had gone to Germany, wrote to know the outcome and was told that the day after the receipt of his letter sums had been brought to them in alms great enough to pay all debts.[20] For more than ten years Codacio carried on his broad

[18] Rib., 2nd Life, 599.   [19] Rib., 588.   [20] Ribad., 2nd Life, 603.

shoulders the heavy burden of the money needs of the
Company and when he was stricken by apoplexy just as he
was entering the room of Ignatius after luncheon, his
brethren asked in dismay: "Where shall we find his
successor for he made all money cares so completely his
own that no one of us knows anything about it?" Not so,
however, Ignatius, who immediately took in ten novices.

In addition to this inspiring example of "the Father" the
brethren were much comforted by incidents which followed
the death of their treasurer.   "The steward of the house
was crossing a deserted place near the Colosseum when an
unknown man appeared who gave him a purse with almost
a hundred gold pieces and went away. When he got home,
told what had happened, and showed the gold pieces, there
were some who feared that the change which takes place
when evil spirits offer money which afterwards turns into
glowing coals, might also occur with this money. But it
was real gold which seemed to be newly minted. It did
not change its form but proved good for the needs of
the house and the payment of debts. A day or two later
when the steward was going to market, as was his custom,
before dawn, another unknown man met him, gave him a
great sum in newly minted gold (some sixty or seventy
pieces) and went away. At about the same time when I
was searching a certain open part of the house where
rubbish and scraps of paper were in a chest, in order to see
if there were any letters there, I stirred up the rubbish and
found, wrapped up in unused paper, a great number of
new gold pieces. So, as many believe, the divine goodness,
by means of the angels, wished to make up to us for the
diligence and skill in his office of Father Pietro Codacio.
When I told this to the vicar of the city he said 'Do not
doubt that also these alms have been procured for your
house by Pietro Codacio for I do not doubt that the charity
of this same Pietro in heaven and the faith and hope of

Father Ignatius on earth have obtained this help directly from the goodness of God.' "[21]

How great the sense of loss was among his comrades, for this humble helper in realizing the ideal of Ignatius, may be judged from the fact that some feared it might be mocked by devils and all believed it was helped by angels.

The ideals and the character of Ignatius were now fully ripened. After this he did not change in any essential respect and few lives have been more self-consistent, more all of a piece, than the eighteen years which he spent, practically without break, in Rome. He was forty-seven years old and for seventeen years since his conversion, external and internal experience and an iron will had been moulding him into a most powerful personality.

But in spite of all his power, Ignatius was not yet clear in his mind what he would do. His plan of going to Palestine first alone, and then with a band of chosen comrades in order to serve God and help his fellow man among the heathen, could not be carried out. He does not seem to have been much disappointed over the blocking of that long cherished plan adopted by his comrades in the oath of Montmartre. He saw the paths of the sea closed by the Turk. Perhaps he saw also, after two years in Italy, that there was much work to be done for the Church among the Christians of Europe as well as among the infidels of Asia. At all events the second clause of the oath of Montmartre must be kept and they were at Rome to put themselves at the command of the Pope and go wherever he might send them.

But the Pope had gone to Nice to make peace between the Emperor and the King of France and nobody knew how long the negotiations might last. So they determined to do whatever they could find to do. Before they could do very much, almost as soon as they were all assembled in Rome, they ran into very serious trouble; the most

[21] Pol. I, 363.

serious of eight inquiries before the Inquisition to which Ignatius had been obliged to respond.[22] He gives an account of this grave affair in the following extracts from a long letter he wrote at the end of the year to his old friend and helper Isabel Roser of Barcelona.

"I can well believe that you are a little astonished that I have not written you more often, as indeed I wished to do, because, if I forget what I owe to Our Lord by your hands with such sincere love and good will, I think that His Divine Majesty will not remember me. The cause of my delay in writing has been due to an affair which has brought us during eight months the rudest opposition or persecution which we have ever met in our entire life. . . . Popular rumours spread abroad without mentioning names have made us suspected and odious to many people and brought upon us great scandal. . . . In order that you may understand the affair from the beginning I will give you some account of it. It is more than a year since three of the comrades arrived here in Rome as I remember I wrote you. Two commenced, by command of the Pope, to teach in the Sapienza. I applied myself to give the Spiritual Exercises near Rome as well as at Rome. We agreed we would do this in order to have some educated men or people of importance on our side; or to speak more exactly on the side of God our Lord. . . . We did this in order not to have so much contradiction from worldlings and so be able to preach His holy word more freely. . . . After we had gained by these exercises (God working in us) some in our favour (and they were persons learned and of much reputation) we decided, four months after our arrival to assemble all the comrades here . . . and we were careful to get from the Legate license to preach, exhort and hear confession. When we had it, four or five of us commenced to preach on Sundays and holy days in different churches.

[22] His letter to the King of Portugal, Letts. I, 296.

. . . We were finally obliged to call our secret de-
tractors before the magistrates.   When one of them
found himself before the magistrates, the others began to be afraid and as they were rich personages,
one with an income of a thousand ducats and the
other of six hundred, all well known in curial circles
and intimate with cardinals and other persons of position in high circles of the Church, they gave us a great
deal of trouble.   But finally the chief among them being
forced to appear . . . said that they had heard us
preaching and teaching and could find no fault in our life
and doctrine. . . . The governor wished to let the matter
lapse in silence but we demanded some written statement of the good or evil in our doctrine, in order to stop
the scandal among the people.   We could not get it. . . .
Finally I went to the Pope's summer castle and talked
alone with His Holiness in his room for an hour.   I told
him plainly all the times process had been brought against
me in Spain and how I had been arrested in Alcalá and
Salamanca.   I did this in order that no one could tell
him more about it than I did. . . . Pointing out how
necessary it was that we should be cleared, not only
before God but also before the public, I begged His Holiness to order a full examination.   The Pope . . . ordered
a formal hearing in our case. . . . Sentence has been
given in our favour.   So we give thanks to God that our
work has never ceased and, now that our innocence has
been finally declared, we hope to do more in preaching
and teaching children."[23]

There was something behind all this which Loyola does
not mention; perhaps because he thought it unimportant.

The little band of poor priests were not the attacked
but the attackers.[24]   One of the most distinguished
preachers in Rome was a certain Augustinian Eremite
Agostino Mainardo.   Six years before the arrival of

[23] Letts. I, 137.   [24] Polanco I, 79.

Loyola and his friends at Rome, Mainardo, while preaching in Asti, had process begun against him and was prohibited from preaching. He had obtained three years
later a papal letter recognizing his doctrine as sound and
forbidding interference with his preaching. Armed with
this, he preached during Lent at Rome with great success. But he was a Lutheran, that is, he held Lutheran
doctrine, though probably he was not aware of it for he
defended his doctrine by the authority of tradition and
of St. Augustine. Some of the comrades heard him preach
and recognized at once Lutheran doctrine such as they
had heard at Paris. They took notes, and, after trying
in vain to convert the preacher by private conversations,
they determined to preach doctrine opposed to his errors
in various places.[25] He had many friends and admirers
and it was by them that the scandals and rumours about
Ignatius and his comrades were spread throughout Rome.
The boldness of Ignatius, above all his frank conversation with the Pope, saved him; for all the comrades wanted
after the imperfect hearing before the legate to take his
advice and let the affair drop.[26] Ignatius was right in
thinking this very dangerous. Ten years later a new
inquisitor at Rome insisted that there had been and was
evidence to prove that the followers of Loyola were sod-
omites, Lutherans and misusers of the confessional. He
expressed the confident hope that Loyola "unless worldly
considerations interfered with a righteous judgment"
would yet die at the stake.[27]

This was, it is true, the sort of prosecutor which re-
gards every acquittal as a calamity; a bulldog type of
court officer known to the history of all courts. But it
was more than usually common among the inquisitors of
the faith; whose processes were not so solicitous about
saving the innocent, if only they might be sure that they
would by no means clear the guilty. The boldness of

[25] Pol. p. 65. [26] Lainez Sc. 374. [27] Venturi I, 637-641. Cited. Boehmer, 233.

Ignatius therefore saved him later from serious danger.

The first heretic opponent of Ignatius finally recognized his own lack of orthodoxy and fled to southern Switzerland where, after long service as a Protestant minister, he died at an advanced age. His two chief admirers at Rome fell four years later into the hands of the Inquisition. One of them, condemned to death in spite of the intercession of Ignatius, escaped from prison and disappeared. His valuable benefices were taken from him, his large fortune confiscated and he was publicly burned in effigy. The other was kept in prison for the rest of his life.[28]

[28] Venturi II, 175. Camara Mem. Scripta I, 307.

CHAPTER IX

THE FORMATION OF THE COMPANY OF JESUS

Up to the conclusion of this affair the impression which Ignatius and his comrades had made upon the city of Rome was slight or unfavorable. The Pope indeed had shown himself gracious. He invited some of them to come every two weeks to talk theology at his luncheon table.[1] They had made also a number of influential friends, like their great patron Cardinal Gasparo Contarini, whose learning, charm and piety had gained him the name of the "ornament of the Italian nation."[2] The tone of uncritical eulogy with which the life of Loyola came to be discussed by his followers of the seventeenth century, led them to exaggerate the first effects of the preaching of his comrades at Rome; as if the whole city had been profoundly stirred or even converted. Ignatius himself speaks very modestly of the results, and Lainez wrote ten years later of their first preaching: "At least it served as a mortification to pride and some souls found profit in our sermons."[3] Ignatius indeed preached in his own language; the others tried to preach in Italian, in which none of them except Lefèvre was very fluent. They made their first strong impression on the city not by education or eloquence—though they had one and soon developed the other—but by practical deeds of Christian duty which dispelled the scandals against them secretly spread abroad by the friends of the popular preacher whose heretical doctrine they had opposed. It may well

[1] Letts. I, 141.   [2] Pastor, V, 105.
[3] Scripta, I, p. 120. Comp. Venturi II, 151 & 152 notes.

130

be that Ignatius used this first experience in mission work to guide him in giving instruction to those he later sent on difficult and varied missions; for no man ever learned more out of his own experience about how to handle other men. It became his habit to instruct his missioners or envoys, whether their special task was to preach, or to teach, or to give counsel, to spend as much strength as they could spare from that special task in deeds of kindness to their fellowmen.

Loyola's first new work of charity at Rome was opening a refuge and a bread line for the "down and outs" of his day. There were many of these in the year 1539. For the winter was very cold and bread was scarce and dear. Driven by hunger the unemployed swarmed into the city where they slept in the streets and squares, starving and half frozen.[4] The heads of church and state seemed not to care. But the ten poor priests went out every night to gather up the hungry and sick and give them food, fire and shelter in the half ruined building where they lodged. For the sick they had a few beds, for the rest straw, for all bread—though sometimes barely enough. The number of these guests whom they compelled to come in from the highways, grew from night to night until finally it mounted to three hundred, and, during the day, the poor priests begged the bread and wood and straw to welcome them. The example was contagious. Arrangements were finally made to shelter and feed these miserable people in the hospitals and poorhouses, until three thousand were cared for every night; a large number for a city of less than 40,000 inhabitants.

Other charity Loyola gave to the poor who were not in the street, but suffering in bare houses. For these he collected large sums of money and, when need was, he diverted to this use money given for the support of the

4 Pastor II, 393.

comrades; until sometimes there was not a penny left
in the house.

The poor priests had already shown a liking for teaching the elements of religion to children and the first work
in which the Pope employed the whole band was instructing all the children of the schools in religion. The governor of the city was ordered to take the necessary steps
to enable them to do this. Later Loyola was to found
in Rome other works of mercy: an asylum for orphans,
a school for Jewish boys, a house of refuge for fallen
women. But just now the attention of the ten under his
lead was turned toward a much greater foundation: the
Company of Jesus.

Most of Loyola's biographers down to recent times[5]
and even one of his three most scholarly latest biographers,
have fallen into an error in regard to this foundation.
There is a natural tendency among the biographers of
men whose lives have wrought great effects in history, to
attribute to them a sort of unhuman prescience by making
them conscious from the beginning of their careers, of the
goals to which they finally attained. Both the enemies
and the friends of Oliver Cromwell, for instance, were
long accustomed to make the false assumption that the
simple country gentleman had cherished for years a plan
to replace the English monarchy by a commonwealth ruled
by the godly under his leadership; or as his enemies said,
had with long sustained malice hypocritically plotted to
kill his lawful king. But usually he goes farthest who
does not try to see the way too far ahead. This was certainly true of Ignatius. He moved as the voice of God
in his soul called him and followed step by step the lead-
ings of Providence. This is not an abstract conclusion. We
have the strongest direct testimony to prove it. Polanco
(Ignatius' secretary) writes that when the brethren took
the vow of Montmartre "it never entered into their heads

[5] See Venturi, II, p. 200.

to found a new religious order." Lainez, one of the original fathers, sustains this by writing, "when we were at
Paris our intention was not to found an order, but to pass
in poverty a life dedicated to helping our neighbours by
preaching and serving in hospitals and to go to Jerusalem
to help ourselves and others, the faithful and the infidel."
A letter written later by order of Ignatius says, "Father
Ignatius and the first fathers did not go from Paris to
Italy to found an order, but to go to Jerusalem and preach
and die among the infidels."[6]   Polanco again writes,
"When in the spring of 1538 our brethren came together
at Rome, they did not propose to themselves in thought
to found any perpetual institution or order, but to devote themselves to the care of souls wherever the Pope
might wish to send them."[7]

We may be glad there is such strong contemporary
evidence against a deliberate effort on the part of Ignatius
"to use reserve and not frankly express his ideas or un-
roll before the eyes of his comrades the plan he had conceived."[8]   If he had practised this kind of silence, con-
cealing for years from his intimate friends at Paris his
real intentions in forming that band of spiritual knights
errant, it would have been a lack of frankness, suggesting grave doubts of the sincerity of the tender and beautiful friendship which bound this little band to him and
united them to each other.

Now that they were finally delivered from the danger of
the Inquisition, had gained by the frankness of their leader
the manifest favour of the Pope, and won by their charity
to the poor the trust of the people of Rome, the question
arose: Since they were not to go to Jerusalem, what
should they do?

In March 1539 the nine poor priests then present in
Rome (one had been added to their fellowship and two

[6] Letts, V, 25. [7] Polanco, I, 51-70. Lainez, Scripta IV, p. 114. Compare
Pol. 79, Letts. V, 259. Venturi, II. 200. Boehmer, 149. [8] Astrain, 115.

sent by the Pope to reform a cloister in Siena) gave themselves up to a careful and prayerful discussion of the problem before them. When their work of the day was done, they met in conference. At first they had to decide a general question: should they or should they not found a company which should not end with their lives? After discussion and reflection the answer was unanimously, yes. The question what this institution was to be called was quickly decided in favor of the Company of Jesus. Ignatius told his secretary, at a time when the name was criticized as claiming for the Company what belonged to all Christians, "that even if all the brethren should wish to change it and all others (except the Pope) should agree it ought to be changed, he would never consent, because he had received such plain signs of God's approval of it that to give it up would be, for him, acting against God's will."[9]

The third question was not so quickly decided. It was: shall we, like other orders, elect a leader and all make to him a vow of obedience? The pros and cons of the question were most carefully discussed in many meetings, and finally it was decided, at the beginning of the year 1539, in the affirmative. In about two months more they fixed the outlines of a plan for the Company of Jesus to be laid before the Pope under five heads. The influence of Loyola's old military training seems to be plain in the trumpet tones of the first phrases of the opening sentence, his experience in helping and teaching men in the latter half of it. "Whoever wishes to be a warrior of God under the banner of the cross in our Company, which we call by the name of Jesus, and to serve only God and His Vicar on earth, must keep in his mind after he has taken the vow of perpetual chastity that he is part of a community founded chiefly to aid souls in Christian living and Christian doctrine, to spread the word of God by

[9] Pol. 73, 79.

preaching, by spiritual exercises, by deeds of neighbourly kindness and especially by the instruction of children and the ignorant in Christianity.

"He must always have God before his eyes and strive with all his might towards the goal shown him by God, keeping always before him those rules which are in a manner a way to God. The decision about the place or position in service which belongs to every man must rest entirely in the hands of the prepositus to be chosen by us. This prepositus shall have power to make statutes with the advice of the brothers in concilium when the majority shall always decide. The executive power and the power to give orders belong only to the prepositus (general).

"All members, so long as life lasts, shall every day bethink themselves of the fact that this Company and all in it are under the command of our holy master Paul III and his successors, so that we are bound to give him something more than the obedience of ordinary clergymen. We are bound by special oath to do whatever he orders us to do; whether he sends us to the Turks or to the new world, or to the Lutherans, or to any other believers or unbelievers.

"Every member shall promise obedience to the general in all things concerning the rule. He on his side must be always mindful of the goodness, the gentleness and love of Christ. Both shall lay it on their hearts to instruct children and the ignorant in Christian doctrine, in the ten commandments and other elementary things.

"We have learned by experience that a way of living as far from greed and as near to evangelic poverty as possible is more edifying to our neighbours and that Christ will provide for his servants. We cannot hold any legal right to any income or real property, but must be content with the simple use of things necessary to life by the consent of the owners.

"All ordained members are to say the breviary accord-

ing to the rites of the Church, not however all together
in choir in order that they may not be turned aside
from the duties of neighbourly love. They shall not
use in divine service either the organ or chanting. For
these things, which adorn the divine worship of other
orders, we have found by experience to be no small
hindrance to us; since we devote a great part of the day
and night to the bodily and spiritual care of the sick.

"We make this sketch of what we do and propose in
order to warn our successors against falling into two errors
we have escaped. First, no one shall ever enjoin upon the
members of our company fasts, scourgings, going bare-
footed or bareheaded, fixed colours of dress and fixed
foods, hair shirts or other ascetic observances. We do
not forbid these things because we condemn them, but
because we do not wish our brethren to find in them an
excuse for withdrawing themselves from the duties we
have undertaken.

"The second error to be avoided is this. No one can
be received into the company unless he has been very
thoroughly tested for a long time." [10]

Having thus reached unanimously conclusions which
could be formulated into a general outline of the institution they wished to found, they left it to Ignatius to get
the Pope's permission and went their several ways to their
tasks already assigned to them. Whether or not Ignatius
was the penman of the capitoli (10), he plainly was the
best qualified man to get papal approval for them. He
sent the document at once to his great friend Cardinal
Contarini, who took the first good opportunity to lay it
before the Pope, who sent it to the master of the holy
palace to give judgment as to whether there might be
unwittingly anything heretical in it. This authority took

[10] From the German of Boehmer translated from the Minuta of Contarini
in Vatican archives, 242 n 3. Italian version Venturi Vol. I, 297.

two months to make up his mind to send word to Loyola that it was "pious and holy." The next day Ignatius forwarded the document to Contarini who at once read it to the Pope. He approved it without difficulty and the affair was sent to the secretariat to prepare the necessary documents.

Cardinal Ghinucci into whose hands the matter came had been a papal secretary since the days of Julius II and was extremely learned in canon law. It was not strange that this veteran of the office, a highly trained bureaucrat, should be disposed to be very critical of this request to found a new order. He suspected first those features of it which were original and unknown to the standard constitution of a religious order. He objected to the prohibition of ascetic rules for the members because it might be used by the Lutherans in their attack on the monks. He objected to the special vow of obedience to the Pope because it might suggest that everybody was not already bound to obey the Pope, etc., etc. In short he and Contarini, who was delighted with the five points as they stood, evidently developed differences of opinion which compelled the Pope to call into their council a third person. He chose Bartolommeo Guidiccioni recently appointed a cardinal. He had been the Pope's vicar when the latter was bishop of Parma, and the Pope had great confidence in him.[11] He took a position on the question of the Company of Jesus which differed from both of the men to whom the Pope had first assigned the matter. Contarini was heartily for it. Ghinucci was against it because he did not like its rules. Guidiccioni said he approved entirely of the suggested rules. If any new orders were to be allowed there could not be better ones. But he believed that no new orders ought to be permitted, and all existing orders ought to be reduced to four: Dominicans, Franciscans, Cistercians and Black

[11] Pastor, V, 135, 123.

Benedictines. This new commissioner therefore, though for entirely different reasons, voted no with Cardinal Ghinucci, and the desire of the ten poor pilgrim priests seemed to be hopeless.

But Ignatius was not a man to give up hope easily in a matter which he believed according to the will of God. This will he felt was now being blocked by the great enemy of truth. It was freely conceded among the poor pilgrim priests that their new opponent was "a good and pious man and very skilled in church law, but Ignatius, recognizing a stratagem of the devil, thought that the Cardinal must be won by prayers and sacrifices, which he took care should be applied to this affair most liberally: for more than two thousand masses were offered to God on his behalf. Chiefly by these (though there were other reasons) the opposition of Cardinal Guidiccioni was changed into approval."[12]

The payment of this spiritual debt vowed by Ignatius took some time for so small a number of priests. A year after the granting of the papal bull, two members of the company on their way towards a dangerous mission in Ireland were ordered to say as many masses as possible on the vow, and to send back a strict account of the number. Some months later Xavier on his way to India wrote back that he and his comrades had said 250 masses for Guidiccioni.[13]

"The other reasons" for the change of attitude by the good cardinal were the skilful use Ignatius made of the influential friends won by his own work and that of his comrades.

The Duke of Ferrara was a warm friend of the poor pilgrim priests, three of whom had worked in his capital. He was very glad to write on their behalf to his friends in Rome and especially to his brother Cardinal Ippolito.

[12] Pol. 72. Lainez, Scripta. I, 122 says 3,000 masses. [13] Letts, I, 197. Mon Xav. I, 245.

Seven years later Ignatius sending to Jay his authorization to go on mission to Ferrara, wrote in a message he manifestly wishes to have quoted: "I can truly say that we are not under such great obligation to any one as we are to the Duke of Ferrara for the foundation of our company: for whose increase may God use, as the prime and most efficacious instrument, the gracious favour and help of His Excellency."[14] Guidiccioni had been for years general vicar in Parma. After he left for Rome two of the poor priests had worked in Parma and made a very strong impression. So the elders of the city government were asked by the missioners to intercede with their former vicar. They did so directly but without effect. Then, by whose suggestion we do not know, they tried an indirect approach. Pope Paul III had an illegitimate daughter Costanza born to him while he was still Cardinal Farnese. She was married to the Count of Santafiore and had very great influence with her father.[15] She did not always use it well. Her son was made a cardinal at the age of sixteen, and his life as he grew older was not an ornament to the purple robe. She was responsible for the naming of four other cardinals whose character and careers shocked the friends of reform. The elders of Parma wrote to her thinking that she might be willing to use her influence not for greed or for ecclesiastical politics.[16]

We do not know just what influences were the most efficient, but Guidiccioni proposed a compromise: that the company should be authorized but limited to sixty members. So on the 27th of September, 1540, a bull of the Pope founded the Company of Jesus on the basis of the five capitoli: certain things being omitted and certain others more definitely expressed. The Company was given power to draw up its own constitutions in accord with these general ideas. Inside of three years the lim-

[14] Letts. I, 569. [15] Pastor, V, 136. n. 6. [16] Printed, Venturi, I, 572. Pastor V, 138.508.

itation on their members was removed by a second bull.

This long wait of sixteen months to get permission to carry out his plan of service to the Church and his fellow men, must have been very trying for Ignatius. He had evidently thought the matter settled when the plan received the hearty verbal approval of the Pope. He wrote soon after to his nephew the Lord of Loyola a jubilant letter: "God has put His most holy hand to this work and, against great adversity, contradiction and opposing judgments, our whole method of procedure has been approved by the Vicar of Christ, giving us entire power to make constitutions as according to our way of life we shall find most fitting." He suggests to his nephew and sister-in-law that they should contribute towards the company. "So since I, although most unworthy, have been enabled by divine grace to establish foundations approved of the Pope for the Company of Jesus (so we have called it), I ought to exhort you and very thoroughly to build on these foundations thus laid, so that you may have no less merit in the building than I in the foundation and all by the hand of God." [17]

This letter to his nephew is psychologically important because it shows unmistakably Ignatius' perfectly clear consciousness that he was the founder of the company. He does not allude to the help of his comrades. He speaks only of the help of God. True, the others had deliberated with him most carefully as to whether there should be any company and as to what the company should be. We know that one of the most fruitful ideas (the idea of conducting colleges) came from Lainez. But nevertheless the Company of Jesus was not the result of mass action. It was the child of Ignatius and without him it would never have come into existence. Every one of the first fathers had been trained in the Spiritual Exercises which was so to speak the slow distillation of

[17] Letts. I 149.

Ignatius' religious life and experience. They were bound to each other through their relation to him. They acted in unison because each followed his lead. It might well have been doubted whether any one could rear the walls save he who had laid the foundation.

Knowing as we do from these letters to his family that Ignatius clearly recognized this fact that he was under God the sole founder of the company, his attitude toward becoming the first general of the company is psychologically hard to understand.

The election did not as might be expected follow at once upon the issue of the bull. The reason is very simple. Seven of the ten were busy away from Rome. This did not block the election, for it had been decided some months before that pressing questions might be decided by the fathers in Rome together with those in Italy who could assemble or send their written votes. On missions of the Pope two of the fathers were on their way to India, one had started for Germany, four were working in Italy and one of these could not leave his work. Seven months after the publication of the bull of institution, six fathers met in Rome, March 1541, to adopt constitutions and elect a general. They accepted various parts of the constitutions already formulated by Loyola and Codure and took action equivalent to appointing them a committee with power to complete the document. They then proceeded to the election.[18] It was determined that after three days of prayerful thought each should bring in a sealed written vote. These votes were to be put in a locked chest, where were already the votes of the fathers in Germany and Portugal and kept for three days "for fuller confirmation of the affair."

When the chest was opened it was found that the votes of all were for Iñigo, except Bobadilla who sent no vote and Loyola whose vote read as follows: "I vote to make

[18] De la Torre, Constitutiones, 313.

him general in our Lord who receives the most votes, except myself. If the company is of another opinion and thinks it better and more apt to the greater honoring of our Lord, I am prepared to appoint the general."

This vote makes evident of course that he expected to be elected, but it also gave notice that he would refuse to accept the office. Of that refusal he himself gives the following account. "Iñigo acted according to what he felt in his soul affirming that he had more will and desire to be governed than to govern. He felt that he was not strong enough to govern himself and how much less could he rule others. Considering this and his many evil habits past and present, his many sins, faults and bodily miseries, he would declare until he had more light that he would never undertake such a task. He begged them to consider for three or four days recommending themselves to God our Lord, in order to find some one who could better undertake the task." At length, though unwillingly, the companions decided to vote again. The result was the same. Then Iñigo said: that to satisfy his conscience he would leave the matter in the hands of his confessor, Father Theodore, a friar of St. Peter de Montorio, making to him a general confession of all his sins, and giving him a full description of all his infirmities and bodily miseries. After that the confessor in the name of Christ our Lord should order him to accept or decline.

The companions when they found they could not do otherwise, agreed to this also, though unwillingly and with dissatisfaction. Iñigo and his confessor then spent three days together by themselves. When Iñigo had finished his confession and asked his confessor what he had decided about his commands, the confessor answered that he (Ignatius) seemed to be resisting the Holy Spirit. With all that, Iñigo asked his confessor to recommend the affair longer to God and then with a quiet soul to write out his opinion and send it under seal to the company. Then Iñigo went back to the house.

The third day his confessor sent a sealed opinion which was read before all. It decided that Iñigo ought to undertake the business and government of the company. He accepted and ordered that the first Friday after Easter they should all make the pilgrimage to the seven churches of Rome and in St. Paul make their vows according to the bull granted by His Holiness.[19]

That Ignatius regarded his conduct in this matter as important is shown by his writing out this full account of it: a thing which he did for no other incident of his life except in letters. His Confessions were dictated, and long after the events described.

It has been suggested that his long hesitation was only a survival of the ecclesiastical code of good manners of the middle ages, which made a deprecatory attitude towards all ecclesiastical honours obligatory as a matter of custom in all well-bred prelates who knew how things ought to be done. This attitude, described by a phrase, *nolo episcopari*, did become a sort of unavoidable convention. But precisely that makes it improbable that Loyola was affected by it. He did not care much for conventions. We have seen how he had worked out of the attitude toward asceticism suggested to him at first by the life of the average mediæval saint, how in spite of his own love of chanting he had put aside the prayers said in choir which for generations had been the regular stock centre of monastery life. He would not have been apt to go back to the past to pick up this piece of ancient clerical manners. To know his life at first hand in his own acts and words and those of his friends, is to be convinced that he was a singularly sincere man. To play, even half unconsciously, a little pious comedy, no

[19] De la Torre, 313.

matter how edifying it had long been thought, would not have been apt to seem to him useful.

The element of sincerity in this long struggle to escape from a burden which after all was inevitable, was his real shrinking from the task. He felt indeed that by the grace of God he had escaped from even mental consent to mortal sin and told one of his companions so. But there was nothing of the pharisee about him. He felt he had those "evil habits, faults and sins" of which he spoke, for he later said to one of his associates that he could "learn something of every inmate of the house but himself." He knew also his feeble strength and weak health and twice during his service as general he tried to resign. There was no self-centred hypochondria about this. He suffered at intervals intensely, and his physicians did not know how to help him. He never expected to live long and it seemed to his intimates little short of a miracle that he was general for fifteen years. He knew that in learning and facility of expression he was inferior to some of his companions. He had felt the call of God to be founder of the Company. He was not sure that he was the best general to lead it into the great future he foresaw for it.

There is another possible reason for the minute description by Ignatius of his own enigmatic conduct, which may be conjectured from his great care to record twice that his comrades were reluctant and dissatisfied to grant delay and did so only because they could not help it. Ignatius had eight times been attacked for heresy or unchristian conduct, and he perhaps foresaw the repeated opposition which the new Company would have to face. He may have felt it better to keep a clear record lest anybody should accuse him of acting out of ambition to become head of a great institution. If this were so it was a weakness; but it was the weakness of a noble mind conscious of rectitude before God and wishing to make it plain before his fellow-men: especially before those who might follow him in the Company of Jesus.

All walking together the seven made their pilgrimage to the churches and then on St. Paul's day Ignatius said mass. Holding in his hand the paten with the consecrated host, he read the following vow to the companions kneeling before him: "I promise to Almighty God and the Pope His Vicar on earth, before His Virgin Mother and the whole celestial court and in the presence of the Company, perpetual poverty, chastity and obedience according to the way of life in the bull of the Company of Our Lord Jesus and contained in the constitutions adopted or to be adopted. Besides I promise special obedience to the Chief Pontiff in regard to the missions mentioned in the bull. In addition I promise I will take pains to see that boys are instructed in the beginnings of faith according to the same bull and constitutions."

Having made this oath he communed. Then he took five consecrated hosts upon the paten and turned towards his comrades. They made the general confession and then each in turn read a similar oath and communed. At the end, after prayer before the great altar, they each in turn embraced Ignatius and gave him the kiss of peace "not without great devotion, feeling and tears."

The Company of Jesus was organized and equipped for its service to the world.

CHAPTER X

THE CONSTITUTIONS

Although the Company had a leader and a commission from the visible head of the Church it had no detailed constitution. The filling out of the first summary sketch laid before the Pope and confirmed in general by his bull, was a task for which the fathers had no time. So they left it to Ignatius and Codure. Codure died within a year [1] and Ignatius was at first too busy governing the Company to write rules for its government. But after the lapse of six years (1547), he began to formulate his experience and in three years he had finished the Constitutions. He then obtained the opinions of some of the older fathers who were easily accessible and spent two years revising the text. He then sent it to all the establishments of the Company and it became law as if it had been formally voted by a general congregation, which was not done until two years after his death.[2] It was not however regarded as finished. He continued to revise its language and it is the clearest and, from a literary point of view, the best of his writings.

The extreme importance he gave to the document may be measured by its last words "and finally let all set themselves to keep the constitutions—for which end it is necessary to know them: at least for each one to know those which relate to himself and so they are to be read or heard read every month."

The Constitutions are preceded by the "first and gen-

[1] Ribadeneira, folio 80.   [2] Preface to de la Torres IX ff. Astrain, 137.

eral examination which must be proposed to all who ask to
be admitted to the Company of Jesus."

Then follow the Constitutions themselves with *declarations;* a sort of running comment declared to be of equal
authority. A short preface says they will be complete,
clear and brief and divided into ten parts.

The first *part* is on Admitting to Probation. The
power to do this resides in the general and in those to
whom he grants it. No one is to examine for admittance
any friend or relative.

Those who have natural gifts and experience are the
best fitted. But temporal coadjutors may be received if
they have "a good conscience, are quiet, tractable, lovers
of virtue, inclined to devotion and content in the Company
with the lot of Martha. People not useful to the Company ought not to be received simply because it would do
them good. Those admitted to probation ought to have
passed fourteen years of age and those allowed to take a
professed oath ought to have passed twenty five."

There are certain impediments which absolutely bar
consideration as a possible novice. These may be arranged under headings [3] *Orthodoxy*—To have denied the
faith among infidels, to have been condemned by public
sentence for heresy or to have been separated from the
Church as a schismatic. *Crime*—To have committed
enormous sins like homicide. *Monk*—To have worn a
monastic habit in a convent or hermitage. *Social*—To
have a wife or to be a slave. *Health*—To be insane or to
show a tendency towards it.

Other impediments not necessarily absolute are strong
passions and inveterate bad habits, suspicion of worldly
motives, an inconstant character, indiscreet devotions
leading to illusions and important errors, lack of education
or brains or memory (except for temporal coadjutors), no-

[3] The headings are the writer's.

table lack of judgment or obstinacy, age too tender or too advanced, debts and social obligations.

There are two probations. The first, when the postulants are treated in a way as guests, lasts from twelve to twenty days; or longer if the superior thinks best. During this time the probationer is to occupy a room apart and he is to be very carefully examined. If he is found not fitted, he is to be helped to serve God some other way. If he seems to be fitted he is to be transferred to the common house and admitted to the second probation which lasts two years.

The second *part* concerns Dismissals. Members of any grade in the Company may be dismissed if their retention is an injury to it and to God's service. The power to dismiss rests in the general congregation of the entire Company and in the general who may communicate it to the provincials, to heads of houses or rectors of colleges. In the case of the higher grades no one may be dismissed without the concurrence of the general.

The causes of dismissal during the probation of two years are quite broad and might be summed up as any sort of unfitness for the work of the Company, ranging from ill health to vice. Dismissals should be made only after prayer, conversation with all whose knowledge of the facts might help to form a fair judgment, and the most careful deliberation. The leaving should be arranged in such a way as to bring no shame on the dismissed and he should be helped to go away in charity toward the house and with the consolations of God in his heart.

Those who leave the Company of their own accord should be allowed to go and no effort made to bring them back if they are thought to be not very well fitted for its service. In the case, however, of promising probationers, every effort should be made to persuade them to come back: especially if it is suspected that they left under some sudden strong temptation or were misled by others. All who leave or are dismissed should be willingly released from their first vow.

The third *part* is on Probation. Both soul and body of the neophytes must be looked after. They are not to talk with any except those whom their superior indicates. Probationers are not obliged to get rid of their property until the probation is over, unless ordered by their superior. This may not happen before the end of the first year. They are perfectly free to choose when to give their property. If anyone wishes to give his property, or a part of it, for the use of the Company, it is undoubtedly a proof of much greater perfection and abnegation of all self love, not to show any tenderness of affection for any one locality, but to give it for general use according to the judgment of the general or provincial; consideration being given not to offend kings and civil authorities.[4] "The probationers must be instructed to guard themselves against the illusions of the devil during their devotions, to defend themselves against all temptations and to learn the means they can use to conquer them . . . It is well that all in the house should practise preaching within it." This exercise might occupy about an hour after dinner, to practise the use of the voice, the method of presenting a topic, etc. Subjects suggested are the virtues; especially self denial and brotherly love. Directions are given for the care of the body and the *declarations* go into some minute details prescribing a rest hour after eating, between six and seven hours of sleep, a careful watch over the aged or those in weak health, etc.

The fourth *part* treats of "Instruction in Letters and in other Means of helping their Neighbours" to be given to those who stay in the Company. It is very much the longest part of the Constitutions and will be considered later in the chapter on the colleges of the Company.

The fifth *part* concerns Admission into the Company.

[4] The reason for this caution is that no ruler liked the export of gold.

Speaking in the broadest way, the Company consists of all who live under obedience to the general, including the novices or probationers; speaking less broadly, it contains three grades; approved scholars, trained coadjutors and professed. Speaking more exactly it consists of the last two classes only. Those admitted as professed must have in addition to spiritual qualities, sufficient education. Besides humane letters and the liberal arts they must be trained in scholastic theology and the holy scriptures. The minimum term of study is four full years of theology after graduating in arts from a university. Postulants must also qualify by the successful defense before examiners of propositions in logic, philosophy and theology. Those found fitted, become professed by taking a vow similar to the one cited on page 145. The oath of coadjutors leaves out the last clause on special obedience to papal orders for missions. The oath of approved scholars obliges only to poverty, chastity, obedience and to join the Company. It is made only to God and not to any man and consists largely of a prayer for divine help and guidance.

In the sixth *part* the element of exhortation comes out very strongly. It concerns " the Members of the Company in their Relations to Themselves." It discusses first the virtues of obedience and poverty. The Constitutions call poverty "the strong bulwark of a special religious profession," and all professed must make a solemn promise not to try to alter the Constitutions in regard to poverty. No house or church of the Company might have an income to which it possessed any legal rights, nor own real estate "outside of that which was necessary or very convenient for their habitation and use." Colleges, as will be afterwards explained, must own property and have income. Houses of probationers might also have an income. "No one of the Company is allowed to persuade any person to give a perpetual alms to the houses or churches of the

Company and if any persons give of their own accord, the Company cannot acquire any legal right which enables it to go to court about it." "Let such things be given when charity inspires it for the service of God." No member of the Company can take any fee or present for saying mass, hearing confession, preaching, reading the scriptures or visiting the sick. "To avoid every sort of avarice" no collection boxes may be in the Company's churches.

The third chapter of the sixth *part* discusses how a member of the Company may or may not occupy himself. He is not to take a parish church because he must always be free to go wherever a pope or his superior wishes to send him. He must avoid as much as possible all secular affairs. The fourth chapter treats briefly of how to aid the dying members of the Company. The last chapter explains that outside of the fourfold oath (poverty, chastity, obedience, and special obedience to the Pope) the fact that any rule of the Constitutions is broken is not in itself a sin unless it is commanded by the superior "in the name of Christ" or "in virtue of obedience"; which he may do if he thinks it best for the member or extremely advantageous to the Company. This is done in order that "in place of the fear of offending, there may rule the love and desire for complete perfection and the greater glory and praise of Christ our Creator and Lord."

The seventh *part* treats of the members "in relation to their neighbours" when they are scattered through the "vineyard of Christ Our Lord." There are four ways of being distributed in "the vineyard of the Lord." The first is when the members are sent on missions by His Holiness the Pope. Such a mission, either among believers or infidels must be obeyed without hesitation or excuse. There is a very strict prohibition against any one, directly or through others, trying to influence a pope or his ministers to send him to one place rather than to another. If a pope wants one or several to go without naming them, the superior is to pick the men. "When a pope makes choice of some one for a mission and it is judged, that if the Vicar of Christ had been well informed, he would not send that man on that mission, the general may give more information about the man chosen; but everything must be finally left to the judgment of His Holiness." The second sort of work is a mission on which a man is sent by his superior in the Company. When possible, it is best not to send one man, but at least two. "The beginners should be paired with the more experienced and the fervent and spirited with the more circumspect and prudent, in such a way that the difference united in the bond of charity may help both." . . . "Because good when it is universal is more divine, those persons should be chosen as objects of work who if they are helped will be centers for extending good to many others who follow their authority or are governed by them. Also spiritual aid which is given to persons of great public influence, whether they are prelates, or princes or lords or magistrates or judges or distinguished scholars, ought to be considered as more important: for the same reason the chance to give spiritual aid to large nations like the Indies, or to chief cities or to universities where many people are wont to be gathered together of the sort who, if aided themselves, may become workers to help others, ought to be preferred."

The members of the Company living in houses or colleges although they have a fixed residence and many duties, can still aid their neighbours in many ways; by good example, prayer, the celebration of mass and other divine worship, hearing confessions, preaching, reading the scriptures in the church of the Company, in other churches or in public squares, pious conversations, good counsel, works of pity for bodily troubles, especially visiting hospitals, in healing quarrels, helping the poor and the prisoners in jails. Those who have a talent for writing should use it, but not publish anything until the general has had it examined to see if its printing would be for edification.

The eighth *part* treats of Aids in Uniting the members with their head and with each other. Unity is necessary to accomplish the objects of the Company, but difficult because its members will be scattered over the world. A great crowd of persons should not be received as professed, nor should any be advanced or accepted even as trained coadjutors or approved scholars except picked men; because "a great multitude of persons whose faults have not been well subdued by self discipline, does not bear order let alone union." That union in Christ so necessary to the work of the Company, is in large part secured by the bond of obedience. Therefore "Whoever is seen to be the cause of division among those who dwell together . . . ought to be separated from that congregation like a pestilence which can spread its contagion if a remedy is not at once applied." The general should for most of the time live in Rome whence communication is easy with all parts, and the heads of provinces should stay chiefly in central positions in easy communication with Rome. "The chief bond for the union of the members with each other and their head is the love of God. . . . The principal enemy of that union is self love which can be combatted by charity and by every goodness and virtue and also by contempt for temporal things. . . . The sending of letters missive, by which, through the efforts of the provincials and the general, news of the entire Company reaches every part of it, is a very especial aid for consolation and mutual edification in Our Lord."

Several chapters treat of the general congregation. For the present it is not convenient that this should meet at fixed periods, but only to elect a new general or to treat matters of great importance. It is to meet usually in Rome. Its members are to be professed and they are normally chosen in provincial assemblies by a majority vote—the provincial having two votes.

There are detailed rules for the election of a general. If any member hears of electioneering he is to report it at once and the offender shall never sit in another congregation. On the day of election the members of the congregation are shut up and they cannot go out or have any food but bread and water until the election is over. Voting is by written ballot without nomination or discussion and a majority of all ballots cast is necessary to elect. If there is no majority, either three or five electors shall be chosen and they, by a majority vote, shall elect a general.

The ninth and longest *part* treats of the General, and the first chapter briefly explains why he should be elected for life.

The first quality desirable in a general is that he should "be closely united to God and very familiar with the use of prayer." Second, he must be one "whose example in all the virtues will help those in the Company. Especially must he shine with the light of charity to all his neighbours and particularly to those of the Company and that true humility which will make him beloved by God and men." He should possess magnanimity and strength of mind and never be dismayed by the opposition of powerful people "being always entirely ready to suffer death if it is necessary for the good of the Company in the service of Jesus Christ."

He ought to be of good understanding and judgment, be cautious, enterprizing and tenacious, have suitable health, appearance and age and be of fair fame outside the Company. "And if some of the qualities mentioned are lacking in him, at least there must not be lacking great goodness and love for the Company and good judgment accompanied by a good education."

The authority of a general is great. He can receive

members into all grades. He appoints and revokes rectors and masters of colleges. He has power to conclude all business contracts, but he cannot sell or disband a house or a college without the consent of the general congregation. It is his duty to see that the Constitutions are kept everywhere and he has power to grant dispensations from their rules "according as the Eternal Light may direct him." He calls the general congregations and orders the assemblies of the provincial congregations. A chapter treats of the authority the Company has over its general and the care it should take of him. He should not be allowed to work too hard or be unduly harsh towards himself. In case of faults, the Company should warn him with due humility through his confessor. He cannot accept any Church dignity without the consent of the Company, which will never be given unless the direct command of the Pope compels it. (11)

If a general is careless or remiss by reason of illness or age, a coadjutor may be appointed by the provincials with the written assent of the rectors of the colleges. "In some cases (which it is hoped in the divine goodness will never occur) as for example actual mortal sin, such as licentiousness, wounding, peculation or heresy," the Company can and should depose a general and if necesary expel him from the Company.

The fifth chapter provides four assistants elected by the congregation and describes the machinery for assembling a council to depose a general.

The sixth chapter emphasizes the need of good superior officers under the general, provides for yearly complete statistics of every part of the Company for his information, warns him against a too particular attention to details, recommends him to have a special secretary to serve "as memory and hands" and to assign certain sorts of things under his care to men expert in them. It also provides for a procurator general who is not to be one of the professed. His duty is to handle the property of the colleges and to defend it when needful. Such an officer was necessary for the members were forbidden to mix in any secular business. Nor could they enter a law court as a witness without express permission of the general, who was not to give it except where the Catholic religion was concerned, or where their testimony could not do harm to anyone. The superior is expressly forbidden to allow a member to give hurtful testimony in any criminal case or to help a conviction which would bring infamy on the accused. "For it is the part of Our Company to serve all men in the Lord and, so far as possible, without doing injury to any one."

The style of the Constitutions is sometimes so artless as to appear naïve[5] and the arrangement is not logical. But they have a power which is their own. They are not so much what we call a constitution as a description of what the Company ought to be: The definition of its different organs and their relations to each other comes in, so to speak, on the side. Ignatius does not over-emphasize machinery but sometimes seems almost to overlook it. He begins, not by a description of the work of his Company or its organization, but by a list of the sorts of men who ought not to be taken into it and an elaborate description of the sort of men who ought to be welcomed to its ranks. His view of the order is personal and not at all mechanical. Men must make it and not formulas. He saw its unity not simply as a similarity of regulations but chiefly as a unity of spirit. He evidently did not look on the rules as iron clad. He provided especially for exceptions and the exceptions he names are manifestly to keep the spirit at the expense of the letter. All through these laboriously wrought-out rules for the guidance of an intricate enterprize for doing good to his fellows, there shines

[5] The editor of the standard edition agrees "Habent enim verba Sancti Patris Nostri, licet simplicia atque interdum rudia, miram vim proprietatemque." De la Torre; Preface VII.

a simple sincerity at times very touching and an unshakable trust in God. This man wishes his followers to be pure in heart, poor in spirit, merciful, to hunger and thirst after righteousness, to strive always to make peace. He is quite sure that men of this sort will carry the Company to great triumphs for God, the Church and man.

CHAPTER XI

THE NEED OF THE TIMES

Just as the Spiritual Exercises incorporate the experience of Ignatius before he founded the Company, so the Constitutions incorporate his experience as general of the Company. The work which he finally set before it is quite different from the vague purpose which had been in his own mind ever since his conversion: the idea of living in Palestine to stimulate his own soul by the memories of Christ and to help his neighbour both infidel and Christian. This purpose he communicated to the comrades who gathered round him in Paris and they recorded their enthusiasm for it in the vow which each one made for himself at Montmartre. This was their only intention when they met at Venice; they were to ask the Pope for work merely in case this plan failed. The forced abandonment of this long cherished plan of going to Palestine and the changing of the voluntary association of friends into a perpetual religious order, seems to have been accepted by Ignatius without any reluctance or disappointment. He had grown used to seeing in the closing of old roads and the opening of new, the hand of God directing his course and, besides that, his year of waiting in Italy had made him aware of the terrible need of work over the entire field. A deep seated wide-spread and very acute corruption had for many years afflicted the Church. Everywhere throughout Christendom "the hungry sheep looked up and were not fed." Ignatius never talked about this. Later he very explicitly warned his followers not to denounce the corruptions of the Church but to work posi-

tively to remedy them. Nevertheless, what he saw and
what he heard made him aware of the facts and he realized
that now, perhaps as never before, the Vicar of Christ
needed faithful servants. He saw the Church beset by
foes within and without and his answer was to raise and
equip the Company of Jesus for her defense.

Let us glance at the situation when Ignatius sent his
followers out to work. All zealous contemporary church-
men admitted that there were gross and palpable corruptions in the Church. None of them in non-controversial
movements could have been disposed to deny the truth
of what Erasmus wrote to a friend in 1521, the year when
Ignatius was converted. "The corruption of the Church,
the degeneracy of the Holy See are universally admitted.
Reform has been loudly asked for and I doubt whether
in the whole history of Christianity the heads of the
Church have been so grossly worldly as the present moment."[1] This corruption seems to have been due pri-
marily to worldliness rather than to the flesh and the
devil: though the latter pair had gotten entrance because
the gate was opened by the first. At all events Pope
Adrian VI who died in 1522 worn out by the herculean task
of cleansing, sent a nuncio to Germany with written instructions about "certain things you can say *viva voce* to
the prelates, princes and representatives of the cities in
Germany when you deem the opportunity fitting" . . .
After full instructions about the heresy of Luther and
what ought to be done about it, the instruction continues "Item: you are to say we openly confess that
God permits this persecution of His Church because
of the sins of men especialiy the sins of priests and
prelates of the Church. . . . The Scriptures cry aloud
that the sins of the people have their roots in the sins of
the priests . . . These were deplorable things in the times
of Alexander VI. And it is no wonder that the disease has

[1] Froude, Erasmus, 284, ctd. Opera, Leyden 1702, d1XXII.

descended from the head to the members, from the chief priests to other lower prelates. All of us prelates and ecclesiastics have turned aside each to his own way and for a long time there has not been one who worked righteousness, no not one, wherefore it is needful that we all give glory to God and humiliate our souls before Him." [2]

Although Ignatius himself was not in the habit of talking or writing about the corruptions of the Church, we may infer that he agreed with Pope Adrian about the cause of the schisms of the North from the text of a speech written six years after the death of Ignatius by his intimate co-worker Lainez who succeeded him as general of the Company. "The corruption of the little of Christendom left demands penitence and emendation. This must begin with the clergy and among the clergy with the Supreme Head and his court, whose bad example and bad use of the power he has from God is the principal cause of the disorders among the members of the Church. How great is the need of such a reformation can be judged by the universal scandal and the hatred among some, the contempt among others, of the Holy See because of the abuses in it. In our day we have seen Germany, Scotland, Denmark, Sweden, Norway and Prussia break away and there is very probable danger that the Kingdom of Poland and the States of Flanders and France will follow. Nor is there any security for those which remain, Spain and Italy, because they are scandalized by the abuses of their Head. . . . The abuses which cause this scandal are first to see the Popes not expecting to do anything in the Papacy except to make great their relatives according to the flesh, and for this reason conceding to princes wrong things and putting unfit men into the college of cardinals." etc. etc. [3]

Here is an extract from a sermon preached at Rome be-

---

[2] Raynaldus, Vol. XII (31) p. 395.   [3] Mon. Lainii, VIII, 800.

fore the Council of the Lateran seven years before the conversion of Ignatius. "If we examine the writings of the fathers and the canons of the Church, do we not find that they tell us to suspend or to depose from priestly orders every flattering and impious priest, every betrayer of his neighbour, every evil speaker, or those who slyly lead their brethren into wickedness, every seditious troubler of peace, the ambitious who sacrilegiously usurp sacred dignities, the envious, the adulterous, the villainous perpetrators of other obscenities, those who are given to cruelty and at the same time revengeful of their own injuries, gamblers, accursed searchers for filthy lucre? Do we not, I say, find that inviolable decrees of ancient canons tell us to suspend or depose this sort of priest? But I ask you, if the benignity of Mother Church did not relax the severity of ancient canons how could such priests exist as they do?" [4]

The Admonition read about thirty years later to the Council of Trent said: "We pastors ought to confess ourselves guilty before the tribunal of God's mercy and take upon ourselves the sins of all because in large part we are the cause of these evils. . . . The prophet Ezekiel describes the living image not only of his own times but of ours when he says, speaking in the name of God: 'The priests have despised my law and polluted my sanctuaries and have made no distinction between things sacred and things profane.' " [5]

Here are some of the phrases from the sermon preached before the same Council by the Bishop of St. Marks. "Look at Rome, France, Spain and you will find no social class, no sex, no age which is not stained, corrupt, putrid. The heathen of Africa and Scythia do not live more impurely and wickedly . . . Oh we pastors who ought to shine more clearly than the sun, we are murdering the

[4] Mansi, vol. 32, p. 895.   [5] Ehses. I, 549.

sheep of the Lord's flock by our example . . . The Apostles and fathers rejoiced in poverty and fled from wealth. We say they were insane. We long eagerly for gold— for gold we turn even to poison and the dagger and we do not hesitate to pillage anything sacred or profane . . . They lived chastely. Our throats burn with the flames of all vices." [6]

The very year that Ignatius arrived in Rome (1538) a remarkable pamphlet had appeared. It was the unanimous report of a commission of nine appointed by the Pope to make recommendations to him about the reform of the Church. Naturally it was intended to be a confidential document but by negligence or treachery it got into the hands of public printers and spread over the world.[7] How outspoken it was may be judged from some of the following summary paraphrases. It says that the beginning of the disastrous conditions of the Church came from the fact that "some popes thy predecessors with prurient ears assembled doctors of theology not in order to learn from them what they ought to do, but so that they might by cleverness discover reasons for doing what they wanted to do. So doctors were found who said the Pope was the absolute lord of all benefices and therefore, since the lord could sell what was his, it was impossible for the Pope to commit simony.[8]

"From this source, most Holy Father there have burst out upon the church of God the many abuses by which we behold her so terribly afflicted as almost to destroy the hope of saving her.

"The first abuse is the ordination of the clergy and especially of parish priests to which no attention is given nor is any care exercised in choosing them. Hence arise innumerable scandals, the priesthood is despised, and rev-

---

[6] Ehses, IV, pg. 557-559.   [7] Pastor, V, pg. 126.   [8] Simony was buying and selling church offices which implied the gift of the Holy Ghost.

erence for Church services is not merely diminished but even almost extinguished.

"Another evil is the distribution of church benefices (bishoprics, etc.) which are given for personal reasons and not for the good of the flock of Christ. Especially Italians ought not to be given benefices in Spain or England, nor Spaniards, nor Englishmen given benefices in Italy . . . The law of the Church, says the sons of priests may not have their fathers' benefices. But dispensations are granted suspending this most holy law. Nothing has done so much to cause that hatred of the clergy from which so many seditions have arisen. ... Another great and intolerable abuse is the system which has grown up to prevent the bishops from punishing criminal clergymen. For wicked clergymen flee to the papal penitentiary officer from whom they find ways to escape punishment: and what is worse by the use of money. This scandal Holy Father disturbs Christian people in a way no words can describe. If equal scandals existed in any merely human state, it would very soon fall—by no means could it long survive.

"Another abuse which must be corrected is in the religious orders because many are so corrupted that they are become a great scandal to those living outside of them in the world and they do the greatest harm by their example. We think that all the conventual orders ought to be abolished: not however in such a way as to do an injustice to anyone, but by forbidding the admission of novices. In this way without any injury they could be quickly wiped out and good monks put in their place. ... Another abuse which troubles pious people is the habit of putting convents under the care of monasteries; whence arises in many monasteries sacrilege, to the great scandal of the people. A great and pernicious abuse is that in schools, especially in Italy, many professors of philosopy teach im-

piety. Bishops should see to it that professors do not
teach impiety to youth."[9]

Ignatius must have heard of this report and it is noticeable that two of its points, the danger of anti-Christian
teaching in schools and the danger of monks taking permanent religious direction of convents, attracted his attention. He met one danger by his system of colleges and
he avoided the other by getting exemption from the Pope
against commands to do it.

These judgments on the condition of the clergy were
confirmed by his own experience. Thirteen years after
the foundation of the Company its missioners wrote from
Corsica that the greater part of the inhabitants of the
island had been led into idolatry because their priests,
ignorant of the proper formula of consecration of the blood
and wine in the mass, were unable to perform the miracle
of transubstantiation. In consequence, when the people
adored the elevated host they were not adoring as they
supposed the true body of Christ but were guilty of idolatry. With a priesthood so careless in regard to the fundamental mystery of their calling, it is little wonder that the
missioners found "the greatest ignorance of God, abundant superstitions, innumerable quarrels, inveterate hatreds, murders committed in every direction, pride and lust
plainly to be seen everywhere . . . Some are very credulous
and accept secret heresies. Many of them do not even
know how to sign themselves with the cross or to say the
Pater Noster or the Ave Maria."[10] . . . "There are six
bishoprics on the island but none of the bishops is now
living in Corsica and so the sheep are scattered and abandoned to the ravening wolves."[11]

An ignorance somewhat less deep was widespread in
other parts of Italy. Preaching by parish priests was
extremely rare. They did not know enough to preach and

[9] Mansi, Sup. 5 p. 539-47. Vol. 35. [10] Pol. III 86. [11] Pol. III 88.

left it to monks sent out from the cloisters. The clergy openly broke their vow of chastity and kept concubines. The brother of Ignatius, priest in Azpeitia, made no concealment of the fact that he had illegitimate children and the case was so common as to excite no remark. Ignatius tells how in Azpeitia it was the custom for unmarried girls to wear nothing over their heads. They "covered their heads" when they were married. But he says,[12] "There were many who became concubines of priests and other men and are faithful to them as if they were their wives. And this has become so common that the concubines have no shame in saying 'I have covered my head for so and so,' and so are known to everybody as mistresses." Ignatius tells how he persuaded the governor to make a law that "all who cover their heads for anyone without being their wives should be punished." This violation of their ordination vow, regarded by most people as venial, was one of the least of the sins that could be found among the clergy in some places. In Lombardy for instance a popular proverb said: "If you want to go to hell, become a priest." [13]

To consult some of the learned and historically minded Roman Catholic scholars who are in recent times doing so much to lift the history and biography of the sixteenth century out of the sentimental fog caused by "edifying" books, or the black bitter mud of controversy, is to find in their pages a mass of equally decisive and unprejudiced testimony to the same effect.

A book written in the beginning of the 16th century and dedicated to the short lived pope Julius III, did not scruple to give the plainest expression to these charges of vice and irreligion among monks and priests. It was entitled the "Anatomy of Vice." Its author asks rhetorically "How many of you priests keep concubines and are

[12] Scripta, I, p. 90.   [13] Cited Venturi, I, 34.

simoniacs full of worldly ambitions? How many of you
carry arms as if you were soldiers? How many come to the
altar of Christ with bastard sons by your side How
many celebrate mass with the poison of hate in your heart?
How many of you loan money at usury and trade in cattle
and horses? How many of you sell the rites of burial, the
tolling of the bell, the carrying of the cross? How many
are unbridled liars? In whom among you can be found
charity, patience, modesty, humility, faith and other virtues which become a priest?" [14]

Of course there was another side to the picture. The
missioners of the Company of Jesus sent to Rome nearly
two thousand letters during Ignatius' generalship and they
write of many faithful priests. But the condition of the
parish clergy in Italy as a whole was deplorable. A visitor
to Naples wrote "the ignorance of the priests here is so
great no one could believe it unless he had seen it. Eight
out of ten priests ought to be degraded from their office." [15]

The bishops, who were supposed to be the pastors of
the pastors, responsible for the character of the parish
clergy, were, in large numbers, indifferent to their duty
and incapable of reforming their dioceses. "In the first
half of the sixteenth century, really excellent bishops were
rare and exceptional, mediocrities predominated and bad
ones, even heretics, were not wanting." [16]   In consequence
a Florentine could write just before Ignatius' death "a
great part of the cities of Italy appear to be infected with
heresy." [17]

How should it be otherwise when so little attention was
paid to the real purpose for which church offices were
given. Caraffa wrote to Clement VII, "There are many
boys and some soldiers who hold at least three parish

[14] Cited Venturi I, 36. [15] Cited Venturi, I, 28. [16] Venturi, I, 348. [17] Cited
Venturi, I, 346.

churches each and to save money they appoint as curates monks who have left their monasteries."[18] Many appointments to bishoprics were evidently made for personal reasons. There were more than 260 bishoprics in Continental Italy many of them with large incomes. A large number of them had become almost infeudated to noble Italian houses and the lists of incumbents of the richest sees show plainly that they were practically family possessions.[19] The succession to the bishoprics of Italy was one of the privileges of the nobility of Italy almost as in Germany; where all the leading bishops were nobles, and had for the most part become prince bishops, independent civil rulers, members ex-officio of the Reichstag or national assembly. If this had not taken place in Italy, it was because the civil princes would not suffer it, preferring to hold the bishoprics as appanages of their houses; and also because the Pope had become a great potentate who frequently put armies into the field. A Catholic writer after a careful survey of the situation sums up his conclusions as follows, "The condition of religion in Italy in the middle of the sixteenth century was in the highest degree wretched. The clergy in all its grades afflicted, in some parts more, in others less, by inveterate evils very hard to cure: the people left at the mercy of their two domestic enemies, ignorance and license."[20]

Astrain says: "Although it is extremely difficult to establish with certainty a comparative judgment between different nations, I do not think it too bold to assert that, at the beginning of the sixteenth century, Spain was in a condition less evil than any other country of Europe . . . Let us say less evil in order to defend ourselves against the opinion of some modern Catholics who have created for themselves an idea of the Spain of that age entirely

[18] Cited Venturi, I, 47. [19] Venturi, I, 162. [20] Venturi, I, 398.

too optimistic; indeed as fantastic and false as the idea of Don Quixote had of the centuries of chivalry . . .

"Catholics and Protestants have agreed in writing the history of the sixteenth century as it is said Apelles painted the portrait of his one-eyed friend—in profile. But with this difference that we Catholics present it from the side of the good eye, and the Protestants show it on the side of the blind eye. So long as history is written in that partial way, it will be impossible for us to understand each other. . . . It is necessary to examine the beautiful and the ugly, the good and the evil. . . . What was in that century the ugly side of our Spanish nation? The frightful corruption of manners. What was the beautiful side? Fixity of mind in the faith, and steadfastness of character."[21]

The condition of Spain in the first half of the sixteenth century though not so corrupt as the condition of most of Europe, was none the less deplorable. The scandals among the clergy began at the top; as for instance an archbishop of Toledo primate of Spain had three illegitimate sons from two mothers. The famous Bishop of Zamorra rode at the head of three hundred armed clergymen of his diocese in the civil wars, assassinated prisoners and after many adventures was hanged in the year of Loyola's conversion. Ten years after Loyola's death, a Venetian Ambassador could write from Spain "The greater number of these prelates live with great pomp and luxury. Very few of them are without illegitimate children whom they publicly own without any pretext."

Many bishops cared nothing for their dioceses except to collect their incomes which they spent at court or at Rome. Five foreign cardinals held in succession the bishopric of Pamplona. No one of the five lived in it and "the first, Caesar Borgia, lived in such a way that the best thing he could do for his diocese was to keep away from it." The enormous riches of some dioceses tended to increase

[21] Astrain, I, LXXII.

the number of worldly or vicious clergymen. The single
diocese of Calahorra had eighteen thousand clergymen;
"the greater part of them doing nothing." "The national
vice of laziness which so disastrously corrupts modern
Spain," brought swarms of applicants around the organization of the Church like flies around a pot of honey. This
weak clergy was unable to do much to stop the violence of
Spanish life, which converted some of the provinces "into
theatres of atrocious crimes or turned them into lakes of
blood." . . . "Knife thrusts and arquebus balls from behind, razing of houses, tearing up the growing crops, assaults on fortresses, raids into cities, arson and tumult"[22]
these were common enough.

Of this need for reform in Spain Ignatius was aware.
You cannot indeed find in him any signs of patriotism in
the sense of a stronger affection for one country than for
another; that was swallowed up in a greater passion for
God and His Church, even as his love of family disappeared in love for the Company of Jesus. But, after all,
to feel that part of his work must lie not at the eastern end
of the Mediterranean but its western end where the only
language he used easily was spoken, could not have
brought to him any impulse of disappointment to be mastered.

If we look across the Alps and the Pyrenees we do not
find the outlook at the time of the foundation of the Company of Jesus more encouraging for the Church. The kingdom of England had followed its king into open schism and
the Pope had replied by a bull deposing Henry and calling upon all Catholic princes to drive him from the throne.

Some years before, Denmark, Norway and Sweden had
broken from the authority of the Papacy and firmly established in national churches the doctrines of Luther.
The majority of the thirteen cantons of Switzerland had
followed Zwingli in a revolt against the Church. Most of

[22] Astrain. Preface.

the states of the German Empire were Protestant, and the influence of the Church even in the nominally Catholic states of Germany was extremely weak. Ignatius wrote, just before his death, to the leader of his missioners to Germany "Pastors, no matter how orthodox Catholic they may be in doctrine, who, by great ignorance and by their evil examples injure the people, should be most severely punished and deprived of the income of their benefices by their bishops. It is better for a flock to be without a pastor than to have a wolf for a shepherd. The ignorance and evil life of such priests brought the pestilence of heresy upon Germany." [23] The heir apparent elect of the Empire, Ferdinand, Duke of Austria "seemed to have persuaded himself that much help for religion was to be expected from our Company in the miserable condition of those regions, although humanly speaking there was no great hope of doing much because obedience to the Apostolic Roman See was not simply lost, it was turned into a sort of deadly hatred. Nor is it easy to believe how much the Sacraments and other sacred things are despised." [24] In consequence of this state of affairs, the early missioners, who had a little of their travelling money left when they arrived in Vienna, were able to make a very advantageous purchase of books because "Thomas Aquinas, Bonaventura and other scholastic fathers were going begging and were bought as they were about to be sold to pharmacists for wrapping paper." [25] They were also able to obtain with very slight expense a building for their college because "There were extremely few monks and the monasteries were everywhere vacant since the monastic calling had fallen into the deepest contempt and scarcely anyone could be found who wished to become a monk." [26]

Perhaps the most sinister thing for the future influence

[23] Letts. VII, 400. [24] Pol. III, 248. [25] Pol. II, 275. [26] Pol. III, 248 and 258, Comp. IV, 234.

of the church in the parts of Germany still nominally orthodox was that "when the King wished to confer bishoprics
and high ecclesiastical offices on fit and chosen men, no
one of this sort could be found. The parishes either lacked
pastors or were occupied by apostates and infamous persons. Young men did not aspire to the priesthood and it
was said (in 1554) that, in twenty years, not twenty
priests had graduated from the University of Vienna.[27]
ٖ "A missioner in Belgium just before the death of Ignatius found himself obliged to attack in the pulpit lust, avarice, gluttony and drunkenness because these vices were
widespread as much among the clergy as among the laity.
Many pastors kept concubines in their houses and some
had to be carried home drunk every day, others held six
or seven incompatible salaried church offices. These vices
were the cause of heresy." [28]

The prospects for the Church in the north were dark.
Besides the ancient provinces in open schism the states
which remained ostensibly in the papal obedience South
Germany, Scotland, France, Poland, the Netherlands were
as the orthodox said, badly infected by heresy.

It was precisely this discouraging prospect which
brought the long demanded and prayed for reform of
which Ignatius Loyola was to be the most outstanding
figure. For what Martin Luther was to the progressive
series of schisms of the various national churches of the
north that Ignatius Loyola was to the revival of the ancient orthodox Church. If that internal reform had come
earlier, it is possible that the national Protestant schisms
might not have taken place. If it had not come at all,
it seems probable that the ancient Church would have
perished of her own internal diseases. That internal reform came when it did, seems to have been due to the
awakening shock of the sweeping success of the northern

[27] Pol. IV, 240.   [28] Pol. IV, 302.

schisms. When magistrates and peoples were not burning heretics and schismatics, but hailing them as heaven sent leaders and when their books were being smuggled into the very strongholds of the authority and faith of the Church, then the words of faithful men like those cited denouncing the judgment of God upon sinners in high places, began to find not a formal but a real hearing.

Venturi says, "For a hundred years people in Rome had been talking about corruption and reform but reform never came. . . . The immensity of the danger, the imperious need of saving the faith and reviving piety were only clear and vivid when in the pontificate of Clement VII (1523-1534) and Paul III (1534-1550) Italy saw itself the target for the attacks of the innovators, who looked forward to a quick and easy conquest." [29]

The orthodox Catholic reform began with Paul III. Before that "the true reform of the Church had not advanced a step. It could not be said that it had even seriously begun." [30]   Pastor says of Paul III, "The profane interests which since Sixtus IV (1471) had with the Popes of the Renascence, decidedly outweighed all others, were still, indeed, very strong with him; but they no longer seemed of the greatest importance. . . . With his pontificate there began to dawn for the Church the hopeful morning of a new era." [31]

The condition of the papal court at his accession was not encouraging. Of the forty-three cardinals who elected him forty were the creations of Leo X and Clement VII and they were mostly true to the type which for more than two generations had been prevalent in the holy college. They were representatives of illustrious families with huge incomes, young lords who had nothing of the clergyman about them except the name and the coat which they did not always wear. They held bishoprics and abbacies (one young cardinal held twelve bishoprics)

²⁹ Venturi, I, 349.   ³⁰ Venturi, I, p. 5.   ³¹ Pastor, VI, p. 3.

which they regarded only as means to fill the purses they emptied by great trains of servants and gentlemen attendants rising to four hundred or by banquets, theaters, hunting, travelling and even war.[32]

There were in the college very few scholars distinguished in the sacred sciences or men conspicuous for their lack of worldly luxury and many of the other sort.[33] For example, young cardinal Ippolyto dei Medici cousin of Clement VII "wore a sword like a cavalier, spent a great part of his time fencing or riding—never put on his robes except when he went to convocation. He was more often seen at races or the theatre, than in his study or at church."[34] This was not astonishing in an age when a chronicler could write: "It was not considered infamous for a pope to have bastard sons and to try by every means to make them rich and powerful."[35] It is certain that the sister of the man who became Paul III, the beautiful Julia Farnese, had been the mistress of Pope Alexander VI.[36] The Venetian Ambassador reports that it was common talk that Alessandro Farnese owed his promotion as cardinal to this fact and he was long called by an indecent nickname because of it.[37] For a number of years he had lived a very worldly life. A son was born to him after he had been a cardinal for ten years.[38] But, under the last three Popes, the dignity and ability with which he attended to the duties of his office had made him popular with the people of Rome. The old Adam of his earlier days as a prince of the Church among fellow cardinals who saw little difference between that princedom and any other, was not entirely dead in him. Within a week of his election to the Papacy, two of his grandsons fourteen and sixteen years old, were made cardinals and he continued to enrich his family. But, in spite of this, Paul III actually did more

[32] Von Renmont, III, 2 p. 275.   [33] Venturi, I, 9.
[34] Cited from Cardella by Venturi.   [35] Segni, cited Venturi.
[36] Pastor, III, 301 n. 3.   [37] Relazioni, Serie II, Vol. 3, p. 314.   [38] Venturi.

for the reform of the church than any of his predecessors for a hundred years. Perhaps the most fundamental thing he did was to make a better choice of cardinals. He created altogether seventy-one: almost all of worthy character and most of them of distinguished ability. From the cardinals of his creation came his four immediate successors; all active in the reform of the Church.

So Ignatius founded his Company of Jesus, at a time when a strong effort was being made by the Head of the Church to reform her crying abuses and vitalize her service to the world.

CHAPTER XII

The most complete summary statement of the work
of the Company is found in the second bull of institution issued ten years after the first by Pope Julius
III in July 1550. "The company is founded to employ
itself entirely in the defense and spread of the holy Catholic faith, and to help souls in Christian life and doctrine
by preaching, public reading of the scriptures and other
means of teaching the word of God, by giving the spiritual
exercises, teaching Christian doctrine to children and the
ignorant, hearing confessions and administering the sacraments. It is also instituted to appease quarrels, help
prisoners in jails and the sick in hospitals and all must
be done by the Company gratuitously without expecting any human wages or salary for its labour."
It will be noticed that there is here no reference of any
kind to reforming the church and only a vague and general phrase, "the defense of the faith," which can be made
to refer to a battle with heresy. Ignatius was perfectly
aware through what he had seen at Paris of how menacing
heresy was to his ideal for the world and his plan of service. Soon after his death, a large part of the energies
of the great and growing army of his followers was absorbed in open battle against it. But his method was
positive. He did not wish to attack error but to proclaim the faith and he had an unconquerable trust that
the sincere ministry of the word and sacraments, the
holy discipline of the Church, would save men from error
and from sin. He thought far less about heresy than his

followers and seldom spoke of it. He felt that the truth
of God was mighty and must prevail if the Company declared it faithfully by word and life.

He could not have been ignorant of the inveterate
abuses in the Church, for the letters of his missioners
told him of the lack of zeal and other evils among the
parish clergy and the head of the papal reform commission, Cardinal Contarini, was his close friend. But to
this corruption he very seldom alludes. Not that he was
in any sense lax in regard to discipline. He was constantly on his guard against his own faults and his standard of character for the Company was so high that he
rejected more candidates than he received.[1] But the
government of the Church was not his affair. He con-
sistently refused to consent to the acceptance by any of
his followers of any ecclesiastical office from parish priest
to cardinal, except a prelacy in Ethiopia under direct
orders from the Pope, a position where authority was
small; while the chief item in the salary was a good chance
for martyrdom.[2] The government of the Church he left
to those God had appointed to rule her. It was the part
of the Company of Jesus to obey implicitly the earthly
vicar of their heavenly captain and to use with unrest-
ing diligence the means of grace God had given the world
in His holy Church. This attitude of positive unques-
tioning obedience he set forth in detail in the last appendix to the Spiritual Exercises. But if without waiting to examine this attitude we put it alongside the Constitutions we find another illustration of that combination so marked in the life of Ignatius, of extreme conservatism and a rather daring tendency toward innova-
tion. Ignatius was perfectly content with all the details
of the ideal of the mediæval Church. Any attempt to
change it, even any failure to praise all its parts, he re-

[1] This is a general impression gained from Polanco. There is no list.
[2] The Pope; cited Pol. VI, p. 6.

garded as wrong. But he was eager to find new methods
for serving that unchanged ancient ideal. He therefore
abandoned a number of what might be called the stock
monastic ideas.

The points on which the Constitutions and the practice of the Company of Jesus differed from all, or most,
of the previous religious orders may be briefly summar-
ized as follows:[3] The oldest orders laid the chief emphasis on saving their own souls and praying for the
world: the Company on helping the souls of their neighbours and working for the world. They were not shut up
so much within the walls of a monastery. They wore no
distinct monk's robe but dressed like clergymen of the
country they were in. They had no fasts, scourgings or
other ascetic exercises imposed on them by rule; these
things might interfere with their work in the world. They
were put through the Spiritual Exercises, a training of
the soul formed by Ignatius before he wrote the Constitutions. Those who wished to enter the Company underwent also a very detailed "examination" to make evident
to them the self denial of the life which lay before them.
The ordinary novitiate or testing time was increased from
one year to two years and once accepted postulants must
pass through various grades before they became full *professed*. During this time they might be, without any
ceremony, summarily dismissed. The Company of Jesus
was consolidated as no other large religious order had
ever been. This was done by destroying the capitular
system which made of other orders a confederacy of chapters whose members were sessile in separate monasteries
which elected their own abbots. The Company of Jesus
was centralized. All appointments of importance in all
the provinces were made by the general. All executives
were expected to take advice, but the final decision was
entirely in their hands subject to revision by their su-

[3] Astrain I, p. LV ff.

periors. The organization was military. No appointments and very few decisions were made by vote. The
rare meetings of the council might be compared to councils of war. The comment of Ignatius on the duty of the
provincials to take advice before important action is:
"This is not to be understood as if the matter were to be
decided by votes but the prepositus is to hear the opinions
and reasons of others and then decide himself." [4]

Finally and perhaps most efficient were two points
established by usage as much as by law: the *professed* became a body of highly educated priests trained for years in
the methods of the New Learning of the Renascence which
the older orders had most bitterly opposed: and secondly
Ignatius, in receiving novices and also in his readiness to
dismiss members from the lower ranks of the Company,
was not only ready, but eager, to sacrifice numbers to
quality.

Not simply the form of the Company was from Ignatius;
the spirit also was his. No founder of a religious order
ever wrote so much to his followers, but the elaborate
system of correspondence by which the whole Company
was kept in touch with every part of it was only very
carefully devised machinery. So long as Ignatius lived
and until those who had known him well were mostly
gone, the living spirit of him who was to his followers
not only the General but "our Father Ignatius," animated the entire company, and the feet, the hands, the
voices of the missioners and teachers were doing his work.

No member of the Company moved or acted without
orders and no soldier of the Company was supposed to
have an attachment to any locality which would make him
reluctant to start instantly for any other place in the
world where he was ordered to go.

Before the foundation of the Company many requests
came to the "poor pilgrim priests" to do work in Italian

[4] Letts. V, 198.

cities and the first of many members of the Company to
go on missions to the heathen started just as the bull of
institution was issued, leaving in writing his vows, his
consent to the foundation and his vote for the general.

To wade through the four thousand pages in which
the work of the Company of Jesus during the lifetime
of Ignatius has been recorded by his secretary Polanco
using the official reports, is to wonder sometimes how so
heroic a tale of devotion could be told in so dull a way.
Perhaps a few scattered lights may make plain the greatness of the labours and successes of these men who carried the spirit of Ignatius over western Europe.   They
went forth on foot, at first two and two, afterwards, when
young men were often sent in migrations to other schools
or houses, in larger bands.   Towards the end of the life
of Ignatius it became the custom to have horses to carry
clothes or books and for the tired to ride in turn.[5]

The old reader of Amadis of Gaul and other romances
of chivalry, liked to review these knights errant of the
word of God before they started and they presented themselves before him that he might see that they were properly equipped for the road with caps, staves and cloaks.[6]
These men were going out to imitate the apostles in proclaiming the gospel by word and example.   Camara wrote
in his memorabilia, "I have often heard our Father say
that he wanted no one in the Company who sought only
to save himself but all must help others to salvation." [7]

Their fundamental work was preaching and, as many
of the parish priests did not preach, they had the same
advantage possessed by the earlier Protestant preachers;
audiences to whom preaching was more or less of a nov-
elty.   The members of the Company were highly educated and well trained, for, from the first, they preached

[5] Pol. V, 28.   [6] I have often seen him do this.   Manareus, Scripta, I, 524.
[7] Scripta, I, 232.

regularly before their comrades in houses and colleges;
but every member did not preach: only those who had
gifts for it. To those picked and trained men zeal gave
power in the pulpit. They roused whole cities as Lainez
did at Venice, Parma and Florence, Domenech at Palermo
and Messina, Estrada at Oporto, Salamanca and Saragossa, Araoz at Valladolid, Valencia and Madrid. They
used street preaching at first, but gradually came to preach
in churches; nor did they neglect smaller places. When
Araoz, a nephew of Ignatius, preached in Basque at
Azpeitia, more than four thousand people flocked from
the surrounding country and climbed trees and roofs to
hear him.[8] In big cities their audiences were even larger.
Lainez preached in the cathedral of Siena on feast days
to eight or nine thousand people.[9] The brilliant young
Strada preached in Spain, sometimes three or four times
in one day, to at least three thousand people, and after
he had preached in the cathedral for two hours it seemed
to his auditors "when his sermon was drawing to a close
that he had just begun."[10] On another occasion ten years
later, at Barcelona, when he preached for an hour and a
half, "No one was seen to move hands or feet or head,
nor to cough nor spit, but they remained hanging on his
lips to the end."[11] Father Miron preached almost every
day and found such thirst for hearing the word of God
that "when he had preached two hours and sometimes
three it seemed to his congregation short."[12] On Good
Fridays sermons even lasted for three or four hours.[13]

They were also fond of using what our forefathers
called expository preaching: reading chapters of scripture with running comments. Their favourite author was
St. Paul, especially the Epistle to the Romans. This may
have come about because he had been the chosen author

[8] Pol. I, 89. [9] Pol. I, 271. [10] Pol. I, p. 196. [11] Pol. V, 381. [12] Pol. II, 95.
[13] Pol. II, 280, III, 31.

of the heretics or because in his youth Ignatius had been especially devoted to St. Paul.[14] At Bastia in Corsica Father Immanuel explained every day the Epistle to the Romans and "when he went to visit neighbouring places, his presence was so anxiously and impatiently awaited by his hearers that every day both men and women came to see him and beg him to come back."[15]

That this interest in the works of St. Paul as a serial was not everywhere so overwhelming, is indicated by the following little sketch which brings a rare touch of humour into the rather heavy pages of Polanco. "It happened once at Perugia that a certain strolling mountebank put up his flag in front of the doors of the chief church and was selling to the people not only his words but his false medicines in flasks and as salves. This was at the very hour when a certain lecturer in the church was explaining the Epistles of St. Paul to some forty hearers; while the mountebank outside had five hundred listeners; among whom were priests and monks. Father Johannes Niger happened to be coming back from the hospital and recognizing the craft of the devil, he sprang on a stone post near the mountebank and began to promise the people that he would give them for nothing much more healthy medicine. When the mountebank saw that his crowd had left him and perceived that Father Johannes was inveighing against the devil the father of lies and all his ministers and saying that they ought to be overwhelmed with stones rather than allowed every day to profane the very temples of the Holy Ghost, he and his comrades became frightened lest things might go from words to those stones he heard alluded to, so, gathering together all his paraphernalia, he fled and as soon as possible left the city never to come back."[16]

The missioners were extremely diligent in hearing con-

[14] Pol. II, 28, 519, 567; III, 42; IV, 83, 146; V, 339. [15] Pol. III, 105. [16] Pol. II, 434.

fessions; for which they were trained by the discussion of cases of conscience. In some cities their confessors had not time to take food; in another "five confessors worked until the third hour of the night with scarcely time to draw breath"; in another "people waited three, four or five days in the church from morning until night to get the chance to confess." [17] They were also very active in promoting frequent communion, preferably once a week, a practice which aroused great opposition among some orthodox people; for example a minister general of the Franciscans tried to induce the vicar of Perugia not to allow frequent communion to those not members of a religious order.[18]

To this positive ministry of the word and the sacraments, they added direct attacks on particular sins. The habit of blasphemy was inveterate in Spain and they founded many fraternities to oppose it. For instance at Gandia they got the people to vote a law fining for the benefit of the poor any one who blasphemed and formed a fraternity whose numbers were sworn to rebuke anyone they heard swear. If the swearer was too poor to pay his fine, he had to kiss publicly a cross marked on the ground.[19]

They did not lack courage to attack profitable sins. Father Frusius found a certain city in Sicily so oppressed by money lenders "that many citizens burdened with intolerable usury had fled to the mountains and were living in caves." He saw to it that all these usurers confessed and were forced to agree to make restitution according to the judgment of the bishop. In consequence one hundred and fifty families came back to the city.[20] Another preacher compelled the restitution in two cities of 6,000 gold ducats.[21] The Church said taking usury was a sin and it meant by usury not excessive interest but any in-

[17] Pol. II, 246; III, 31; V, 306. [18] Pol. IV, 155. [19] Pol. V, 371. [20] Pol. II, 36. [21] Pol. IV, 213.

terest. The law of the Church was by this time as badly kept in Italy and Spain as the prohibition law is in America and all sorts of legal quibbles had been devised to make the profession of a banker one a good Catholic could follow. The members of the Company did not hesitate to proclaim the law of the Church to a great trading city like Genoa which would have been ruined by its strict application.[22]

The members of the Company did a great deal to help the poor, not only by collecting money for them, but by courageously standing up for them against oppression. For example, in Monreale the fathers of the College of the Company became aware that there were two magistrates who plundered the poor almost openly and by threats prevented all resistance to their exactions. These two corrupt officials had great influence with the governor and he gave more heed to the lies they told him than to the complaints of the poor about the oppression they suffered. Sometimes he even answered appeals by punishment instead of redress. The governor perished in a shipwreck and was succeeded by his brother. These two evil magistrates began to act the same way under the new governor and no one, not even the suffragan bishop, dared to talk with him about it. But the fathers of the college brought certain facts to the governor's attention and urged him to make a thorough investigation. He found a great deal of wickedness, removed the offenders, replaced them by good magistrates and ordered suits opened for the restitution of the large sums gained by grinding the faces of the poor.[23]

One of the favourite good works of the Company was to attack vice by opening houses of refuge for repentant magdalens, after the model of one founded by Ignatius in Rome. For these they got houses from the city or

[22] Pol. I, passim II, 620; III, 84, 310; IV, 33, 213; V, 105.
[23] Pol. V, 210.

used some vacant convent where the women could stay until they were either married (with dowries provided by charitable people) or decided to express their penitence by becoming nuns.[24]

The members of the Company brought about many restitutions of ill-gotten gain; either won from young men at play or gained by dishonest, but not illegal, practices in business. A man, as a result of frequently taking communion, went back twenty years in his accounts to make restitution to those he had wronged and in addition "imitating Zaccheus, gave a large part of his goods in alms for the poor."[25]

The members of the Company expressed its spirit, not only by proclaiming repentance, faith and good works from the pulpit and by the sacraments, but also by their example. They were active in founding and extending asylums for orphans.[26] They were very assiduous in visiting the sick and, in preparation for this service, every novice must spend at least one month as an ordinary prentice attendant in a hospital, doing the most menial services. If he showed the least unwillingness he was rejected. Imprisonment for debt was then everywhere common and the condition of many of these poor debtors was deplorable. The members of the Company visited them in prison and in many places made collections, paid their obligations and set them free.[27] They visited other prisoners also and often accompanied the condemned to the scaffold. The cruel criminal code of the times caused continual executions, and the fathers saved many from utter despair; for instance, a Sicilian nobleman, who when sentenced "offered himself to all the devils and tried to commit suicide in his cell," was brought by them to a repentant frame of mind.[28]

[24] Pol. II, 234; III, 204: 222. [25] Pol. IV, 392; V, 468, 517. [26] Pol. III, 203.
[27] Pol. I, passim II, 233.   [28] Pol. II, 233; V, 210; 374.

They were peacemakers; one of their most common and fruitful efforts was to inculcate in preaching, and also by private conversations, the fundamental precept of Christ, "If ye forgive not men their trespasses neither will your heavenly Father forgive your trespasses." [29] Certain parts of Italy and Spain were plagued by feuds as deadly as those which for the last few years have filled, and are still filling, the streets of Herrin, Illinois, with cowardly murder. In those places where public opinion held these legacies of murder sacred, the ordinary influence of the Church was as powerless to create an effective general detestation of the hatred, cruelty and treachery of these feuds as the influence of the churches has been powerless in our own day to stem the tide of murder and revenge in central Illinois. But the members of the Company were continually reconciling quarrels. Sometimes these were not very serious, as when, for instance, two respectable women quarrelled, and one hit the other. For this she had been five months in jail where she had fallen ill. The fathers induced her opponent, who had her arrested, to go to the jail and nurse her. But many of these quarrels were deadly; like the enmity between two Sicilians each of whom had a son murdered in the feud. They had long kept away from confession and one had refused to say the Lord's prayer "as we forgive our debtors." Yielding to the teaching of the members of the Company they publicly forgave each other. Another feud the fathers healed had lasted seven years and cost many lives, while another one had involved two whole villages in deadly hostility.[30]

In healing domestic troubles, also, they were very active as when they reconciled a husband with his wife, from whom he had been separated for nine years. They solved some very complicated troubles: for instance, "A

---

[29] Matthew, VI, 15.   [30] Pol. II, 8-24; II, 197, 226, 530, 650; III, 394, 414, 84, etc.

certain woman, a servant to a married couple, was driven by the evil spirit to tell the wife that her husband planned to poison her. The wife fled to her father's house. Whereupon the servant told the husband that his wife had plarned to poison him, and mixing something with ashes and brine, gave it to the cat. The cat died and the servant, though twice put to the torture, persisted in her lying accusations of the innocent; so husband and wife were separated. Some years afterward the servant came to a neighbouring city where a father of the Company so moved her heart that she confessed her sin." [31]

Such good deeds as these were obligatory on all members of the Company no matter how important their mission. When at the request of the Pope, Ignatius sent two of his best theologians as advisers to the Council of Trent, he gave them detailed instructions that, so far as possible, they were to preach, "never touching on points where Protestants and Catholics differ," expound the scriptures, hear confessions, teach children, talk with men about salvation and visit the poor in the hospitals.[32]

The tone of life which the followers of Ignatius recommended in the pulpit and confessional and in their private talk, was decidedly serious. They seem to have been opposed to most, if not all, popular recreations. "In a town in Spain when an exhibition of tight-rope walking had been made ready in the market place and the people and the magistrates were met together to see it, Father Baptista sent his associates who begged the magistrates in his name to order the acrobat to go away and not to suffer that sort of amusement to be offered to the people; because there was in it as much danger to the soul as to the body." [33] In the city of Cordova, a certain magistrate who had been a great supporter of giving bull fights and other games to the people, began after he had confessed to a member of the Company, to oppose this sort of spec-

---

[31] Pol. V, 145-160.   [32] Lett. I, 388.   [33] Pol. IV, 348.

tacle "most offensive to God." Finally by a threat of
leaving the city he procured the suppression of bull fights;
"and anyone who knows the zeal with which the nobles
of that city were addicted to these spectacles will understand how difficult was this victory." [34] Macaulay's sneer
at the Puritan suppression of bull-baiting in England in
the seventeenth century that they did it "not because it
gave pain to the bull but because it gave pleasure to the
spectators," is both literally true and utterly untrue in
spirit. Both the English Puritans and the Spanish Jesuits
opposed bull-fighting because it seemed to them a frivolous amusement, unworthy of a true Christian and one
which brought other evils in its train. The Jesuit missioners frequently got women to cut their hair and give
up wearing jewels. They sometimes refused to let jewelry be sold for the benefit of the poor lest it should
become a snare to others; so the earrings and bracelets
were broken and sold as gold. The good fathers do not
seem to have reflected that the broken gold could be
easily melted down and formed into new jewelry.

They made very active war on the popular books of
chivalry—Amadis of Gaul and others of that sort, so loved
in his youth by Ignatius. In the Company's church in
Gandia, Spain, the preacher exhorted his hearers to bring
all such books to the courtyard of the college and receive
for them missals, prayer books and edifying works. On
one occasion, in the midst of the university, while boys
dancing round the pyre chanted the Christian doctrine,
over fifty romances were burnt. These romances of chivalry though intolerably prolix, are mostly so harmless
morally compared to many modern novels, that one wonders why they were so eager to destroy them. Probably
the modern commentator on the Chronicle is right in his
conjecture that they were afraid "the people would waste
their time in reading these useless books, and once accus-

[34] Pol. V, 517.

tomed to them, would be kept away from pious and more serious works." [35]

This chanting of Christian doctrine was a device for making the straight and narrow road more pleasant. Two hundred boys were trained in it, and they taught many others. It would surely be a very difficult task to turn into popular songs the answers on the ten commandments in the shorter catechism by which many of us were trained in our youth. But something very like this seems to have been done by the early missioners of the Company of Jesus in Gandia. "In the whole city day or night nothing else was sung by big or little except the Christian doctrine. The workers at trades in the city and the farmers in the fields solaced their labours with this song and mothers did not blush to learn it from their sons. . . . Four hundred boys (no small number for that little city) met on Sundays and feast days to recite the catechism. They were keen to point out the mistakes of their comrades; and those who said it best had prizes, rosaries or pious books, and so many learned it well that sometimes it was necessary to give seventy or eighty prizes." [36]

The preachers and confessors of the Company opposed cosmetics and paint for their women penitents even in the Kingdom of Naples where the use of such aids to beauty was taken as a matter of course. [37] Questions about the costume of women have always been puzzling to preachers, even to those as downright and unafraid as the members of the Company. It is not surprising therefore that this question of cosmetics was referred to "our Father Ignatius." He replied, "So far as the use of cosmetics by the Neapolitan women is concerned: if they do it as an aid to some evil action, it is a mortal sin and they cannot have absolution. If they do it because their husbands want them to, they may be given

[35] Pol. IV, 352, n. 3.   [36] Pol. IV, 350.   [37] Pol. IV, 174; V, 174.

absolution. But it is good to persuade them to persuade
their husbands not to make them use that vanity. If they
do it out of vanity and to appear beautiful, although
they have no other intention of mortal sin, using cosmetics
is not a mortal sin. Nevertheless it is a great imperfection
and not without sin; although not mortal sin. And
though it can be absolved, it seems better for the confessors of our Company (which desires the perfection of
everybody) to act as follows: If the first exhortation
does not stop it, to say to these women plainly, that if
they wish to remain in such an imperfect religious attitude, they do not wish to have anything more to do with
them and that they may go where they will elsewhere to
make their confession. Nevertheless, either because it is
a small matter, or for any other reason, discretion may be
used in some special cases and this ought not to be made so
strict a rule as not to leave any room for exceptions." [38]

It would not be right to say that the Company of Jesus
wished the world to be entirely without amusement. Even
the novices were left, as we shall see, at least one game,
but they wished these amusements to be of a serious character. As for example, the students of the college of
Medina del Campo gave "amid the greatest applause and
to no small edification, the tragedy of Jephthah killing his
daughter, written by one of the brethren, which set forth
moral instruction in opportune places." [39] . . . The students of the College of Cordova gave a Latin comedy
based on the parable of the prodigal son, "those passages
being cut out which were not well fitted for pious ears."
Together with the introductory oration it lasted for three
hours. Each act was explained by Spanish verses to which
was added a brief comment drawing its moral lessons.
"Those who knew Latin said they had never seen anything
which pleased them more." [40] The Company even endorsed a special pious game of cards. This was invented

[38] Letts, VIII, 337, Compare IX, 266. [39] Pol. V, 421.

by the ex-duke of Gandia, a descendant of Pope Alexander VI, who had given up the wealth and state of one of the leading grandees of Spain to fight for God in the Company of Jesus. When he urged the Infanta of Spain, then engaged to the Prince of Portugal, to banish the inveterate card playing of her future husband's palace, he had promised that he would teach her a better game. A year later in the palace at Lisbon, she reminded him of his promise. He took forty-eight blank cards and ordered that on twenty-four the names of virtues should be inscribed and on twenty-four the names of vices. On each there was written a sentence condemning or commending. At the bottom of each card was a phrase to be read aloud by him who drew it. In the case of the virtues this expressed the holder's confusion because of his lack of that virtue—in the case of the vices, the holder of any card found a sentence of self condemnation because he was interested in such a vice. Whichever side got the most virtue cards won. Each of the other side was obliged to read aloud what was on the bottom of his card to the great confusion of any who were known to practise these vices.[41]

The game had an immediate success. (12). The Princess and her ladies played it, and the chronicler says that the excitement was as great as if a large stake were to be won or lost. Ignatius heard of it and approved.[42] It may be doubted whether the gentlemen of the suite of the Prince were drawn to adopt permanently this game of the virtues and vices instead of whatever took for them the place of bridge, but it shows at least that the good father was willing to try to combine instruction and amusement.

The serious and noble attitude toward life which lay behind all this that we call Puritan, is essentially the same serious and noble attitude which inspired the ideal of men

[40] Pol. V, 522.   [41] Pol. III, 357.   [42] Letts. X, 381, 649; XI, 45.

like Cotton Mather and Jonathan Edwards in New England two hundred years ago, or of men like John Knox in
Scotland four hundred years ago. We have changed. Who
dare say that we are stronger or wiser? But we have
changed: both Catholic and Protestant. What would
Ignatius Loyola or Franciscus Borgia have said about this
notice posted throughout a modern pious Catholic
community? "On such and such a date the Sodality of
the B. V. M. will give a euchre party and dance in aid of
the Church of Saint X at eight o'clock."

CHAPTER XIII

Ignatius Loyola almost from the time of his conversion up to the very eve of the foundation of the Company, met menacing suspicion in Spain, Paris, Jerusalem, Venice and Rome. That may be explained by two facts: it was an age when the Church was in danger, and Ignatius was very independent and entirely unknown. But why serious opposition and bitter attack continued after he and his Company had been taken under the special protection of the popes, is more difficult to explain: for this opposition did not come, while Ignatius was alive, from the Protestants. Up to the time of his death the Company of Jesus had not yet occupied so conspicuously the forefront of the battle, as to draw upon themselves the concentrated fire of the opponents of the Church. Nor is any allusion here made to the accusations from almost all Roman Catholic countries which brought about their suppression by the Pope more than two hundred years after the death of their founder. With these charges this book has nothing whatever to do. It has been already pointed out that, if the charges for which the Pope suppressed the Jesuits in 1773 were true, they must have entirely departed from the spirit and broken the explicit commands of their founder. The continued, one might say uninterrupted, opposition to the Company on the part of many Roman Catholic people, is a puzzling phenomenon which demands at least an attempt at explanation. For one who knows Ignatius at all in his writings and letters, it is hard to understand how good Catholics could have opposed the work of a

man so entirely loyal to the Church. How did it come
about that highly orthodox preachers and theologians
accused of heresy the writings of one who said that if the
Church called white black we should believe it was black
because the Church was the organ of the Holy Ghost? [1]
The only answer possible is to point out and illustrate
from the early history of the Company, some of the traceable causes of this opposition.

In the first place it ought to be said that the common
Protestant assumption that the Roman Catholic Church
has always been a huge semi-hypnotized mass of human
beings accepting by rote without any exercise of intelligence, whatever is said or done by their superiors from
priests to bishops, a common dead level of uniformity
where everyone must agree with everyone else about everything, is not true and has never been true. Great controversies have agitated the Church; such as the controversy
over conciliar supremacy, or the age long debate over the
immaculate conception of the Virgin Mary. Terrible
criticisms of her condition or administration have been
boldly uttered by sons of the Church who never dreamed
of leaving her. The orthodox Dante puts popes in hell.
Deep and strong differences of opinion have sometimes
centered about men. Savonarola, executed as a heretic
and schismatic at the urging of papal commissioners, was
held to be a saint in the Dominican convents of North
Italy and venerated by St. Philip Neri the intimate friend
of Ignatius.[2] Erasmus, solemnly cursed in hundreds of
pulpits as the cause of the Protestant schism, was patron-
ized by Pope Clement, urgently called to Rome to help
him by Adrian VI and offered the red hat of a Cardinal
by Paul III.[3]

There is nothing therefore unique in the history of the
Church, in the mere fact that very great differences of
opinion should be expressed openly in regard to the use-

[1] Spiritual Exercises, Regulae p. 556.   [2] Villari, II, 417.   [3] Froude, 419, 420.

fulness of the Company of Jesus.

Opposition to the Company came from a number of very different causes. The most obvious source of dislike was bad men whose gain or pleasure was interfered with by the efforts of the fathers. For example, very bitter opposition was stirred up in Rome by Ignatius himself some six years after the founding of the Company. A certain man had led a wife to run away from her husband. Ignatius persuaded her to come to his house of refuge for women. Whereupon the man began to stone the house of refuge at night. He even had pamphlets printed and distributed which contained accusations of horrible impurity, impiety and crimes, so that the fathers could hardly appear in public without "being reviled by some impudent scoundrel or greeted with curses." When patience had ceased to be a virtue, Ignatius asked the Pope to investigate. He appointed the governor of the city and his vicar to examine the charges. They pronounced them false and would have severely punished the slanderer if Ignatius had not intervened on his behalf. Touched by this and healed of the "disease of his insane passion," the slanderer became a friend and benefactor of Ignatius and the Company.[4]

Nevertheless, as scandal is for many people more interesting to talk about than virtue, incidents like this left a certain taint, often unconscious, in some people's minds. Puritans who denounce sin without fear or favour are always apt to suffer in this way.

Another cause (sometimes an unconscious one) was the jealousy of monks of other orders. The rivalry between different orders of monks is very familiar to all readers of the history of the Church. It sometimes takes naïve and amusing forms rather resembling the rivalry which may exist between two loyal regiments of an army. Anybody who talked with members of the two infantry regi-

⁴ Ribad. f. 100.

ments, who, in the Great War, fought in the neighborhood of Belleau Wood, remembers their caustic comments
on the marines getting all the popular praise for those
glorious actions; because the regulations permitted news-
paper correspondents to write about the marines but not
to mention the numbers of the units in any engagement.
The Jesuits have always been extremely proud of their
regiment in the army of God and apt to feel that what
"ours" did was a little better done than what others did.
And the others did not altogether like it. For example,
a certain official of the Franciscans tried to persuade the
vicar of Perugia to stop the missioners of the Company
from giving the communion very frequently and "that
good monk said in the course of his argument; 'there was
nothing in all this talk about the wonderful deeds of the
Company in India because there were few of the Company
there, while the King of Portugal had sent hundreds of
Franciscans to India.' "   It hardly seems necessary to
bring in as the chronicler does, the devil as the special
instigator of this rather natural piece of human weakness.[5]
A letter written by order of Ignatius recognizes this monastic jealousy as one of the Company's difficulties. "The
matter of getting license from the Emperor to hold real
estate in lower Germany, will soon be arranged by God's
help. That the religious orders oppose it, is not to be wondered at. They are our sharpest opponents, while on the
other hand we do our best to deserve well of them. May
God forgive them." [6] When the Company tried in 1555 to
establish themselves in Nymwegen the members of other
religious orders in the city said they would leave if the
Company was permitted to enter.[7]

The chronicler seems to have the feeling that the Company had a type of religion a little more precious than anyone else had, for, relating how Father Franciscus Borgia
had affected the palace of the Princess Joanna at Lisbon

[5] Pol. IV, 155.   [6] Letts. IX, 587.   [7] Pol. V, 279.

so that "whoever entered it seemed to be entering a religious house, where noblewomen and their servants went to
weekly lessons in Christian doctrine as willingly as they
had been accustomed to go to vain spectacles," adds "and
they seemed to weep for the lost time when they had lacked
this doctrine of the Fathers of the Company of Jesus." [8]

There are indications that Ignatius himself was not free
from this feeling that the Company was the first among
the religious orders. This may have been the reason why
he refused to amalgamate the Company with three other
comparatively new orders, also mendicant priests of similar aims, who wished at different times to join it—the
Somaschi, the Theatines and the Barnabites.[9] Ignatius
very politely but very firmly refused all consideration of
these suggestions.[10] Nor did he ever care about coöper-
ating with other orders. For instance one of the Company
was taken prisoner in Sicily by a raid of Turkish pirates.
When the friends of the captive could not raise three
hundred gold pieces for his ransom, the Turks carried him
to Africa. Ignatius was much concerned over the effort
to ransom him or exchange him for a Turkish prisoner.
There was a congregation for the redemption of captives
which offered to coöperate in redeeming this man.
Ignatius refused their request "lest a door might be opened
for 'ours' to mix in the affairs of that congregation." [11]
The rules of the Company, indeed, forbade receiving anyone who had worn any monastic robe or even had training
in another order. Exceptions were made,[12] but generally
it did not work well. Many of those received as exceptions
to this rule were dismissed and the society was satisfied
that the rule was a good one.[13] (13)

It is true that there are many instances in the life of
Ignatius and his followers of friendship with individuals of
other orders.[14] With the Carthusians as a body they had

[8] Pol. III, 359. [9] Ribad. Dicta, Scripta I, 439-440. [10] Letts. I, 475, 476; IV,
495, 496; Pol. II, 429. [11] Pol. III, 184; Comp. Letts. III, 357, 355-452; Also
Letters Ig. to Salmeron. [12] Pol. III, 116, 334. [13] Pol. III, 333. [14] Pol. II, 282,
378; V, 91; V, 72.

very friendly relations. But nevertheless, in general, the attitude of the Company might be called a "stand off" attitude. Their official chronicler even says, "It must be confessed experience teaches that a very close friendship with priests who are not of the Company, even though in other respects they are good and spiritual men and active in helping their neighbours, is not to be cultivated." [15]

The only explanation of a curious episode in the life of Ignatius would seem to be this subconscious attitude; for, in spite of his constant self examination, Ignatius, like everybody else, must have had a subconscious psychology. Ribadeneira writes, "One day after dinner our Father Ignatius and I were walking in the garden where many others were. While we were talking of various spiritual things, the Father stopped suddenly and said, 'Who are those walking over there?' When he had made out that it was a certain priest of ours talking with a novice, he called the priest and asked, 'What were you talking about with the novice?' He said, 'Father, we fell into talk on the subject of humility and self mortification and I was telling him of what I had seen or heard of these virtues in regard to friar Texida (a certain man of great reputation with some people),[16] in order to exhort the young man to imitate him.' To this the Father answered; 'And is there any lack of examples of this sort in the Company of Jesus which you could set before a novice without seeking others among outsiders?' And he rebuked the man with very severe words and ordered his name taken off the list of those who were allowed to talk freely to novices." [17]

It may have been on the part of Ignatius a prevision of the need of defense—but it must have been mixed with the feeling that the Company ranked very high amongst the many orders which served the Church—that he ordered

[15] Pol. IV, 112.   [16] He was a Franciscan.   [17] Scripta, I, 365.

the two members sent at the request of the Pope to the
Council of Trent, to get for the Company the approbation
of the Council. An influential bishop "extremely friendly
to the Company" thought it ought by no means to be
attempted; partly because "no religious order had ever
before been approved by any general council of the
Church.' [18]

Out of this intense love of the Company came a habit
of the fathers which could not have been placating to those
disposed to question their methods. For example, we have
seen that when one of the cardinals opposed the foundation of the Company because he thought there were too
many orders already, Ignatius thought "the good and pious
man was tricked by the devil." [19] The cardinal finally
withdrew his opposition, but if he had known the Company
was attributing to the devil his careful opinion on an
abstract question of Church policy, it can hardly be
thought it would have hastened his consent. The same
evil spirit worked in the house and at the table of the
Archbishop of Toledo against the Company.[20] This
charge was retorted against the Company by some of the
most bitter of their enemies. At the University of Salamanca a learned and distinguished preacher said that
Ignatius and his friends were the "precursors of antichrist
bearing his banner." [21]

There is of course nothing peculiarly Jesuit or Roman
Catholic in such bitter quarrels between sincere people
working for the same end. These hatreds among pious
people have their roots in human nature and their growth
is helped by the simple logic that as God is with us, the
devil must be with our opponents. That Protestant of
Protestants, John Wesley, when he had broken with his
earlier friends, the Moravians, in the middle of the eighteenth century wrote, "I found it necessary openly and ex-

[18] Pol. II, 254.   [19] Pol. I, 72.   [20] Pol. IV, 415.   [21] Pol. I, 298.

plicitly to warn all who fear God to beware of the German
wolves falsely called Moravians." [22]

Another sort of opposition came from some parish
priests who disliked to see their churches emptied to fill
the churches of the Company and their penitents flocking
to the Company's confessors.[23]   When the schools of the
Company began to flourish the teachers who lost pupils
sometimes expressed hostility.   In Perugia one of these
came into a public examination and a little incautiously
criticised the Latin theme of a scholar, saying no Latin author would have written certain phrases. But when he was
shown that Cicero used similar constructions he packed up
and left the city early the next morning.[24]

During the lifetime of Ignatius politics did not become
a cause of opposition to the Company.   He writes for
instance to a missioner in Corsica who had sought advice
"to attend to preaching the doctrines of the Christian
life and not to become involved in any way with affairs
of state.   Prudence and holy discretion demand this and
besides it is expressly ordered in our Constitutions." [25]
Ignatius said once to Ribadeneira, speaking of some zealous members of the Company "who wanted to reform the
world and thrust themselves into the affairs of government
like men of the state, that he did not approve of it.   That
when similar things came to him he was wont to think
about what he should have to give account of to Our Lord
at the Last Judgment.   It seemed to him he would not be
asked whether he had a plan to reform the whole world,
but whether he had obeyed the laws of his Company,
hearing confessions or preaching or reading the scriptures
or governing the Company; in short, helping souls like
a poor monk."[26] Fifty years after the death of Ignatius,
a clear record that suspicion of political intrigue by the
Jesuits was widespread, is found in one of the criticisms

[22] Journal, III, 499. [23] Pol. III, 272 and passim. [24] Pol. IV, 149 et passim.
[25] Letts. V, 442. [26] Scripta, I, 435.

made on Ribadeneira's life of Ignatius by Father Manareus, a younger contemporary of the founder. He says
Ribadeneira uses the phrase "the Company ought to
employ itself in *large things* and the Spanish translation
says in *great things*. It would be better in my judgment to
expunge both of these phrases; because, generally, in every
nation among all peoples we are falsely accused of mixing
ourselves in great affairs rightly belonging to princes or
states. Let us not therefore give occasion for carping."[27]

But, while we see by this example that political action
on the part of its members, or the suspicion of it, became an
active cause of opposition to the Company of Jesus within
two generations of Ignatius' death, it was not an active
cause during his lifetime and his authority was used
strongly against it.

For centuries the privileges of monks, who were not
under the ordinary jurisdiction of the episcopate, but
owed direct obedience to the Pope had, from time to time,
become a source of trouble with bishops and this happened to the Company. Ignatius tried in every way to
avoid this friction. For instance, when he found that
the Bishop of Modena was raising questions as to the
technical validity of the "faculties" or permissions from
Rome to preach, confess, etc., he sent word that they were
not to be used in any way displeasing to the Bishop; but
according to his advice and wish. In cases where episcopal attack on the society became acute, Ignatius was not
in favour of appealing to the Inquisition against a defier
of papal orders. He used the less violent action of canon
law by procuring inhibitions of local judgment and citations to Rome; where the rights of the Company were
always sustained.

Several of these conflicts with episcopal authority were
rather desperate. At Saragossa the Archbishop excom-
municated anybody who should hear mass, or preach,

[27] Scripta, I, 723.

in the chapel of the Company. The Augustinian friars paraded around the college of the Company, bearing a crucifix covered with black cloth and chanting the imprecations of the one hundred and ninth psalm against the enemy of the righteous: "Let Satan stand at his right hand . . . and let his prayer become sin. . . . Let cursing come into his bowels like water and like oil into his bones, etc." Posters were put up in the city representing the four chief fathers of the Company surrounded by devils with flames beneath them and derisive mottoes.[28] To avoid riot they withdrew from the city, but were finally reinstated by the orders of the Princess Juana, regent of Spain for her brother Philip II. She forced the Archbishop to withdraw his excommunication by broad threats of the Inquisition. It is characteristic of the way Ignatius handled these affairs, that he wrote directing the head of the college to visit the Archbishop "and kiss his hands in my name; because, when properly informed, he showed himself so favourable to us and beg him to consider us all his sons and servants."[29]

Perhaps the worst and most illuminating of these struggles was with the Bishop of Cambray. Father Bernard Olave went to show him the letters of the Pope. The Bishop was very indignant, received "ours" with many contumelious words and ordered his officials, if they found any of the Company preaching in his diocese, to put him in prison at once. He said the reason for this action was that all the mendicant orders of monks were going to bring suit in the ecclesiastical courts because the Jesuits did great injury to the parochial clergy and the religious orders by refusing to accept any fees either for preaching or for hearing confessions.[30] A second interview was even more stormy. The Bishop scarcely glanced at the papal letters presented to him. "What," he burst out, "do you want to do here preaching? Don't you know we have

plenty of preachers and learned ones too? Why don't you
go to the Germans, the Turks or the Indians, or even to
the English, to become martyrs for the faith if you are
so good as you wish people to think? But you are only
hypocrites, vagabonds, seducers and floating scum. If
you want to preach why don't you join the Franciscans
or some other approved order?" But Bernard answered:
"Our order is approved by the Pope. Read it in the
letters." "But you," said the Bishop, "have fooled the
Pope by your lies. I forbid you to preach in my diocese.
If you do I will order you to prison." There was nothing
to be done with a man in this mood and Cardinal Pole,
a great friend of the Company, advised Bernard to quit
preaching while he tried to placate the enraged Bishop.[31]

But all these causes of trouble were probably less
potent in creating in some places an atmosphere hostile
to the Company, than a single practice of theirs; defending against parents the right of young boys to join the
Company. That this was a very strong cause of hostility
in many places is not emphasized by the biographers of
Ignatius, but, to put together passages from the earliest
chronicle of the Company and the repeated instructions of
Ignatius in regard to it is to become aware how much
trouble it caused them.

When Jay went to Vienna in 1551 he found that "the
devil before their arrival had scattered rumours that the
Jesuits were hypocrites who shut people up in rooms with
closed windows and compelled them to undergo long fasts
in order that the Holy Ghost might come upon them and
so they seduced young men and compelled them to take
vows."[32] Ignatius had word in 1551 from the College of
Cologne that "the parents of boys who wished to serve
Christ rose against us like raging lions and tried to draw
their boys back from our rule of a more perfect life and,
when neither threats nor blandishments prevailed, they

[31] Pol. IV, 304, 313.   [32] Pol. II, 278.

even sought help from the law; for they thought it insanity and a dishonour to the family for their sons to renounce the world and submit to the yoke of obedience." [33] The Jesuits were accused before the senate of "lying in ambush for the sons of patrician families, snatching them from the very arms of their parents, luring them by subtle arts into the Company and then sending them to remote places whence they could hardly be brought back." [34]

In Rome itself, when two boys had disappeared their mothers came to the "church of the Company while mass was being celebrated, crying out and making a great disturbance, which they continued at the college and in the houses of some of the cardinals, saying that we had founded our colleges to steal boys and we had hidden theirs —while the truth was neither of them had ever entered either our house or our college." [35]

Some of the struggles of parents to keep their sons out of the Company became *causes célèbres*.

Octavian Caesar was the son of a man high in the government of Naples. When he was fifteen years old the boy asked the rector of the College of Naples to receive him into the Company as a novice. The rector refused because he had not the consent of his parents. The boy then tried to run off to Rome but his mother caught him and kept him shut up at home for some time. When he was free he suddenly joined some members of the Company on a ship to Messina in Sicily "where seeing his zeal and perseverance he was accepted." [36] His mother moved heaven and earth to have him brought back to Naples. The Viceroy of Sicily questioned the boy and found he did not want to go back because he was afraid his mother might break down his loyalty to the call of God. The Viceroy said the boy could stay in Sicily. The lad withstood the visit of his father, who returned to Naples satis-

[33] Pol. III, 266. [34] Reiffenberg, ctd. Pol. III, 267. [35] Letts, IV, 111, [36] Letts. VII, 674.

fied his son was called of God. But, to placate his wife, he first tried vainly to procure papal letters ordering the boy's return and finally got the Duke to write to Ignatius. To satisfy him, Ignatius wrote that if Octavian were to come to Rome "(which I do not know that he ought to do) he would be made to pass by Naples." "Nevertheless he wrote to 'ours' not to send him to Rome,[37] but to take the first opportunity of sending him to a college in Spain." [38] Some months later, his father came to Rome and got the Pope to refer the matter to Cardinal Caraffa. He was Archbishop of Naples; no friend of Ignatius or the Company and a great friend of the parents of Octavian. He ordered Ignatius to restore the boy to his parents. Ignatius, however, going to see the Pope, quickly obtained permission not to obey these orders.[39] The mother, who loved Octavian more than any of her other sons, came to Rome and stirred up much sympathy among some of the cardinals. The case was again heard by other cardinals and Ignatius wrote to the boy giving him permission to come to Naples to see his parents and forbidding the rector and the provincial of Sicily from preventing his departure.[40] This of course did not touch the root of the trouble from the point of view of the parents, because the boy did not want to come and would not use a mere permission to come.[41] Two months later another letter was written by Ignatius' secretary, "The mother of Octavian has come to Rome and stirred up much gossip in the city by her tears and pleadings among distinguished ecclesiastics and by saying publicly that we have stolen her son. The Cardinal of Carpi, our protector, has spoken three times to our Father Ignatius and twice to me, urging us to bring Octavian to Rome, so that, being examined personally in his house, the boy may be returned to us and there will be nothing left to say. Our Father was content to order a

[37] Pol. III, 190.   [38] Letts. V, 709-712.   [39] Pol. IV, 18.   [40] Letts. VII, 421.
[41] Letts. VII, 675.

letter written that Octavian should come to Rome soon, so that we may get this trouble off our backs." To this letter there is a postscript which says that "our Father, after having ordered this letter written, has reconsidered and, taking into account what a bad example it would be, as well as the dangers of the journey, orders that the boy should not be sent no matter what letters are written; unless the letter is written by order of the Pope, whom we are bound to obey. . . . We hope however that His Holiness will not command any such thing." [42]

For three years Octavian persevered in preparing to become a member of the Company and his superiors were very content with his constancy and his diligence in study. But he became ill and was sent to his home in Naples to be nursed back to health. He behaved so severely towards his parents at first that they complained to the rector; who ordered him to be more gentle with them. After a month at home he returned to college improved in health but soon fell into a fever and became extremely melancholy. He was then sent to a villa of his father for two months where he improved in health, but conceived such a hatred for the college that he could not bear to hear it mentioned. He wrote to Ignatius to say he was not fitted either in mind or body for the society and applied for admission to the Theatine fathers who refused to receive him. A letter of Ignatius had no effect upon him and he joined his father and mother in talking very freely against the Company saying he had been led astray, had written to please his superiors, had taken vows without knowing what he was doing and other things of the sort.[43]

During the lifetime of Ignatius these causes, of which only sample instances (14) are given, created in some extremely orthodox Roman Catholic circles a critical atmosphere towards the Company which even the full patronage of the popes did not dissipate. Even their

[42] Letts. VII. 670.   [43] Pol. VI, 252-255.

popular name of Jesuits (which the early members of the Company did not use) was made a ground of attack upon them. In pulpits and in pamphlets it was said that this name was a mark of presumptuous pride which implied a claim to be the only true followers of Jesus. (15) In the middle of the eighteenth century Wesley raised a similar objection against the Moravians. "They commonly style themselves Brethren. Now this implies that they are the only Christians in the world or at least that they are the best Christians in the world." [44] It seems rather hard, however, that the early members of the Company of Jesus were attacked for calling themselves Jesuits, a name given by their opponents which they did not use. Ignatius explained that the "Company" was called by the name of its Commander; as was usually the case.[45]

We do not get a true picture of the life of Ignatius if we fail to understand that it was passed not only amid affection and admiration, but amid constant criticism and active opposition. He bore this opposition with patience and joy; pointing out to his followers that Christ warned His disciples that men would speak evil of them. This opposition made trouble for the Company in many localities like Perugia, Bologna, Valencia, Strassburg, Cambray, Salamanca, Alcalá, Saragossa, Rome, Paris, Toledo, Cologne, Vienna, the Netherlands, etc. How bitter and how dangerous it was may be judged from two examples in which feeling against the Company expressed itself through mouthpieces so conspicuous that it became known in all centres of intelligence.

Melchoir Cano was a very learned Dominican friar who at the age of thirty-five was appointed to the first chair of theology in the University of Salamanca—a position which gave him a sort of intellectual leadership in Spain. He was evidently very conscious of his duty as a watchdog of the Lord to give warning in regard to heresy

[44] Journal, III, 52. [45] Letts. XII, 615.

no matter how distinguished the person tainted with it.
Soon after the death of Ignatius he attacked Bartholomew
Carranza, a brother Dominican who was Archbishop of
Toledo; the richest and perhaps the most powerful prelate
in the world. The result of Cano's attack was that the
Archbishop spent seventeen years as a prisoner of the
Inquisition.[46]

A few years after the formation of the Company, Cano
attacked it in the pulpit and soon after wrote a pamphlet
in which he suggested that the apparent good fruits of the
Company were merely "the pits of plums and were to be
suspected as tricks of the devil who often disguised himself
as an angel of light." [47] Ignatius showed no signs of anger
at this attack. He wrote that Cano spoke out of good zeal
rather than with due knowledge.[48] His reply was to procure a letter from the General of the Dominicans to Cano
exhorting him to let the Company alone, and a letter from
the Pope naming two Spanish bishops to take action
against those who slandered the Company. Cano then
accused the Spiritual Exercises of heresy and a commission was appointed to examine the book. They blamed
everything about it, from the fact that it was originally
written in Spanish and not in Latin, through the fact that
the Exercises lasted thirty days, to the name of the Company of Jesus. They did make one criticism which seems
clearly in the theological field. The Latin translation
says: "even though it were true that no one could be
saved unless he were predestinated" and the examiners
said this plainly implied that a man might be saved who
was not predestinated: which was the heretical opinion of
a certain Catarino.[49] They called it "erroneous, rash, scandalous and even heretical." [50] The Provincial of Spain
pointed out that there was no ambiguity in the Spanish
original which read "even though it is true that no one

[46] Cambridge, 410. [47] Astrain, ctd. 325. [48] Letts. II, 317-213. [49] Astrain, 373.
[50] Pol. III, 524.

can be saved unless he is predestinated" and caused the Latin version to be changed. Ignatius blamed him very much for changing the Latin version because it had been approved by the Pope and added "he never would defend those opinions but the Church would defend him." [51] He also wrote that the idea, that some not predestinate can be saved, was not officially declared heretical. "For in the last council the work of Chaterino containing that opinion was presented and nothing was determined against it." [52]

In spite of this serene confidence, the approval of popes could not merely in itself save Ignatius from virulent attack. The voice of the foremost theologian of Spain echoed through the ecclesiastical world and probably had much to do in determining the denunciation of the Company by the Sorbonne, the theological faculty of the University of Paris.

This question came before the Sorbonne in the following way. Ignatius obtained from the King license to open a college at Paris. This had to be registered by the Parliament. In the committee of the Parliament, Father Broet of the Company found at once violent enemies—one said the devil was the author of the Company.[53] The Committee referred the matter to the Bishop of Paris and the faculty of theology. They were even more unfriendly. "Throwing such envenomed darts as could hardly be believed by one not present at the hearing." [54] The faculty finally decided that this new Company claiming in some peculiar sense as its own the name of Jesus, had abandoned the usual marks of religious orders, enjoyed privileges which injured episcopal authority, and other orders, princes and states and had abandoned the practise of the monastic virtues, abstinence, common religious ceremonies and ascetic discipline. Therefore it seems dangerous in matters of faith, disturbing to the peace of the Church,

[51] Scripta, I, 308. Memoriale. [52] Letts. VI, 598. [53] Pol. III, 289. [54] Pol. III, 292.

subversive of monastic religion and greater in destruction than in edification.[55]   Ignatius' answer to this was, not to appeal to the ecclesiastical courts, but to ask the friends of the Company to write their opinions of its work. A great mass of such written testimony in favour of the Company was collected from kings, princes, city councils, universities, bishops and other witnesses.   But the formal entry of the Company into Paris was long postponed.

[55] Pol. IV, 329.

CHAPTER XIV.

IGNATIUS AS THE GENERAL OF THE COMPANY.

In spite of all this widespread and bitter opposition the Company grew rapidly. It grew from the bottom upward. For eight years after its organization only two new professed were added, and during the next eight years of the life of Ignatius only thirty-five more were received to full vows.[1] This small number must have been extremely busy in carrying the responsibility for the work which was being done. Eight years after its organization the Company was located in twenty-two places organized into four provinces; Portugal, Spain and India were separate provinces and Sicily, Italy, Germany and France formed one province under the direct leadership of Ignatius. It had only seven houses of its own. Three years later it was established in forty-three places and Italy, outside Rome, was made a province. At the death of Ignatius twelve provinces contained eighty establishments of which forty odd were colleges, nine in Asia and South America and the others in Europe. About a thousand members in the various ranks of the Company carried on its work. This was only the beginning. The plant now firmly rooted continued to grow with great vigour. Five years after the death of Ignatius, Pope Pius IV wrote to Philip II of Spain: "It is something almost unbelievable to see how in a short time that Society has spread and how useful it has already become to the Church of God through its many colleges and with what zeal it opposes the pest of

[1] Pol. VI, 40.

heresy."[2] This growth was due to the confident and skilful leadership of Ignatius, but it continued vigorously
after his death and, when the Company of Jesus was suppressed by the Pope 200 years later, it had 41 provinces
and 22,000 members.

Great confidence in success on the part of their
commander is a large element in the morale of any company, especially if it is organized in a military fashion.
His intimates were very fond of telling after his death
striking instances of the confidence of Ignatius in the
future services and triumphs of the Company. In the
early days at Rome when their college was leading a
peripatetic existence in hired houses, he stood out for the
purchase of a large piece of ground, saying, "the time will
come when you will need even more land and very quickly
you will be lacking two square feet rather than having one
too much."[3] None of his followers was ever so dismayed
that a letter from him could not restore courage to the
remote struggler.

One of the most skilful provisions of Ignatius for carrying on the government and maintaining the morale of the
Company, was a very elaborate system of letters, which
kept its different establishments constantly in touch with
their general and enabled him to keep them in touch with
each other. "No founder of a religious order was ever so
labourious in writing to his followers"[4] as Ignatius. He
took the greatest possible pains over important letters,
reading them again and again, spending sometimes two or
three hours on a single letter.[5] This huge correspondence
became a terrible burden. Quite early in his service he
reckoned that "the letters we send amount to two hundred
and fifty."[6] He wrote much about the importance of
this correspondence. Establishments in Italy and Sicily
were to write every week, in Spain, France and the Neth-

[2] Cited Rocquain, p. 20. [3] Rib. 642, Edition 1593. [4] Prolegomena, Letts. I, 6.
[5] Memoriale, Scripta, I, 225. [6] Letts. I, 238.

erlands every month, in the Indies every year. They were to receive answers in Italy every month, outside every four months; besides the general letter of news three times a year.[7] These letters were not to be diffuse, nor filled with trivial things. Two copies were to be sent; one in Latin and the other in the vernacular.[8] Things not for general edification were to be put in a separate letter or in a postcript.

Criticism has been made of this regulation providing for two sorts of letters, "private" and "showable," to be passed on to the entire Company. It could be foreseen that, as the Company grew and spread, things would naturally happen which it would be cruel and foolish to make widely known. The idea that everybody has an inherent right to know all about everything that happens to everybody else, comes out of a false idea of democracy and has no roots in morals or religion. It is the spawn of the practice of yellow journalism in its merciless and mercenary pandering to impertinent curiosity. This provision for private letters might of course be abused. Almost any good rule may be abused, but it takes a rather strong prejudice to see in it an outcome of excessive craft or of anything else but the shrewd common sense of Ignatius.

Ignatius' confidence that his work was of God, who would "give the increase," did not tend in the least to make him dispense with the use of wisdom in directing the work of his followers. We have seen how after arriving at Rome, he rapidly escaped from the exaggerated quakerism which impelled him to trample under foot the usages of human society. He soon came to feel the wisdom of considering, especially, the relation of the Company to what in modern Protestant missions and evangelism are known as "strategic points" and "leaders." Ignatius never allowed his followers to neglect helping the poor, teaching the ignorant, nor the care of the sick in hospitals, but when the

[7] Letts. II, 550.   [8] Letts. IV, 439.

King of Portugal wished the first member of the Company in his kingdom to become the tutor of his heir, Ignatius made him accept the King's offer.[9]   He himself made a journey from Rome to Sicily to reconcile Duke Colonna with his wife, Joanna of Aragon.[10]   He wrote letters which persuaded the daughter of the Viceroy of Sicily to marry according to her father's wishes.[11]   When the somewhat rash and free spoken Father Bobadilla [12] had offended the Emperor by openly opposing the Interim (a futile attempt to reconcile Lutherans and Roman Catholics) and had been sent out of Germany, Ignatius received him in such a way as made it evident he did not endorse Bobadilla's attitude.[13]   Ignatius would have approved the idea of his secretary that, just as it seemed to be providential that the Company at its beginning had important friends in Rome, so it was by God's direction that the earliest members of the Company in Spain had made friends at the royal court among the men whose favour and help was necessary to their establishment in the provinces of that country.

It was said of William Pitt the elder when he was directing the mighty effort of England in war which all over the world turned victory into defeat, that every officer who talked with him in his cabinet came out full of the hope of success and the energy to gain it.   This was the effect Ignatius had upon the missionaries he sent out to fight for the Kingdom of God.   His power of inspiration came from the fact that he let them see the horizon, and his horizon was broad.

He was sending missionaries to two continents, he was organizing Europe into skeleton provinces and looking forward to the day when the nations should be covered with a network of schools, he was training in the German college the preachers who were to stay the great tide of Protestantism, he was writing the Constitutions

[9] Pol. I, 156.   [10] Pol. II, 427.   [11] Pol. II, 554.   [12] Pol. II, 554.   [13] Pol. I, 294.

for a Company which was to be strong on four continents, but, amid all this, he found time and zeal for details. He wrote letters about buying wheat at reasonable prices and searched for wholesome cheap wine for the table. He discussed stuffs for robes, saw that the rooms were properly swept, and made rules to guide the cooks in the use of salt. He was neither a dreamer, letting his hopes make him forget small duties, nor a martinet, seeing only the mechanics of life. His genius like that of every great executive, included, but was not mastered by, a capacity for boundless painstaking.

In any labour or controversy Ignatius wished always that positive rather than negative arguments or methods should be employed. When any establishment was wronged by its neighbours, he abhorred lawsuits and always advised patience or a peaceful compromise by the aid of common friends.[14] Members of the Company were directly advised to preach positive doctrine and to avoid controversy with the heretics.[15] This was not only wise tactics in itself, but it had a second result of which Ignatius may or may not have thought. It saved the Jesuit preachers and writers, at least during his lifetime, from the terrible acrimony which prevailed on both sides in so much of the discussion between Catholics and Protestants. Luther used against his opponents the entire vocabulary of coarse abuse he had learned in his youth among the peasants. Calvin, whose nurture had been more gentle, could write a pamphlet which seemed to a calm and tolerant contemporary historian "filled with the most venomous lines."[16] Their Catholic opponents did not lag behind in this contest of bitterness. For example, the clergy of a great church had carved on one of the stalls in which they sat around the high altar for solemn worship, the figure of a boar preaching, with the inscription, "This is that swine Calvin" and this proof

[14] Rib. 552, Ed. 1593. [15] Letts. I, 388. [16] De Thou, III, 74. Confirmed by Lenient, I, p. 181, ff.

of how Christians loved one another in the sixteenth century still exists in St. Sernin at Toulouse.[17]

We have seen already a specimen of the readiness of Ignatius to ignore the past hostility of a bishop when a settlement had been made by what might be called friendly pressure instead of law. The most striking instance of this sort of wisdom is perhaps the attitude Ignatius ordered to be taken not long before his death, when his old opponent Caraffa became Pope Paul IV. Ribadeneira tells how he was sent to Flanders "when things looked stormy. Our Father advised me to be careful how I talked about what the Pope did and to take into account that everything I said would get to the ears of His Holiness. And because he had done things which seemed very hard to excuse, our Father said that what I had to do was to praise the actions of the previous Pope, Marcellus, and the good will he showed toward the Company, without saying anything at all about the present Pope."[18]

Ignatius was extremely anxious to avoid all causes for slander, hence the prompt punishment for any infringement about the rule for going alone to see women,[19] although among his earliest and most faithful friends there had always been numbers of pious women. Immediately after the foundation, women, both individually and in convents, had been under the religious direction of the Company, but a few years later Ignatius got from Paul III a brief forbidding this.[20] In this again he learned by experience. His old friend, Isabel Roser of Barcelona, to whom he had written fifteen years before, "I owe you more than any one in this world," [21] had lost her husband. She made a cession of all her property for the use of the Company and came to live in Rome under the direction of Ignatius. For two years the Company provided

[17] Lenient, I, 183. [18] Rib. de Actis, Scripta I, 389. [19] Pol. III, 167. [20] Pol. I, 211. Letts. I, 517. [21] Letts. I, 85.

her and two women of her household with lodging, food, clothes and service, through an old noble, Estevan de Guia, who acted as majordomo. She proved a most intractable person who would not keep her vows of obedience, nor separate herself from worldly friends and relatives who kept spreading scandals about the Company and saying that she was kept under the Company's care by force.[22] Ignatius, who had caused her property to be given back to her about a year after she made cession of it, released her from her vows of obedience, writing that he could no longer consider her as "a spiritual daughter but as a good and pious mother which she had many times shown herself to be to him."[23] She made a hysterical scene with Ignatius before a number of his friends and hers. She said she had intended to give a large sum to the house of refuge, but, if the Company was no longer to receive vows of obedience from women, she would not give it. Ignatius replied he would not change his mind about what seemed to him for the greater glory of God, whether she gave or did not give. "After several hours the show (fiesta) came to an end."[24] There was much ugly talk and the matter got before the ecclesiastical courts which decided for the Company. Isabel Roser went back to Barcelona, wrote to Ignatius asking pardon for the past and expressing her love for the Company, and shortly afterward entered a religious order.[25]

Ignatius was particularly anxious to avoid the charge of greed. The members of the Company were forbidden to take any fees, to ask money from any one with whom they had talked of religious things and especially prohibited from telling any one by whose bed of illness they were in attendance to give or leave money to the Company. They could not be present when wills were made nor be

---

[22] Letts. I, 401. Comp. 441, 488. Scripta, I, 645-658. [23] Letts. I, 424.
[24] Letts. I, 439. [25] Letts. I, 439, N. 9, cited Epist. Mixt. IV, 148.

executors.[26] The houses of the Company could not own property—the real estate was held by trustees and the Company had no title to it defensible by law. But the colleges, none of which made any charge for instruction, must have foundations sufficient to feed and care for their students, and there were minute rules to keep the Jesuits of the house in any city from taking meals in the college, or otherwise profiting by their foundations. When an income-bearing property had been given to found a college at Padua, Ignatius wanted to fix on it an annuity for the nephew of the giver,[27] and he did similar things in other cases.

Ribadeneira wrote that, although in the beginning Ignatius was not difficult about novices or new members, he became so and said that if anything made him wish to live, it was that he might be difficult about admitting members to the Company.[28] He wrote a good deal about the choice of novices. He said "a man who was little use in the world was less use in the Company." [29] To the five bars to admission in the Constitutions, he adds others: indomitable passions, inconstancy, dullness unfitting for study, weakness of body of any sort. "Other external gifts like nobility, as they do not suffice if the rest are wanting, so they are not necessary if the rest are present. Nevertheless, so far as they help to edification, they make those apt for other reasons, better fitted to be accepted."[30] He wanted boys of good appearance and was displeased with a father who accepted a novice who had a broken nose.[31] He sent around a measure to prevent the acceptance of undersized candidates. (He was himself a small man). He evidently sought noble boys as students for the colleges, but he lost no time with well-born ne'er-do-wells and once summarily dismissed the heir of a dukedom and ten of his companions. When twenty-two lads

---

[26] Constitutions, Vī, Cap. III, 7. [27] Pol. I, 275. [28] Rib. de Ratione Gubernandi, Scripta, I, 444. [29] ib. [30] Letts. IV, 36. [31] Scripta, I, 445.

came down from Germany to the German College in Rome, he wrote word to send better picked youths the next time. What he particularly wanted was, first, devotion, and, second, brains; though men strong in the first, even though lacking in the second, might be extremely useful as temporal coadjutors, who did most of the manual labour, because "their simple faith and good example were most useful to others inside and outside the houses."[32]

Many who wished to be novices were refused and many were dismissed because they were found inapt, either during the two years' novitiate or in the lower grades. In 1552 one hundred and thirty were dismissed in Portugal, where there was a mutiny in the Company, and during the next four years at least two hundred were dismissed in the other provinces.[33] These dismissals were without fear or favour; the sons of princes or a younger brother of the member who succeeded Ignatius as general, went like any one else. A certain number left also of their own accord. Perhaps the most solid reason for the success of Ignatius' ideal, next to his extraordinary personality, is that in recruiting the Company he tried for quality rather than numbers. He despised mediocrity and always demanded aspiration toward perfection in religion. What he wanted was what he described as "that rare and excellent achievement which is worth six hundred common ones."[34]

He gave little weight to the objections of the parents of young lads who wished to follow what he thought and the Church thought, was a higher way of living. This angered many people of his own age and seems to many more of our own day incredibly heartless. But to place ourselves at his point of view, without any attempt to decide whether that point of view is wrong or right, is to see that such an attitude seemed to him simply doing

[32] Scripta, I, 232, Memoriale.   [33] Boehmer, 289, cited Nadal II, 37.   [34] Cited Hughes 118, from Letter on Obedience.

his duty toward God and the lads who said they heard the call of God in their hearts.

Ignatius writes "in regard to young men from eighteen to twenty such as you write about, no wise man who is a good Catholic ought to doubt that they should be admitted to probation in religious orders even without the consent of their parents." He gives two examples out of many he might cite. "The son of the first noble in Portugal after the King, finding himself seriously and continually called of God in his heart, scaled in the middle of the night the wall of the college where he was locked up and came to *ours* at Coimbra. His family took this very hard and did everything to get the young man out of our house. They persuaded the King to order him sent somewhere else to decide about his plans in life. He, however, refused to come out and was afraid of danger to his soul if he left our house. Ours defended him before the King with such Christian reasons that all attempts of his family were vain and the young man remains in our Company to this day." A young noble was received in the Roman House and sent to a college in Sicily to escape the worldly importunity of his relatives. The uncle, who had friends among the cardinals, and who was a bishop, appealed to the Pope to order the young man back to Rome where his relatives could talk to him. The Pope answered: "Far be it from me to expose him to the danger of losing his soul through being persuaded to refuse to obey the call of God in his heart."[35]

Ignatius felt that boys of fifteen, or nearly fifteen, were old enough to hear the call of God to give up ordinary life in the world and look forward to entering the Company. If they were mistaken, he felt it would appear during the two years of their novitiate, or the long years of study at a university before they took the full vow. He believed that the danger of their making a mistake under

[35] Letts. IV, 93.

the training and influence of the Company, was less than
the danger of denying the call of God under the influence
of parents more ambitious for their children in the things
of this world than in the things of God. He refused a
suggestion from Vienna to lower this limit of age set by
the Constitutions, so as to admit from Germany boys between twelve and fourteen; but said he would use his
power of dispensation in special cases and give it to his
correspondent.[36]   It seems that in this matter of age he
resisted the zeal of some of his followers, for he laid it
down as a practical rule that " a very tender age was an
impediment to reception" and added "fifteen shall be
considered a very tender age to admit even to probation."[37]

The attitude of Ignatius, in this matter, was quite similar, only reversed, to the attitude of the Protestants, who
strenuously justified resistance to parents on the part of
children who did not wish to enter monasteries. It was a
common practise in pre-reformation Germany for parents
to force daughters into convents to avoid the expense of
keeping them and giving them marriage portions. Luther
preached one of his most powerful sermons against parents
who cast their children into hell by vows they could not
keep, as idolaters of old had thrown their children into
the fire of Moloch.

In defending the right of young people to choose for
themselves between the call of God to join the Company
and ordinary life, Ignatius was of course not taking a
position in the least new. He quoted Thomas Aquinas,
Jerome and many other doctors of the Church on the
sinfulness of trying to withdraw our fellow men from
the path which led to a more perfect Christian life and
a more complete service of God. Even in mediæval times
cases like the bitter opposition of the parents of St. Francis of Assisi had been not uncommon. But the recruiting of Ignatius for his Company raised much more opposi-

[36] Pol. IV, 252.   [37] Letts. IV, 37.

tion. Times were changed. Not only had the Protestant schismatics renounced the whole monastic ideal, so that the monk Martin Luther deliberately and dramatically broke his vows by marrying a nun, but, even among orthodox Catholics, the monastic ideal of life no longer held its unique and powerful supremacy: as witness the infrequency of new foundations and the cardinals who thought there were too many religious orders already.

It is very difficult for most of us moderns to put ourselves in the place of men who felt that life in a religious order was undoubtedly a more perfect Christian life than any life in a family could possibly be. To resist the call of God to this higher life seemed to them the worst possible sort of religious apostasy. This is precisely what Ignatius and his followers believed with all their hearts. Hence, very naturally, they came to be afraid of family affections as a danger to that complete surrender to doing the will of God and helping their neighbour, for which they strove. Not indeed that they bade any one neglect a family which imperatively needed him. Married men were not eligible to the Company. A man, not professed, who asked to be dismissed to help the needs of his family, was sent away in peace and afterwards readmitted in the same grade. A Neapolitan who had taken the vow was ordered by Ignatius, on the advice of the members of the Company in that city, to live at home because both of his parents were old and needed his help. He did so, subject to the call of the Company when his duty to his parents was over.[38] But though they admitted family duty as a bar to service in the Company, they feared family affection as a danger to those whose hearts ought to be wholly given to God and man.

Father Adrian was sent home by the physicians because he was dangerously ill. At the end of two months the physicians had done nothing for him and he went back

[38] Pol. III, 188; IV, 181.

to the college, where, beginning with the very day he gave up the doctors and all their works, he began to enjoy the best health he had ever known in his life. During his stay at home, his sister and mother showed the greatest piety, confessing and taking communion every week. His sister, learning that certain books were needed for the students, bought them. His mother gave much money to the college and precious ornaments for the church, while other members of the family showed other signs of piety. "Nevertheless Father Adrian, knowing that domestic entanglements even with pious relatives ought to be guarded against like poison, returned as soon as possible to Louvain." [39] There was a boy in the College of Valencia, extremely pious and very brilliant, who wished to go with Father Miron to Portugal. The head of the College would not let him go without the permission of his parents. They were unwilling to give permission but the boy, "using spiritual rhetoric brought them over so completely to his way of thinking that they begged Father Miron with tears to take him along. But when, with a placid and joyful face, he said goodbye to his mother, who was dissolved in tears, she cried out, 'Oh, my dear son, don't you know that I am your mother that you can leave me with a heart so untouched?' The boy answered he left in order to serve God more perfectly and so he did it with a joyful mind. But when the boy said goodbye in our college to his spiritual brethren he wept copiously. Thus he caused all to admire the way in which he put off mere human affections as well as the way in which he put on spiritual affection." [40]

Such anecdotes as these, recording what they praised and what they feared, show better than pages of description the attitude of Ignatius and his friends towards family affection. He who finally enlisted in the Company of Jesus must forget all other ties. To those who wished

[39] Pol. II, 591.   [40] Pol. II, 351.

"to postpone or refuse the state of higher perfection, because of carnal affections to please their parents," they quoted the saying of Christ to the young man who wished to bury his father before following him: "Let the dead bury their dead," and they pointed reluctant parents to the words: "He that loveth father or mother more than me is not worthy of me"; or: "if any man come to me and hate not his father and mother . . . and brethren and sisters . . . he cannot be my disciple."[41] As a soldier marching off to almost certain death for his country said a last goodbye to his family, so Ignatius wished his recruits to answer the call of their invisible Captain, leave behind them father and mother, brother and sister, and follow Him in a lifelong fight for God.

Nevertheless, family feeling was so strong and wide spread that Ignatius found himself obliged to take practical account of it. Parents began to fear that the schools of the Company were used like nets to gather members and boys were taken out of schools, especially boys of noble families.[42] So Ignatius issued a rule that no one should be received as a novice from among the scholars in the colleges, without the consent of the parents; explaining that the loss suffered by parents withdrawing boys from the schools and their alienation from the Company, would be greater than the gain from the admission of their sons. This rule was enforced.[43] But Ignatius had a letter written to explain that little attention should be paid to the objections of a father, when the young man was not a student in one of the colleges of the Company, for the parents' consent was not necessary in that case.[44]

To the letter to superiors ordering that boys from the colleges of the Company should not be received without their parent's consent, there was added this notable phrase: "And there will not be lacking ways of helping

[41] Pol. IV, 272; Letts. V, 167; Mt. X, 37; Luke XIV, 26. [42] Pol. IV, 58; V, 109, 1417. [43] Pol. II, 421; V, 114, 497. [44] Pol. III, 198; Letts. IV, 41.

the good desires of any one who wishes to enter the Company—sending them to other places or as God shall inspire."[45]

Allusion has already been made to the fact that many of those who have written about Ignatius with the motive, perhaps unconscious, not of giving a true picture of him, but of expressing their dissent from what he taught, are apt to accuse him of indirection. The phrase above is called notable because it seems to the writer unique in the letters sent out by Ignatius. There is nothing else in the original sources of his life which can be fairly or seriously cited to support a charge of indirection. Certain facts and letters in connection with the cases of Octavian, young Ricasoli [46] of Florence, and others, arouse the strong suspicion that the suggestion of this postscript was acted upon. That the suggestion was sent out with a good conscience appears not only from its last words, but also from the whole attitude of Ignatius in the matter. But its lack of frankness is as evident as the baselessness of the charge of craft brought against his conduct in general.

[45] Letts. IV, 112; Pol. II, 421. [46] See note (14) to page 205.

CHAPTER XV

OBEDIENCE

Monks of all orders bound themselves by vow to poverty, chastity and obedience. Ignatius wished to lay a special emphasis on the last of these monastic virtues. He wrote: "although all orders hold obedience to be necessary, we ought to desire particularly that the members of our Company should be distinguished by this virtue, because we do not match many other orders, either in the austerity of our dress, or in fastings; or in the mortifications of our common way of life. Therefore we desire much in our Lord we shall all be truly distinguished by obedience and real abnegation of our own will and judgment."[1] The most quoted of the phrases Ignatius employed in regard to this virtue which he called "the firmest anchor of the soul,"[2] are not particularly significant because they were stock figures of speech; often employed before him by monastic writers: for example they ought to let themselves be wielded entirely by their superiors "like a staff in the hand of an old man," to assume a lack of personal choice about all things "like that of a dead body which goes wherever it is taken without any repugnance whatever."[3]

The ideas of Ignatius on obedience are to be found in his celebrated letter to the Jesuits of Portugal, thought by some of his followers "the most admirable of all which

[1] Letts. II, 63, compare III, 509.   [2] Letts. II, 57.   [3] Letts. III, 502, Constitutions, VI, cap. 1.

came from his pen." [4] Its teaching is supported by many citations from scripture and the fathers [5] and the latter show that no point in it was new.

St. Benedict, who, in the sixth century, began the organization of monasticism, wrote in his celebrated Rule: "When the monk receives a command he should obey it immediately as if it came from God himself." Ignatius begins his explanation of obedience by saying that a superior should be obeyed not because he is good or wise but because he is our superior and as such he is to the man he commands, the Vicar of Christ. The first and lowest grade of obedience is execution, i.e. doing what is commanded; which does not deserve the name unless it is joined to obedience of the will. Whoso does not make this surrender makes his own will the measure of God's, instead of making God's will the measure of his. But entire and perfect obedience requires also the surrender of the understanding, so that we not only wish the same thing as our superior, but think the same as he does (in the matter ordered) "subjecting our own judgment to his so far as the devoted will can control the understanding.

"Because, although the understanding has not the freedom of choice possessed by the will and naturally gives its assent to that which appears to it true, nevertheless, in many things wherein the evidence of known truth does not force it, the understanding may be inclined to one side or the other and, in such things, every obedient brother should incline himself to think what his superior thinks. Certainly, since obedience is a sacrifice in which the man, without any division of himself, offers his entire being in the fire of love to his Creator by the hand of His ministers . . . it cannot be said that obedience comprises only doing what is commanded or contentment of the will in doing it. Obedience also includes the judgment;

[4] Astrain, 611.   [5] Letts. IV, 669.

thinking what the superior orders so far (as has been said) as the mind can be inclined by the effort of the will. . . . Just as among the heavenly bodies there can be no movement without subordination of one body to another, so in the movement of a rational being by another (which is obedience) subordination is necessary for transferring the influence and virtue from the mover to the moved and this cannot occur without conformity of will and understanding.

"The understanding may be misled as well as the will. The scriptures say 'Lean not upon thine own understanding' and also, in other human affairs, wise men know it is true wisdom not to trust one's own wisdom. This counsel is even more necessary in regard to spiritual things and persons . . .

"He who has not this obedience of judgment cannot have a perfect obedience which is to obey with love and joy. He loses perseverance, promptness and skill. He loses the much praised simplicity of blind obedience, questioning in himself if the command is wise or unwise, perhaps blaming his superior because he commands that which is not to his mind. He loses humility and fortitude in difficult affairs.

"Unless the understanding is subjected in obedience there arise discontent, pain, delay, slackness, murmuring, excuses, which rob obedience of its value and merit.

"Lack of surrender of the judgment disturbs the peace and tranquillity of the one who obeys and differences of judgment disturb the peace and union of the congregation; hence St. Paul urges let all think and speak the same thing.

"Finally to subject the judgment in obedience, is to offer to God the noblest of oblations: not keeping back anything of oneself and conquering by love for Him the natural inclination all men have to follow their own judgment.

"Three rules will help towards this perfect obedience. First: Do not look on the superior as on a man subject to errors and miseries, but look at what you obey in the man, which is Christ the highest wisdom, the highest goodness, infinite love; . . . so, using the inner eyes of the soul rather than the outer eyes, you will be able to conform your will and judgment.

"Second: Always be ready to look for reasons to defend what a superior orders, and not for disapproving it; third, assume that the order is in accord with God's will and begin with enthusiasm to obey it."[6]

The hopes Ignatius built on this virtue as the cornerstone of his work are seen very plainly in a stinging letter of rebuke he wrote not long before his death. A man who had been disciplined on account of lack of obedience had kept badly the promise he made "to obey like a dead thing." Evidently he had been talking about the interpretations and limits of the doctrine of obedience, saying that men "ought not to be homicides of themselves, etc." "That," burst forth Ignatius, "is the most pernicious doctrine which can be taught for the union we seek in this Company and the perfection of obedience based on love. It has the power of the pestilence to infect quickly a whole college. That spirit is the very essence of pride of intellect and corrupts the entire simplicity and magnanimity of obedience. Its end is voluntary apostasy or being summarily dismissed to save others from infection—however, so far as that is concerned, the Company will consider the charity that may be shown towards an individual without danger to the general good."[7] Frequent dismissals of novices and probationers shows how firmly he believed in the necessity of obedience.[8]

The chronicler gives instances of the zeal with which novices tried to attain this perfect obedience. Once when a number of them were cleaning the mud from a street

[6] Letts. IV, 669.   [7] Letts. XI, 276.   [8] Pol. II, 169, 697.

in front of a house, one said they had got down to solid
bottom and another said they had not yet got to it.   Their
father superior who was present said they were on solid
bottom "and then he who had just denied it said 'We
are on solid bottom and if you father say it is mud, I
will confess it is mud.' "[9]

A novice of eighteen years lay dying and his brethren
begged him to pray for them when he got to heaven.   He
said, "Yes, I will gladly do it if permission is given me to
pray to Christ for you, for I shall not be able to enter
the heavenly mansions nor to pray for you there without
obedience to the Father in Heaven.   Because if here in
this world we must obey, how much more there, whence
all obedience descends to us! . . . and this purity,
obedience and simplicity *ours* could not help but ardently
admire."[10]

In one of the novice houses a young lad died "who
had set an example of great patience and obedience and
at the end he did something of great edification by asking from the master of the novices permission to die."[11]

A special attack has been made upon Ignatius for his
teaching of obedience on the ground that at least by in-
ference it obliged members of the Company to commit sin
like theft or murder or perjury when ordered by their
superiors.   In the first place this, if it were true, would not
be *especially* chargeable on Ignatius for his doctrine was
not his invention—every point in it can be sustained by
citations from the fathers of the Church.   In the second
place the charge is false.   In the section of the Constitutions which treats of obedience he expressly repudiates the
idea that his men are to obey a command to sin,[12] and he
does the same in several of his letters; twice in the celebrated letter on obedience.[13]   There can be no doubt that
if Ignatius had heard that any of his followers had drawn

[9] Pol. V, 434.   [10] Pol. II, 229.   [11] Pol. IV, 198.   [12] Part IV, Cap. 1.   [13] Letts. I,
228; III, 501.

such a conclusion from his teaching, he would have echoed the judgment of Paul about those who sinned that grace might abound—"whose damnation is just." (16)

In spite of the fact that Ignatius found in the doctrine of obedience the spiritual basis for a government of his Company as absolute as that which a general and his hierarchy of officers impose upon an army in time of war, he was not a tyrant; even a benevolent one. He sought advice; though he had strict ideas about the way it should be offered to a superior. When Lainez whom he chose as his successor, wrote "a little freely" criticizing the withdrawal of needed men from provincial colleges to strengthen Rome, Ignatius was much displeased and replied, pointing out that he had preferred local good to general good, and admonishing him to think the matter over until he had realized his fault and, when he had realized it, to write what penance he was prepared to undergo. Lainez replied thanking Ignatius for the correction and begging to be used wherever he was needed. Meantime he proposed, "with many tears," three penances, all so heavy that Ignatius would not impose any of them. Nor did he impose any other; accepting this humble self condemnation of Lainez as an ample penance for his fault.[14]

Later he wrote rules on the "Way to Consider a Subject or Negotiate any Matter with Superiors," which made evident that he by no means wished to shut out the offering of information or advice by inferiors who had received orders; but only to forbid beginning a discussion in the place of doing what one was told to do.[15]

As years went on Ignatius came to dislike "innovations" in the Company and he seems to have had a natural liking for uniformity even in details; but he was free from the weakness of those rulers of men who trust no one's judgment but their own and so want to do everything themselves. He frequently noted that things he

[14] Pol. III, 61. [15] Letts. IX, 90, 93.

suggested were only by way of advice and not ordered by his authority as general which it was sinful to disobey.[16] At other times after expressing his opinion, he adds, "Nevertheless I leave the matter to your prudent consideration."[17] An old father recalling how he begged Ignatius for minute instructions when he was sending him to become rector of a distant college, wrote that Ignatius replied " 'Oliver, do as you think best: fit the rules to the place the best way you can.' And when I begged to know how to distribute the staff he was sending with me, he answered with few words 'Oliver, cut your coat according to your cloth and your needs.' "[18]

"In the same way our Father wished the provincials to have in their provinces all the liberty possible in governing them."[19] When he sent Nadal as special envoy to Spain and Portugal, he gave him a number of blanks sealed and signed with permission to write over the signature any letter, private or public, he might believe to be useful in the Lord.[20] He was very insistent that by the virtue of obedience men expecting to be assigned to duty should be entirely ready to go cheerfully anywhere they were sent, but, in making his assignments, he carefully considered not only the aptitudes but the inclinations of his men.[21] For Ignatius did not look on obedience as an iron rule to crush individuals into a mass. He meant it to be a spiritual grace to unite the hearts and minds of men whose individuality was highly developed, into a living organism devoted with a single will to a common object: the service and glory of God and the helping of their neighbours.

The celebrated letter on obedience of which a brief paraphrase has been given was addressed to the "Comrades of Portugal." It was called forth by the gravest internal difficulties which Ignatius had to face in gov-

---

[16] Pol. III, 440; Letts. V, 127. [17] Letts. V, 674. [18] Scripta, I, 519. [19] Scripta, I, 285, Memoriale. [20] Pol. III, 439. [21] Scripta, I, 209, Memoriale.

erning the Company. Those difficulties were caused by the character and conduct of the only one of his nine first fathers who ever acted disloyally toward him. Nothing can show more plainly that the discipline of Ignatius, though severe was not heartless or iron clad, than his conduct toward Father Simon Rodriguez; guilty not only of forgetting the spirit of the Company but even the sense of honour and the feeling of affection toward an old friend. Indeed the attitude of Loyola towards this disobedient son is so indulgent as to suggest at one point to one of his recent biographers the question, "How can this letter so opposed to the habitual prudence of our holy Father be explained?"[22]

Simon Rodriguez started for India with Xavier, but was detained in Portugal by the King, over whom he soon came to exercise considerable influence. Ignatius allowed him to act for six years as if he were provincial of Portugal. Although some disquieting reports had come to Rome during this period about the Company in Portugal, Ignatius appointed Simon Rodriguez provincial of that country in 1546.[23] The year before, he had called Simon to Rome. But the King so strongly opposed his leaving that Ignatius, who never unnecessarily opposed the highest civil or ecclesiastical authorities, rescinded the call. Five years later Simon joined some of the principal fathers assembled at Rome to give advice about the Constitutions Ignatius was writing.

Outwardly the Company in Portugal, its first province, was extremely flourishing. It had two well established colleges and three hundred and eighteen Portuguese had entered its ranks in eleven years.[24] But Ignatius was troubled by what he heard from the inside and not pleased with the spirit shown by Simon; who went back to Portugal in the spring of 1551. At the end of the year Ignatius felt certain that he ought to be removed from

[23] Astrain, 614.   [23] Letts. I, 449.   [24] Astrain, 586.

Portugal. To do this easily, he divided Spain into two
provinces, Castile and Aragon, and ordered Simon to take
charge of Aragon.   Then he appointed Father Miron as
the Provincial of Portugal. Ignatius sent Dr. Torres as
his personal representative with full powers to carry out
these changes.   In case Simon did not want to go to
Aragon, he was to be allowed to go to the Brazilian
mission; as he had asked two years before. The King
was now willing to let him leave.   But Simon Rodriguez
said that his health would not permit him to go to Brazil
or to Aragon and so he had determined to stay in retire-
ment in Portugal. Dr. Torres, who had kept in the background, now filled out one of the signed blanks given him
by Ignatius with orders to Simon to go to Aragon at
once "by virtue of holy obedience."   The King backed
this by a letter and the reluctant Simon had to go.

Unfortunately Father Miron, who had been sent to Portugal by Ignatius to succeed Simon, although a man of
very great piety, proved himself incapable of government.
He was stern, impetuous, changeable, without tact or
judgment and he helped the splitting up of the Company
which had already begun.   There were scores of ex-
Jesuits; almost all talking against the Company. Simon
himself by letters secretly furnished one of his chief ad-
herents outside the Company with slanders against
Ignatius.[25]   These slanders accused Ignatius of being a
man of worldly ambition, who had used the wealth of the
Duke of Borgia (recently admitted to the Company) for
the benefit of his family.   They went on to say that
he drew money out of Portugal, that he sent the ablest
sons of Portugal to other countries and replaced them
by novices and foreign students who would never be of
any national use.   These calumnies made considerable
impression at court until they were disproved. The harm
done to the ideals of Ignatius may be indicated to some

[25] Astrain, 601, note 2.

extent by figures. The province had sent a number of
missionaries to Brazil and India, but, when these troubles
became acute the Company in Portugal still numbered
some two hundred and fifty. When it was over, about one
hundred and thirty members in various grades had left or
had been dismissed.

When the situation was at its worst Simon got permission from Ignatius, on the ground of feeble health, to
go back to Portugal. None of the houses of the Company would receive him and he spent his time on the
estate of a powerful patron, the Duke of Aveiro.

In May 1553 Ignatius summoned Simon to Rome "by
virtue of holy obedience." Two months later, having
heard nothing, he wrote again, a gentle and affectionate
letter urging him to come. At the same time he sent to
the provincial, documents enabling him to give Simon
three warnings and then if he did not obey, to dismiss
him from the Company.[26] If Simon said he was ill, competent physicians of the order of St. Dominic were to be
consulted. At last they got him started and, six months
after he was first summoned, he arrived at Rome.
Ignatius gave him a cordial welcome and the best apart-
ment in the house. He would have been willing to bury
the past in silence, but the hard headed Simon insisted
that his conduct should be examined solemnly by four
fathers.[27] Several of the fathers who had been in Portugal had for more than five years suspected that he was
led astray by "el demonio,"[28] and they gave testimony by
word and letter. The commission of inquiry—it might
almost be called a court martial—decided that he was
guilty of undue confidence in his own judgment; unedifying self indulgence and luxury in living, ambition, etc.[29]
The evidence to sustain their judgment, and even a charge
of deliberate personal disloyalty, is abundant. They im-

[26] Scripta, I, 674, 675.   [27] Astrain, 627, Note.   [28] Scripta, I, 667.   [29] Scripta,
I, 677.

posed a penance that he should write letters to Portugal
acknowledging his faults to several named people within
and without the Company, that he should never go back
to Portugal, that he should say every day the Lords
Prayer and Ave Maria asking God to pardon his pride
and disobedience, that every week for seven years, unless
his health was too feeble, he should say a mass for Portugal and inflict strict discipline on himself, that for two
years he should fast once a week and converse with no
one outside of the list given to him.[30] Of this penance
which the fathers judged very small, Ignatius remitted all
but the first part.[31] To accompany Simon's letters of
penitence, he wrote a circular letter to say that his dear
son, although he had failed in some things, had acted without evil intentions. He added, "From his conversation
and company, I have every day more and more satisfaction."[32]

This satisfaction could not have lasted very long, for
Simon began to complain of Ignatius and he also savagely
attacked his judges.[33] Ignatius confined him to the house
and sent to Naples for Salmerón and to Ancona for
Bobadilla, hoping that these old comrades of Paris
would bring him to a better frame of mind. But Simon
treated them little better.[34] He appealed to the Pope
for a dispensation to spend two years as a hermit with
the intentions of choosing a hermitage near Lisbon. This
was blocked with the help of a letter from the Ambassador
of Portugal, to the Pope, saying that the King did not
want Simon in Portugal. Simon then tried to persuade
Ignatius to give him permission to go to Portugal because
his health demanded his native air. Ignatius refused, but
gladly gave him permission to make a pilgrimage to Jerusalem. Simon changed his mind again and Ignatius sent
him to Venice with permission, if he wished to spend

[30] Scripta, I, 678. [31] Scripta, I, 680. [32] Scripta, I, 680. [33] Scripta, I, 681.
[34] Scripta, I, 681, 683.

the summer at Monreale in Sicily "which is the best air and the most beautiful position of all the establishments of the Company." Simon showed a very bad temper. He opened letters addressed to others, "an act very evil even among secular people," and wrote Ignatius a sour rather insulting letter.[35] In short he acted like a wilful and pettish child. Ignatius continued to treat him like an affectionate modern parent who believed the trouble had some physical nervous root. Certainly the attitude of Ignatius toward Simon is in marked contrast to his severity at the very same time to his old comrade Lainez and his faithful helpers, Polanco and Nadal. It may be conjectured that he feared lest harshness might drive Simon into apostasy and the loss of his soul. As a matter of fact, Simon Rodriguez did good service to the Company for more than twenty years after the death of Ignatius: eight in Italy, twelve in Spain and the last years in Portugal.

He did such good service that, when a candid account of his conduct was printed in 1616, the Jesuits of Portugal were very much scandalized and wrote protesting to the editor of the book in which it appeared.[36] He wrote a reply in regard to the duty of the historian which ought to be rescued from oblivion, because it sets forth so clearly the danger of that willingness to be edifying at the expense of frankness, which has been the curse of religious history and biography; Protestant fully as much as Catholic. He says complaint may be made of a historian either because the things he relates are not true, or because even if they were true, they ought not to have been told. Under the first head he points out that the things objected to rest on the written testimony of seventeen named witnesses of the highest character. Under the second head he says, "If things are true no historian can,

---

[35] Scripta, I, 698.
[36] Father Sacchini publishing the manuscript of Father Orlandini.

without violating the laws of history and his own conscience, keep silent about them. . . . The reason is that
since the essence of history is to narrate outstanding
things either good or evil, . . . (which in the case of a
biography help to form a true judgment of the man)
he who publishes a history relating only good things
writes himself down as willing to deceive. . . . Truth is
rightly called the soul of history. If she is absent because
writers keep silent about what should be told, history dies.
For it is against the truth not to say those things which
ought to be said." [37]

[37] Scripta, I, 703.

CHAPTER XVI

THE COLLEGES OF THE COMPANY OF JESUS

Perhaps the effort of the Company of Jesus which finally exercised the greatest influence was their work in education. Long before Ignatius thought of founding the Company he believed in the necessity of education for those who desired to help their fellowmen. At the age of thirty-three he joined small boys in the study of Latin grammar and spent the next eleven years of his life in gaining a university education. He found his first comrades at the universities and he looked for them nowhere else.

In spite of Ignatius' evident inclination toward learning, the germinal idea of founding a network of colleges came not from him but from Lainez,[1] and the famous Ratio Studiorum or method of the Jesuits was formed more than fifty years after the death of Ignatius.[2] He saw only the beginnings of Jesuit education. At his death, the Company had nine schools and colleges in India and America and about thirty-five in Europe.[3] Two hundred years later, there were seven hundred and twenty-eight Jesuit universities, colleges and schools attended by some 200,000 pupils.[4]

Although Ignatius did not suggest the beginning of this great educational system, nor establish its final form, he left his impress upon it.

The ideas about education which he approved are to be seen in the fourth *part* of the Constitutions, which

[1] Scripta, I, 220. [2] Hughes, 154. [3] Pol. VI, 42. [4] Hughes, 70, 74.

occupies a quarter of that document.   It is characteristic
of Ignatius that it is not labelled "On Education" but
"Of the Means of Instructing those who are Kept in the
Company, in Letters and other Means of Helping their
Neighbours."   The preamble sets forth that, as the object
of the Company is to aid the souls of their neighbours,
not only a good example, but knowledge of doctrine and
skill in teaching it, are needed in its members.   Therefore, as soon as young men have shown that they have
the foundation of self denial and growth in virtue, the
next step must be to give them knowledge and train them
to use it.

The comment goes on to explain that it is very difficult
to recruit for the Company among men already educated.
Because most learned men want ease after they have
gotten their education and are frightened away by the
great labour and self denial required of members.   So it
seems best to admit young lads who by their good habits
and abilities give hope of becoming both virtuous and
learned enough to work in the vineyard of Christ.

The core of the students are those under vows, but poor
students who do not look forward to joining the Company may be received if they suggest good hopes that they
may make workers in the vineyard of the Lord.   The convenient age is from fourteen to twenty-three.

The spiritual training of probationers must be carefully
looked to, so that on the one hand, zeal for learning
does not make them slack in their religious life, nor on the
other hand, prayers or meditation take too much time
from study.   They must study humane letters in various
languages including rhetoric, logic, metaphysics, natural
and moral philosophy, and then go on to scholastic and
positive (patristic) theology and holy writ.   Orderly progress in the sciences should be arranged.   Holy writ may
be studied with or after positive theology.   When the
languages in which the Bible was written are studied, one

of the objects set before the learners shall be the defense of the translations approved by the Church.

At least every Sunday, leaders appointed by the rectors shall briefly defend propositions they have posted the day before and anyone, either from the house or outside, may take part in the debate. All, but especially the students of liberal arts, must ordinarily speak Latin and once a week after dinner, one of the most skilful must make an address in Latin or Greek. Students, who cannot learn or do not want to, should not be allowed to waste their time. They must be sent from college and replaced by others who will profit by their opportunities.

Students from outside ought to be instructed in Christian doctrine, to go to confession every month and frequently to hear sermons; in short be trained not only in letters but in habits worthy of a Christian.

Much emphasis is laid on training the probationer scholars for their future work in helping their neighbours. They should have practice in preaching and public reading of the scripture; they should be shown how to teach Christian doctrine to children, etc. "They should be taught to help their neighbours to die well and what should be done in that crisis which may achieve or lose the final end of eternal happiness . . . They should be instructed how to adapt themselves to a great variety of persons and warned against possible mistakes. For although that wise tact can only be taught by the Holy Spirit . . . it is at least possible to give hints which help and prepare for the result which the grace of God must bring about."[5]

According to the papal bulls the superintendence of the colleges is in the hands of the professed of the Company whose executive is the general. He appoints the rectors from among the spiritual coadjutors (a professed might

---

[5] It is easy to guess that these paragraphs came from Ignatius; that skilful fisher of men.

be rector only temporarily). A rector's first duties are
to sustain the morale of his college by prayer and holy
desires and to see that the Constitutions are kept: therefore he is advised to read the *part* concerning colleges
publicly two or three times a year. He appoints all
officers of the college and, with the help of a council, provides for everything.

About a third of the *part* devoted to educational establishments is given to the universities Ignatius hoped the
Company would some day manage.

Theology is the study which best prepares a man to help
the souls of his neighbours. The principal effort of the
universities of the Company should therefore be to have
very good teachers of scholastic and positive theology and
the sacred scriptures, but without trying to teach ecclesiastical law. "Because the use of theology in these days
demands a good knowledge of humane letters and of Latin,
Greek and Hebrew, there should be good teachers of these
subjects. . . . The natural sciences prepare the mind for
the perfect understanding of theology and they also should
be taught together with logic, metaphysics and mathe-
matics. As medicine and law have little to do with the
objects of the Company these faculties shall not be included in its universities."

Attention must be paid to the formation of Christian
habits by the students of the universities. No student not
under vows is to be compelled to attend religious exercises,
but all lectures must be opened with prayer and every occasion which arises for exhortation to love and serve God
is to be improved by the lecturers. The vicious or lazy
are to be punished, the incorrigible dismissed. Every year
each member of the council shall write to the general a
letter about the rector, and twice each year similar letters
must be sent to the provincial. Every third year all members of the Company at a university, down to the grade
of approved scholars, shall write about all the others,

and the rector. These letters must be sealed so that no one knows what the others have written.

There are a number of details about the management of the colleges which Ignatius learned by experience. Some of these are mentioned in the Constitutions and some not. It was found best not to be too ready "to send scholars who made trouble in one college to another," and not to mix novices and ordinary scholars, nor allow outsiders to teach in the schools of the Company.[6] Students should not be allowed to beg for the care of the poor, nor to engage in any good work which interfered with their studies. Students unable to read and write were never to be admitted. Nor was Ignatius willing to allow the Company to be saddled with responsibility for foundations so small as to be hopelessly inferior. Not long before his death he wrote to Lainez, "Speaking truly it is impossible to call any thing even a mediocre college, which has not at least two priests, three or four masters and two assistants, together with two servants, in all ten at least."[7] (17) The expenses of these institutions were much reduced by the fact that their staff received no salaries except their food and lodging.

There was one item however on the budget of some Jesuit colleges which does not appear in that of any modern institution of learning: the salary of the corrector or whipper. In those days the rod was regarded as a necessary and normal instrument of education, and Ignatius believed, like most people of his own and succeeding generations, that boys could not be properly educated without it. But he also forbade any member of the Company to punish a student.[8]

This rule was strictly enforced. In the College of Naples one of the teachers lost his temper in class and whipped a student with his own hands, instead of telling him to go to the corrector. His superior ordered him as a pen-

[6] Pol. III, 161-166.   [7] Letts. V, 733.   [8] Pol. III, 23.

ance to eat his meals sitting on the floor and to drink only water. The penitent, who had been weak and unwell for a while before the incident, went to his rector and said he conscientiously felt that drinking nothing but water would impair his health. He was told that obedience would serve him instead of medicine. So he drank water. This not only did not harm but rather helped him so much that he became strong and well "which thing ought strongly to commend to everybody the advantage of carrying out strictly all imposed penances."[9] There were two ways to get around the difficulty about the use of the indispensable rod. The first was to employ a corrector from outside the Company to do the whipping. But correctors were hard to find. In Modena, though the bishop spoke to several about it and offered them a salary, none could be found to exercise the office which was considered somewhat like that of an executioner.[10] Ignatius had also suggested appointing a student corrector. But when they tried that in some places the parents of the boys whipped objected. In other places the boys objected still more. At Venice a student chased with a drawn knife the fellow student appointed to whip him and at another college, when several boys had been whipped by their fellows, they came the next day armed to avenge the insult in blood.[11] But in spite of all difficulties Ignatius continued to insist that it was "very indecent and improper for a member of the Company to punish any scholar with his own hands."[12]

The schedule of work in Jesuit colleges in the days of Ignatius would start an insurrection in the average American college today, but it was probably mild in comparison to other institutions. Here for instance is the programme at the College of Montaigu, the first Ignatius attended in Paris. At 4 arise, 5 to 6 lesson, at 6 mass followed by breakfast, 7 to 8 recreation, 8 to 10 lesson, 10 to 11 dis-

[9] Pol. II, 525. [10] Pol. III, 150 e. g. [11] Pol. IV, 127, III, 38. [12] Letts. X, 403.

cussion and argumentation, 11 dinner, during which the
Bible or the life of a saint was read aloud, 12 to 2
revision of lessons, 2 to 3 recreation, 3 to 5 lesson, 5 to 6
argumentation and discussion, 6 supper, 6½ examination
of day's work, 8 in winter, or 9 in summer, bed.[13]

The directions in the Constitutions frequently repeated
in letters to rectors, to see that the students had sleep
enough and were not overworked, imply a programme
somewhat less grinding than this. Besides, the scholars of
the Company had great advantages over the unfortunate
pupils at Montaigu which had two nicknames: one was
Bean College and the other was Flea College. Rabelais,
an old student, gives a vivid description of what these
names meant. Even more revealing is this tragic record
from a petition for amendment written by Jean Boulaese,
professor of Hebrew at Montaigu. A *"poor"* drowned 29
Jan. 1573. A *"rich"* threw himself out of a window 16
April 1573. A porter killed by blows and another badly
wounded, 14 May 1573. A *"poor"* goes mad, 2 June
1573. Another *"rich"* jumps out of the window, 8 July
1573. And on the 25th of October others are beaten into
illness and death.[14]

Ignatius was very insistent on care for cleanliness and
sufficient food and he set the example by his careful in-
spection of the Roman establishments. When he saw from
the reports an increase in cases of illness in any college, he
ordered a careful revision by physicians of all the conditions of living; including the dietary.

The care for morals in the colleges of the Company was
real and never formal; whereas, at many colleges, there
is strong reason to suspect that outward strictness masked
great laxity. At Sainte Barbe at Paris, while Xavier was
there, a knot of students went out frequently on debauches
led by one of the masters, who finally died of syphilis.

[13] Lefranc, p. 65, cited Félibien.   [14] Godet, 296.

The strict supervision of Jesuit colleges rendered such a condition hardly possible.

No tuition fees could be charged and Ignatius would accept no foundation for a college unless it provided for the entire expenses of a certain number of scholars. Modern governments use the same principle of free instruction and living expenses in providing for a succession of trained men to fill the higher ranks of their armies. Most Protestant denominations in America use a system of scholarships and fellowships in recruiting for their ministry and a large percentage of the students in our theological seminaries do not pay either tuition or their living expenses. It may be conjectured that the ideal of Ignatius for his colleges would have been to fill them with selected students who paid nothing for living or studying there. But he found difficulties, not simply about getting money enough—from the beginning the Company found wealthy and generous friends and patrons—but also because gratitude compelled him to receive the sons of these friends and patrons. So, apparently rather reluctantly, this permission was given in the Constitutions, "sometimes, for good reasons, the sons of rich or noble parents may be admitted to the colleges when their parents pay their expenses." [15]

That paragraph became the basis of the establishment, in response to a growing demand, of boarding colleges, which finally impaired the gratuitous character of Jesuit education. Such a change would perhaps have been inevitable, simply because of the enormous spread of the system; for it would hardly have been possible to maintain more than seven hundred establishments with over two hundred thousand students, on a purely gratuitous basis.

This fact that Ignatius and his comrades intended their colleges to train men for the Company, and, in the case of outside pupils, to form good workers in the vineyard of

[15] Board and lodging only.

the Lord, must be kept in mind by those who wish to understand them. They were exclusively teaching institutions. Nowhere in the Constitutions is there the smallest suggestion that the faculties must try to be investigators or discoverers of truth. Indeed the writer is unable to recall in the letters and works of Ignatius or the reports of his conversation by his friends, a single phrase which suggests a hope that new truth was to be discovered. He did indeed once recommend the scholastic theologians as better fitted than the patristic fathers "to define for our time the things necessary for our salvation because they are more modern." [16] But of the three doctors he cited as examples of "more modern" teachers, two had been dead over two hundred and fifty years and the third nearly four hundred years.

Acquaviva, who in the closing years of the sixteenth century succeeded Ignatius as general, laid down in the new "Method of Studies" this rule. "Let no one defend any opinion which is judged by the generality of learned men to go against the received tenets of philosophers and theologians or the common consent of theological schools." This order would make all teachers instructors only in "definite matter," which is judged by other men to be in accord with tradition in philosophy and theology.[17] Whether this is wise or not ought not to be here discussed. But it ought to be pointed out that this later rule is undoubtedly in accord with the ideal and spirit of Ignatius.

The object of Loyola then in founding a college was not at all the search for new truth. It was exclusively the defense of old truth. Intellectually this son of Basque nobles was by inheritance, by temperament, by experience and training a typical conservative. His lack of interest in the discovery of truth was caused by his absolute cer-

[16] Spiritual Exercises, Regulae 554.   [17] Hughes, 149.

tainty that the Church had all necessary truth, and his consequent absorption in spreading or defending it.

But this extreme conservative on the theoretical side was, on the practical side, inclined to be an innovator. We have seen the innovations he introduced into the Company and how they were attacked by men who were more conservative than he; because they feared not only any truth which claimed to be new, but any custom or method which was new. This willingness of Ignatius to adopt new methods if his reason or experience commended them to his judgment, appears in his ideas about his colleges, under circumstances which make his frank adoption of a new method very surprising in a man of his extreme conservative position.

Ignatius always retained "respect and love for that university which was the mother of the first fathers of the Company." [18]   It was known that Paris was a very expensive university. For instance a student wrote that he was paying more just for his room "and a little dirty one at that," in Paris, than he could live for luxuriously at the University of Louvain in the Netherlands. Nevertheless Ignatius wrote from Paris to his brother, who was considering sending a younger son to a university: "Don't think about the cost. You gain on it in this university because the lad will learn more here in four years than in any other in six."[19]

To anyone reading the chronicle of the early Jesuits it is evident that Ignatius got at Paris most of his ideas about methods of teaching[20] and it must have been there that he learned to prefer the methods of the New Learning to those of the Old Learning.

Some readers may be glad to have a further definition of terms perfectly clear in the days of Ignatius. Before the beginning of the fourteenth century a movement is visible in the records of human taste, feeling and thought

[18] Letts. IX, 451; XI, 452.   [19] Letts. I, 78.   [20] Editors of Polanco, III, 243 n.

which, it is commonly assumed, found its first conscious leader in Petrarch, who died something over a century before Ignatius was born. He was a strenuous critic of the methods of education his generation had inherited— the so-called scholastic system. His followers, called *humanists* in distinction from the *scholastics*, became, together with their artist friends, one of the chief influences in what historians have come to speak of as the Renascence; meaning a rebirth of the human spirit, a more complete consciousness of individuality, a new sense of the beauty of the world we live in and the value of the life we live in it, a love of classic art and literature, a revival of the critical impulse, which inevitably came into conflict with the ascetic ideal of the middle ages.

Ignatius learned, by reading the lives of the mediæval saints, the mediæval ascetic ideal and for a time practised it fully. But when he founded the Company, he forbade rules imposing ascetic practices. It would however be a very great mistake to attribute this change of attitude toward asceticism to the influence of the spirit of the Renascence. To the spirit of the Renascence in general he was totally opposed. The change in his attitude toward extreme ascetic practices, came simply from his practical judgment. He learned by experience, as he wrote to Theresa Rejadella fifteen years after his conversion, "with a healthy body you can do much, with a weak body I do not know what you can do."[21]

The struggle between the New Learning of the *humanists* and the Old Learning of the *scholastics* was one special phase of the conflict of the spirit of the Renascence with mediævalism. The old orders, especially the Dominicans and Franciscans who at the time of Ignatius' birth furnished many of the professors of the universities of Europe, were the leaders in the defense of the Old Learning and they were always ready to denounce their antag-

[21] Letts. I, 108, compare II, 235.

onists as heretics and threaten them with the stake. But the New Learning found powerful protectors. By the middle of the fifteenth century, it had won the ear of all the princes of the Italian states; and popes friendly to it like Nicholas IV and Pius II began to appear on the throne of St. Peter. In the sixteenth century the rulers of the great transalpine states became its patrons. Cardinal Ximenes, regent of Castile, Maximilian, Emperor of Germany, his grandson, Charles V, Henry the Eighth of England, the "Defender of the Faith," Francis I of France, etc. In short, long before the middle of the sixteenth century, the New Learning was the mode. This did not happen without desperate battles on the part of the advocates of the Old Learning and the question came to a point over the place to be given to the study of languages.

In Germany, early in the sixteenth century, the Dominicans attempted to get an order from the Emperor that all Hebrew books except those in the Bible, should be destroyed. When Reuchlin, the first German to know Hebrew thoroughly well, objected, they threatened him with the stake and after a long struggle the case against him was quashed at Rome. All higher instruction was given in Latin, but the scholastics had grown indifferent to its quality. The three languages therefore, Latin, Greek and Hebrew, became the banner of the New Learning. At the birth of Petrarch (1304) there were few born west of the Adriatic who knew Greek and when its study began to prevail north of the Alps the men of the Old Learning were especially opposed to it. Sir Thomas More, Chancellor of England, wrote to Oxford this letter:

"I heard lately that either in some fools' frolic or from your dislike to the study of Greek, a clique had been formed among you calling themselves Trojans and that the object was to throw ridicule on the Greek language and literature. . . . I have been informed that one of

these Trojans has been preaching sermons denouncing
not only Greek classics but Latin classics too and all liberal education. A fool's speech comes out of a fool's
head. . . . He calls those who study Greek heretics. The
teachers of Greek he says are full grown devils, the learners of Greek are little devils. . . . It is not for me, illustrious doctors, to defend Greek. . . . The finest writings
on all subjects are in Greek. . . . The New Testament
was written in Greek. . . . The King's Majesty, our Sov-
ereign, has himself more learning than any English sov-
ereign ever possessed before him. Think you that he will
look on in silence when worthless blockheads are interrupting the cause of sound instruction in the oldest university in this realm? . . . Your wisdoms therefore will
find means to silence these foolish contentions."[22] The
patrons of the New Learning took positive steps to support it. The Emperor Charles V called Erasmus, to form
at Louvain "a college of the three languages." The Car-
melites tried in vain to block it and declared publicly,
"Luther has fallen into his terrible heresies by studying
the New Learning."[23] In 1517 Francis I asked Erasmus
to come to Paris to found a college of the three languages
like that at Louvain. The King's plans were delayed but
in 1530 he made the beginnings of the Collège de France
by establishing lectureships in the three languages. The
faculty of the Sorbonne opposed the plan as long as they
dared and indirectly attacked it in the following utterances. "First proposition: The holy scripture cannot
be well understood without Hebrew and Greek. Censure.
This proposition is rash and scandalous. Second proposition: A preacher cannot truly explain the epistles or the
gospels without the said languages. Censure. This
proposition is false and impious. Either of these prop-

[22] Jortin, III, App. LXIII No. VIII, Froude's translation.
[23] Froude, Erasmus, 287, 266 cited.

ositions renders him who asserts it extremely suspect of Lutheranism."[24]

Now it would have been quite consistent with his attitude in general if Ignatius had been frightened away from the New Learning by this battle. For he was extremely suspicious of heresy and very much afraid of its influence.

This appears very plainly in his attitude toward books. Camara writes "Ignatius himself told me that, when he was a student at Alcalá his confessor advised him to read 'The Christian Soldier's Handbook' of Erasmus. But he would not do it, because he had heard some preachers and persons in authority blame that author. So he answered that there were plenty of books of whose authors no one said any evil." [25] (18) He prohibited the books of Savonarola in the Company. To one who asked why, he wrote, the reason was "not that some of his books were not good—like 'The Triumph of the Cross' and others— but because the author is a subject of controversy. Some hold him for a saint, others think he was justly burnt; and that is the more common opinion. So the Company, inasmuch as there are so many good books free from all controversy, does not wish to use controverted authors: It does not however condemn them or even blame them."[26]

This natural tendency to keep away from everything suspected of heresy, must have been emphasized, so far as the denounced New Learning was concerned, by what Ignatius saw in Paris during his student days. There were few scholars among those burnt by Francis I. But those who fled the University, like Cop, the Rector of Sainte Barbe, and John Calvin, were all humanists. Indeed it was commonly said at the time "qui graecizabant, lutheranizabant";—those who became interested in Greek became interested in Lutheranism."[27] It seems like the final

[24] Lefranc, Le Collège de France, 122. [25] Scripta, I, 201, Memoriale. [26] Letts. V, 180, XI, 104. [27] Bobadilla, 614.

proof of the shrewd commonsense of Ignatius that in this matter of the New Learning he escaped from his natural fear of anything that anybody accused of heresy, saw that there was not necessarily any heresy in a cultural education, and realized that the Company must have the new weapons to fight the battles of their own day.

Just how he learned in Paris his respect for the three languages and humane letters as the base of all special training in theology, cannot be traced exactly. It seems hardly possible that he learned it at the College of Montaigu for Beda, its principal, was a leader of the Old Learning. It is possible that he transferred to Sainte Barbe after a year, because he did not like the instruction at Montaigu. At all events Sainte Barbe was the most progressive of the colleges in the University and was winning its nickname of the "Athens of Paris." "New textbooks were being used and many of the faculty were men of the new ideals in studies."[28] During Ignatius' stay there "the object toward which these teachers had so long aspired was attained; genuine classic instruction was installed in all the chairs."[29]

Wherever it came from, certain it is that the colleges of the Company founded their education on that training in humane letters and in Latin, Greek and Hebrew, which was the sign of the New Learning. They often applied to their new institutions the name "trilingual colleges,"[30] and the public exhibitions sometimes ended with the recitation of verses by the students in Hebrew, Latin and Greek.[31] In all this Ignatius was extremely active, now advising a correspondent to tone down his Latin style, and now sending a long letter to the Duke of Bavaria to explain that the Company does not wish to undertake theological instruction in the Academy of Ingolstadt unless, "according to the method of our other

[28] Brown, Buchanan, 19-60. Revue Rabelaisienne. VII, 304. [29] Ouicherat, I, 132. Comp. 44, 202. [30] Pol. II, 551, 122. [31] Pol. I, 283.

colleges, provision is made for teachers of humane letters to give the preparatory training in Latin, Greek and Hebrew literature."[32]

It was this progressive step of conservative Ignatius, frankly adopting the method so many of his orthodox contemporaries feared, which after his death, enabled his followers to fight Lutheran and Calvinist on equal terms, to halt the progress of schism and actually win back heretic territory for the ancient Church. It was because the Jesuit schools were, in method, up to date, that influential people wished to send their sons to them. If Jesuit fathers had not been so well trained in polite learning and the elegancies of literature, princes would not have been so eager as they afterwards became to seek them as tutors for their children.

Four years before his death Ignatius founded what was to become perhaps the most influential of all his educational institutions—the German College at Rome. The idea of this establishment was not his own invention. It was suggested by Cardinal Morone[33] who had been papal legate in Germany and knew the desperate condition from the point of view of the ancient Church, even in the nominally Roman Catholic states of the Empire.

Soon after its foundation Ignatius had a letter written explaining its purpose. "I did not write in my last letter about a work of great Christian charity to bring back Germany to the faith and religion of the Catholic Church by erecting a college to which youths shall be brought from all parts of that region, including Poland, Bohemia and Hungary: lads of ability endowed with good natural parts and nobles among their own people. The idea is that these lads leaving those countries before they are depraved by the vicious habits and heretical opinions customary there, may be instructed in sound doctrine and a virtuous life, and, leaving the College as fit workmen for

[32] Letts. VIII, 659. Letts. VII, 540. [33] Rib. p. 453.

the vineyard of the Lord, may go back to those countries —one with a bishopric, another to take a parish, another as canon of a cathedral, etc., in order to preach and help by doctrine and example those who speak his own tongue. For there is a great lack there of faithful and good workers and an over-plentiful supply of bad and perverted workers."[84]

[84] Letts. IV, 185.

CHAPTER XVII

THE BEGINNINGS OF MISSIONS AMONG THE HEATHEN: THE APOSTLE TO THE INDIES

Francis of Jassu and Xavier was descended from a race of Spanish country gentlemen. His father had risen to wealth and position in the service of the Kings of Navarre and married the heiress of a family of higher rank, from whom Francis took his name. The fidelity of the family to their old sovereigns during the wars of conquest, which added the crown of Spanish Navarre to the other crowns of Ferdinand the Catholic, King of Aragon, dilapidated the family fortune, and the castle of Xavier was dismantled. In its half ruinous walls Francis was born about fifteen years later than Ignatius, whose family seat was some sixty miles distant. About two hundred years later it came to be asserted as an unquestionable fact that Xavier was born in a stable like Jesus, but there was never any particular reason to believe it to be true and we now have very good reason to know it to be false.[1]

Francis had no taste for arms and at the age of nineteen went to Paris to qualify for a comfortable benefice. After he had been there eleven years, he was elected to a canonry in the Cathedral of Pamplona which was as much of a sinecure as he chose to make it and opened the way for that career in the Church which he had chosen as a boy.[2] But already he had set his feet upon another way of life. After he had been four years at the Univer-

[1] Cros. I, 49. The same baseless legend grew up about Ignatius.
[2] Cros. I, 140.

255

sity of Paris, his fellow Basque, Ignatius Loyola, became
his roommate and, by a long struggle of three years,
finally decided him to take the vow of Montmartre: to
live all his life as a poor priest without benefice, to go to
Jerusalem, to teach the infidel or if that were impossible,
to do whatever the Pope should order him to do. This
intimacy with Ignatius caused evil reports that he was
a heretic and these had gotten home. So when Ignatius
started for Spain in 1535, he carried a letter from Francis
to his brother, the head of the house. It points out that
Ignatius had often helped him with money and, so far
from being a heretic as scandalous tongues said, had saved
him from associates whose heresy "is now plainly known
to all Paris." He asks his brother very delicately to send
him some money.[3]

Soon after the pilgrim priests arrived at Rome, Father
Gouvea, who had been principal of the College of Sainte
Barbe, of which Ignatius and Francis were students, suggested to the King of Portgual that the pilgrim priests
would make excellent missionaries to the Portuese conquests in India: now some thirty-six years old. The
King, who probably believed what he wrote, that "the
principal end both of my father and of myself in the conquest of India . . . has been the propagation of the holy
Catholic faith," ordered his ambassador to see the Pope,
and the outcome was that Ignatius agreed to send a
Portuguese and a Spaniard from his scanty force. He
first chose Rodriguez and Bobadilla, but the latter became ill and Xavier started on twelve hours' notice for
Lisbon. To separate from his comrades was evidently
a strain upon his affections and before leaving Italy he
wrote to Ignatius the first of many touching phrases of
love. "I believe that in this life we cannot see each
other any more except by letters. To see each other face
to face with many embracings—that will be for the other

[3] Mon. Xav. I, 201.

life. Let us then for the little time which remains to us of this life, visit each other often by letter."[4]

In order to match this affection for his brethren by willingness to mortify his affection for his family, local tradition built up the legend adopted by many of his biographers, that he refused when passing close to his home to turn aside to say goodbye to his mother. There is no need of discussing whether this would be a high stage of self-abnegation necessary to evangelic perfection, or a misunderstanding of the spirit of Him whose dying lips commended His mother to the care of the disciple He loved. As a matter of fact, when Xavier went through Navarre on his way to India, his mother had been dead more than ten years.[5]

Rodriguez, whom Ignatius named as the comrade of Francis, was retained by the King of Portugal, and so the "Apostle to the Indies" left Lisbon with two young companions. From Goa, the capital of Portuguese India, he wrote his first Indian letter in September, 1542, and in ten years he died. Few men have lived so much in so short a time and some hundred letters,[6] written during those ten years, show a vivid, lovable and powerful personality; different from that of Ignatius but almost as extraordinary.

He was sent out to evangelize India, and it was his own idea to preach in Japan and to push on to China. His original task might seem a terrible one. The Portuguese conquests, defended by a chain of forts, extended along the western coast of India from Goa to the southernmost point of the great promontory; a distance of two hundred leagues. It was a long, thin strip, and they controlled inland little farther than the cannon of their fleets could carry.[7] The Portuguese were conquerors and traders, and, in the forty odd years which had elapsed

[4] Mon. Xav. I, 208.   [5] Cros. I, p. 161.   [6] See remarks of Cros. II, XXX.
[7] Cros. I, 208, 424.

since their first appearance on the coast, they had proved not only the superiority of their artillery, but their greed for gold. John III and his father may have sent their admirals, governors and captains across the sea out of zeal for Christianity, but very few of those sent made plain any other motive but a desire to gain money, and history shows few greater instances of the impossibility of serving God and mammon. Every decent man who has left his impressions of Portuguese India denounces their immorality, their injustice and their cruelty to the natives. The spirit which animated them as a whole was not superior to the spirit of Cortez and Pizzaro. If they did not steal so much as those cruel, wholesale bandits, it is only because they lacked opportunity.

The Franciscans and Dominicans who preceded Xavier as missionaries to the Portuguese conquests had been able to make little real progress against the bad example of the rulers and the fear and hatred it bred in the natives. Besides, the natives were of a low order of intelligence and character and would at best have been difficult to evangelize truly. To both of these facts, the great corruption of the Portuguese and the low order of the natives, we have clear testimony from Xavier himself. He wisely forbade his followers to attack in the pulpit the sins of men in authority. Tha⸳ was to be done in private conversation and through the confessional. But, manfully, he wrote the plain truth to the King and bade him reform the administration of his colonies, if, at the Day of Judgment, he would not hear himself condemned to hell. As for the intellectual capacity of the natives, he wrote from Goa: "Those received into the Company in these countries should not be used for anything more than the work of domestics in the houses where the Portuguese fathers live (temporal coadjutors), because they can never be ordained as priests for lack of the necessary qualities. Every year fathers must be sent from Portugal." In all forty-two fathers were sent out to him.[8] Considering the limited personnel of the Company and the great demands on its resources during these years, this number indicates great interest in the work in Asia. Personally Francis had no reason to fear any direct hindrance from the civil officials. His gentleness and tact made it hard for them to quarrel with him and besides he was directly backed by the King, who gave him liberal supplies of money and great authority. In addition he was a papal nuncio and, under the circumstances, entirely outside the scope of the authority of the civil officials.[9]

He exercised civil power when it was needed to help his teaching. He sent a magistrate to the Malabar coast with the promise of a sum of money for every woman convicted of drinking arrack (the penalty was three days in prison) and bade his helper tell the municipal authorities of the City of Punicale that, if he learns that arrack is being drunk there, "they will pay for it very dearly to me." He ordered that disobedient Christians should not be allowed to join in the pearl fishing and levied upon that chief industry of the coast, taxes to provide schools for children. He ordered that a certain Portuguese wrongdoer should be banished from the coast. These and similar acts indicate the power given him by the support of the King.

But while the government did not interfere with him at all, Francis thought it was failing utterly in its first duty. When he had been six years in India, he wrote to the King of Portugal to say that there was only one way to spread religion in India and that was for the King to lay the duty directly upon each governor; giving him command of all the members of religious orders ("the King should name here in the first place the Company of Jesus") to evangelize the country. To enforce this duty the King ought to take "a solemn oath that, if any gov-

[8] Cros. II, 233, I, Appendix.   [9] Mon. Xav. I, 815.

ernor did not make many converts, he would have him put
in irons and kept long years in prison with confiscation of
all his goods." Francis adds: "If every governor was very
certain that this oath of Your Majesty would be kept,
the Isle of Ceylon, many kings of Malabar, and the Cape
of Comorin would be Christian in a year."[10]

It was not by such dangerous plans as this that
Francis Xavier deserved his title of Apostle to the Indies.
His work was ceaseless, frequently left him short time to
eat, and kept him on foot until he dropped with fatigue.[11]
He had a wonderfully winning manner and one of his
early biographers said he did more good by talking than
in preaching. His example and his wise words made all
men love him. Under his gentle influence jealousy between the Company and other orders all but disappeared,
for he ordered "Charity, friendship, and love with the
blessed friars of the order of St. Francis and St.
Dominic."[12]

The principle which underlay all his action was love.
He wrote to Ignatius: "The rector you send for the college at Goa should have two qualities above all. The
first is obedience, so that he can win the friendship of the
magistrates and clergy. Besides that he must be, not
grave and severe, but affable and of a sweet disposition.
By that quality he will win the hearts of all and especially
of his brothers, the students. The Company of Jesus it
seems to me, is nothing but a company of love. Harshness on one side, fear on the other, ought to be far from
us. No one ought to be retained by any constraint. On
the contrary, those lacking the necessary virtues ought to
be rejected even though they wish to stay: and those
who have these virtues—it is love alone which should
bind them together."[13]

The letter of Francis written to the fathers and brothers

[10] Mon. Xav. I, 450. Compare letters to Rodriguez, 455, also Pol. I, 346.
[11] Cros. I, 226, II, 276, cited Letts. Francis.
[12] Cros. I, 450, cited Letts. Francis.　[13] Cros. I, 423.

of India giving an account of his mission to Japan is called by historians "The Great Letter." It was intended not only for Goa but for a wide circulation in Portugal among young men who might be future missionaries.[14] It ends as follows: "I beseech you that there may be among you a true love which allows no bitterness to be born in the soul. Turn part of your zeal into loving each other and part of your desires to suffer for Christ into conquering all dislikes which may stop the growth of that love; because you know Christ says that in this He knows His disciples 'If they love one another.'" Ignatius doubtless read these passages with pleasure and approval, but if he has written many paragraphs in precisely the same tone, the writer has missed them.[15]

The love which filled the heart of Francis Xavier, was no weak complacency. He could take strong active guided by shrewd common sense which reminds us strongly of the method of Ignatius in handling similar situations. The man sent by Ignatius to serve as Rector of the College at Goa was "a good preacher and a good man, but, by the unanimous judgment of all the fathers in India, incapable of governing."[16] In the absence of Francis in Japan, the rector did great harm by action impelled by zeal without knowledge and exceeding his authority. On his return Francis reprimanded and punished him and when he showed pride and obstinacy dismissed him from the Company and stood by this action firmly in the teeth of the Viceroy and the nobles of his court. Francis had trouble with his secretary, a young man of influential family who apparently could not forget that fact. So he wrote to his vicar just before starting for China: "If André Carvalho does not go this year back to Portugal, dismiss him from the Company. Don't let him be ordained in India, for I forbid it. . . . Tell the Bishop of

[14] Cross. II, 3. [15] There is one similar passage: Letts. I, 507. [16] Cros. I, 439, Lett. Father Lancilotti to Ignatius.

Goa that I beg him to grant me the grace not to let him be ordained even to the diaconate." But he wrote to Father Simon at Lisbon: "I have thought it best that André Carvalho, who acts as my secretary, should be sent to Portugal. . . . Here the climate is unfavourable to his health, perhaps his native air will suit him better." Many speak highly of him. "For my part I cannot say much good of him, but I hope in God that, when he shall have acquired more knowledge and more virtue, he will be very useful in the Company."[17]

He could use the whip of small cords but reprehension was not the easiest thing for him. After writing Father Cyprien: "You are so accustomed to following your own sweet will that you scandalize every body and then excuse yourself by saying it is the result of your temperament," Francis bursts out in a postscript: "O Cyprien, if you knew with what love I write such things to you, you would remember me day and night and perhaps you would weep at thinking of the great love I have for you. If the hearts of men were visible in this life, believe me, my brother Cyprien, you would see yourself plainly in my heart."[18]

Francis has left no record of visions and ecstasies like that of Ignatius, but everybody who came close to him knew his life was pretty well divided between trying to help his neighbour and intercourse with God. There is very strong evidence, including his own and that of intimate friends, that there were associated with his preaching phenomena of recovery from illness similar to those for which abundant and manifestly honest affidavits can be today obtained in connection with cures wrought at pilgrimage shrines, e.g. at Ste. Anne de Beaupré, Canada, at Lourdes and Lisieux in France. Let Francis tell of these himself. "I lived for four months in a large Christain community. . . . So many people came to ask me to go

[17] Cros. II, 249, 252.   [18] Cros. II, 241, 243.

to their houses to recite certain prayers over the sick and so many of the sick themselves came to me, that, without any other work, it would have given me enough to do . . . and I was teaching children, baptizing, translating prayers, answering endless questions, burying the dead, etc. Nevertheless I could not reject such holy demands without peril to their faith. . . . So I ordered the boys who knew the prayers to go to the houses of the sick. There they united the family and neighbours and all repeated several times the creed, telling the sick man to believe that he would be cured. Then followed other prayers. . . . Our Lord rewarded by many graces of healing the faith of the parents and neighbours and that of the sick themselves."[19]

Seven years after his arrival at Goa, Francis was the head of a string of mission stations stretching a thousand leagues to the Malay Archipelago. But he was not content. The adventurous spirit of the man inclined him to answer with joy a Macedonian cry to come over into the little known Empire of Japan and begin new conquests for the kingdom of Christ.[20] So, feeling that his presence was no longer necessary in India, he started on his long voyage, taking with him a young Japanese from the College at Goa. He found the Japanese, like the Athenians, anxious to hear some new thing, and he founded missions, which, thirty-five years after his death, furnished thousands of converts who died for their faith. Even before he had gotten back to Japan he had determined to go to China. The introduction of foreigners into China was forbidden under pain of death and Xavier arranged to go in the suite of a merchant ambassador, bearing very handsome presents for the Emperor. The captain of the fortress of Malacca, moved by political jealousy, broke

[19] Mon. Xav. I, 284. [20] "The Japanese have sent ambassadors to the King asking for fathers to teach the Christian faith." Letts. Francis, Cros. I, 470.

up the expedition. Xavier, however, persisted in his mission; now become extremely dangerous. He got to the half desert Chinese island of Sanchoan, where foreign merchants landed secretly to trade with Chinese; living during this furtive visit in huts built of straw which they burnt when they left.[21] For a very large price Xavier bribed the captain of a Chinese merchant ship to run the risk of smuggling him into Canton.[22] But the man was slow in coming back with a smaller vessel and, after two months of waiting, Francis took a fever. We have a confused account of his stay on the island from a young Chinese convert from the College of Goa who was with him to the end. We learn from it that, after five days of high fever, this great wanderer across strange seas to uncharted lands saw his "pilot face to face."

He was a strong and noble personality, a born leader of men who became an inspirer, a path finder, for those who came after him.

No one who reads with a candid mind the letters of Francis Xavier and the recollections of those who knew him, will think of attributing the chief glory of the extraordinary missionary work in Asia of the Company of Jesus to any one but him. If Ignatius wrote him many letters, they have not survived. The last letter of Ignatius summoned Xavier back to talk with the King of Portugal and the Pope and to select and inspire men for the Asian missions. It crossed the news of his death.

It was not the distance that kept Ignatius from sending orders, for he wrote Xavier that he could govern the Indian mission just as well, indeed much better, from Portugal than from Japan or China. It was again the common sense of Ignatius which kept him from interfering in matters where he had no experience and hampering by orders a great lieutenant who needed no guid-

[21] Cros. II, 341.   [22] Cros. II, 331.

ance. Nevertheless the glory of Xavier is part of the glory of Loyola. Ignatius worked for three years in Paris to win Francis from the vulgar ambition of a younger son longing for a rich and distinguished ecclesiastical career, to an ideal of poverty and humblest service. He kept him from heresy and remained through life his greatest inspiration. Whenever Xavier wished to recommend anything especially by word or pen to his brethren in India, he was wont to add: "I beg, or recommend, or order, this by the love, or the reverence, or the obedience we all owe to our blessed Father Ignatius."[28]

Francis, in the last year of his life, wrote a letter whose opening words show what strength he drew from the friendship of Ignatius. "Most truly my Father, I received a letter from your holy charity at Malacca on my way back from Japan and God knows how my soul was consoled to get the news it so longed for that you were alive and in good health. And, among many other holy and consoling words of your letter, I read those which close it, 'All thine without ever being able to forget you, Ignatius.' These words I read with tears of joy as I now write them down with tears; remembering the days of the past and how much love you have always had and still have for me, and also thinking how God has delivered me from great labour and peril in Japan in answer to your holy prayers. . . . You write of your great desire to see me before you die. God knows how great an impression was made upon my soul by these words of such great love and how many tears they bring to my eyes every time I recall them to mind. . . . The least of your sons but the oldest in exile. Francis."[24]

Somebody has written on the documents of the process of canonization of Ignatius and Francis this epigram:

[28] Mon. Xav. II, 807. Teixeira to Rib. [24] Mon. Xav. I, 668, 674.

"Very many and very great
Are of Xavier the miracles:
But one miracle of Ignatius
Is the greatest: namely, Xavier."[25]

During the lifetime of Ignatius a beginning was made
of the Jesuit missions to South America by sending six
comrades to Brazil. At his death seven years later Brazil
was a separate province of the Company with establishments in three centres.

An attempt to renew unsuccessful efforts of other
orders to bring into the Church the monophysite heretic
Ethiopians who acknowledged the authority of the Coptic
Patriarch of Alexandria, met with no lasting success.

The missions to the Indians of Canada and the Middle
United States, the heroic story of which is told in the
Jesuit Relations, were not begun until seventy years after
the death of Ignatius.

[25] Cited, Stewart, 342.

CHAPTER XVIII

THE SPIRITUAL EXERCISES

The most efficient means Ignatius had for gaining suitable recruits for his Company were the Spiritual Exercises. The accumulated force produced by these powerful psychical efforts during a period of complete separation from ordinary human intercourse, must have tended to create a current in the soul which drifted sensitive and noble natures—and Ignatius wished no others—powerfully toward a life completely absorbed by the direct service of God and their fellow men. That general decision once made, gratitude for help in reaching it would impel those most apt toward the Company of Jesus. The Directory of Ignatius, a sort of appendix dictated by him "in substance" shortly before his death, says:[1] "It is not desirable to advise everybody to shut himself up to take the Exercises. . . . He who begins them ought to be educated or capable, free and fit for the Company. . . . If he is apt but not disposed to take the Exercises, aid him with familiar conversations, but cautiously, so that he does not suspect there is any craft; though it is the holy craft spoken of by St. Paul to the Corinthians when he wrote 'being crafty I caught you with guile.' Remember that it is contrary to the rules of the Exercises and the purity of the spirit of the Company, to urge anybody to join it."

Although all members of the Company were given the Spiritual Exercises (temporal coadjutors only in part) it must not be assumed that they were given only to those

[1] Pg. 751, 785-786 Mon. Ig. Series Secunda. Vol. I.

who were expected to enter the Company if they stood the test. On the contrary, a great many people took them who were not expected to join the Company, but in such cases usually only the first week was given.

The arrangement of the little book appears somewhat clumsy. It seems more like a mass of pieces put together than an organic work. In spite of his long years spent in study, Ignatius never acquired facility in logically arranging his thoughts in writing, or in expressing them with elegance. He does not always write even with clearness. The Exercises contain nearly five hundred words in a form peculiar to itself or at least very unusual, and the Catholic historian Johannes Janssen says of it, "From a literary point of view the book is entirely without charm."[2] Its power will seem the greater to those who put themselves in the place of the giver and receiver of the Exercises.

In spite of the fact that a good deal of the Spiritual Exercises comes from other books, it is an extremely original work. The name had been a common term for a long time. Twenty-one years before Ignatius was converted, the Benedictine Abbot of Montserrat, Garcia de Cisneros, had printed a book entitled Ejercitatorio Espiritual (Method of Spiritual Exercise). Ignatius while he was at Manresa, close to Montserrat, would be very apt to read this book and a comparison suggests strongly that he did. Parts of the Spiritual Exercises may have been derived from Cisneros for example, four of the twenty *Annotations*, three of the ten additions, etc. But it is in no sense dependent upon Cisneros either in thought or language and the most striking and powerful things in it are not to be found in his work. The Spiritual Exercises also made use of the Life of Christ by Ludolph, which was one of the books read by Ignatius while he was recovering from wounds. It was to that bed of pain that he him-

[2] Longridge page VI, Introduction.

self traced the beginnings of the Exercises. At the end of the Confessions[3] he said, in answer to a question, he had not "written them at one time but some things which he had observed in his own soul and found useful seemed to him perhaps fitted to be useful to others and so he put them in writing. For example, the way of examining the conscience, etc. Especially he told me that the section about *Choices* he had drawn from the conflict of spirits and thoughts which he went through in the castle of Loyola when he was suffering with his leg." When he was arrested in Salamanca, six years after his conversion, he gave to the judges for examination a manuscript book which was undoubtedly the beginning, perhaps contained the most striking parts, of the Exercises. There is a translation into "very barbarous Latin,"[4] made in 1541 which contains the complete book as we know it. During these twenty years therefore from 1521 to 1541 Ignatius wrote the Exercises in Spanish. Whatever materials he may have found in his memories, conscious or unconscious, of things he had read in a few other books, the inspiring and moulding element is his own experience and this makes the book his.[5]

It was first printed eight years before the death of Ignatius (1548). The preface of the book explains that it is not meant for popular circulation, and therefore is not to be sold. It is not intended to be an ordinary manual of devotion like the Imitation of Christ so loved by Ignatius. It is to be put only into the hands of those who are directing the exercises, as a guide in giving them. At the beginning of the more modern editions there is the beautiful old prayer Anima Christi, as well known as the Our Father or the Ave Maria. Ignatius did not place it there but he recommends its use later in the Exercises. (442.)

[3] Scripta, I, p. 97. [4] Astrain, 148. [5] For its sources see Watrigant; also Int. to Mon. Ig. Series Secunda, I, pages 10-136.

Soul of Christ sanctify me.
Body of Christ save me.
Blood of Christ lift me out of self.
Water from the side of Christ wash me.
Suffering of Christ comfort me.
Oh! good Jesus, hear me:
Hide me in Thy wounded arms:
Let me not be separated from Thee:
From the wicked enemy save me:
In the hour of my death call me,
And bid me come to Thee,
That with the saints I may praise Thee
To all the ages. Amen.

The main body of the Exercises consists of forty-four pages. It is preceded by twenty pages of annotations and followed by thirty-four pages of addenda. The Exersises proper are divided into four weeks, but the director has power to shorten or lengthen them in actual days if he thinks best. The object is said to be "To conquer self and order life without being decided by any exaggerated affection."

The first week is preceded by a meditation on the principle and foundation from which all progress must come; that principle is the object of human life. Ignatius states it most succinctly thus: "I am created to praise God in word and deed and to save my soul;" which is equivalent in different words to the Westminster Catechism: "What is the chief end of man?" "To glorify God and enjoy Him for ever."

The use of all things in life should be controlled by the object of life and the purpose of meditations on it is to make ourselves "so far as possible indifferent; not desiring health more than infirmity, riches more than poverty, honour of men above contempt, a long life more than a short one, but only desiring and choosing what will best lead us to fulfil the true purpose of life." This preparatory meditation is followed by two sorts of examinations of conscience.

The first is a "particular examination." Beginning on rising in the morning, the man must determine to guard himself against the sin that easily besets him. After the midday meal he ought to go over carefully every hour since morning and mark by a point on a diagram the number of times he has fallen into that sin. After supper he must do the same. Ignatius gives an example of the sort of diagram to use for this record of sins and recommends that day should be compared with day and week with week to see if there is improvement.

This *particular* examination is joined to a *general* examination of the conscience. The director should point out that we have three sorts of thoughts, one our own and two which come from without; one from the good spirit and the other from the evil spirit. He must then explain the conquering of evil thoughts. Sins of word are then discussed; blasphemy, slander and idle words, i.e., "any talk not intended to profit me or anyone else." Under sins of deed are included disobedience to the ten commandments, the precepts of the Church and things commended by superiors, like indulgences or bulls of crusade, "for we incur no little sin by opposing or causing others to oppose such recommendations of our superiors."

Five things are then recommended to the penitent, thanks to God, a prayer for grace to know his sins, to demand an accounting from his soul, to ask pardon of God, to determine by His help to improve. A general confession covering the whole life is then to be made to a priest, but not to the director who is giving the Exercises. After this preparation the first exercise opens with a prayer. Two *preambles* begin it, the first is what Ignatius calls: "*Composition; seeing the place.*" This is continually used and means an effort of the imagination to clothe the idea with a visible form. In the case of sin it means trying to see with the eye of the imagination. "My soul imprisoned in this corruptible body and my whole self living like one banished from his true country in this vale of misery among brute beasts." The second preamble is "to demand of God what I wish and desire; in this case shame and confusion of face over my sins." Then follow the three *points* of the *meditation* to which must be applied the three faculties of the soul: the memory, the understanding and the will. The points are the three sins. First that of the fallen angels "considering that while they have gone to hell for one sin, I have deserved it for many sins;" second, the sin of Adam and Eve "bringing to my mind how great corruption came by it upon the human race, so many men going towards hell"; third, "the particular sin of some one person who for one mortal sin has gone to hell, and many others without number who have gone to hell for fewer sins than I have committed."

The Exercise ends with a *colloquy*. Imagining Christ on the cross, the taker of the exercises is to ask Him "about His becoming man and dying for my sins." Then he is to ask himself "What have I done for Christ, what am I doing for Christ, what ought I to do for Christ?" This colloquy should be made "as a friend speaks to a friend or a servant to a master."

The form of this exercise is that of all the others. The prayer, the two *preambles* that is *composition* and *fixing* the *object,* the *points,* the *colloquy,* appear in all the exercises.

The second exercise uses all these forms in a meditation upon the man's own sins ending by a colloquy with God on mercy. The third exercise is a repetition of the first and second but it closes with three colloquies: one with Our Lady, ending with an Ave Maria, the second with Christ, ending with the Anima Christi, the third with the Father ending with the Lord's Prayer. The fourth exercise is a resumption of the third; ending with the same three colloquies.

The fifth exercise is "a *meditation upon hell*." It opens with a prayer followed by the *preambles*. The *composition* is "to see with the eyes the length, breadth and depth of hell." The thing asked for of God is "a realizing sense of the pains of the damned, so that, if through my faults I forget the love of God, at least the fear of the pains of hell may keep me from sin." A sort of exercise which Ignatius called the application of the senses and often used follows on five *points*. 1. "To see with the eyes of the imagination, the great fires of hell and the souls as it were in fiery bodies. 2. To hear with the ears the laments, the groans, the cries, the blasphemies against Christ Our Lord and against all his saints. 3. To smell the smoke, the brimstone, the sewer filth and putrid things. 4. To taste by the palate bitter things such as tears, melancholy and the worm of conscience. 5. To feel by the sense of touch how those fires burn the souls."

The *colloquy* is with Christ recalling to memory the souls which are in hell, some for not believing in His coming, some for believing but not obeying. It is to be divided into three parts; those lost before the incarnation, those lost during His life in this world, and those lost since. It ends with thanksgiving "because I am not in any of these classes."

It would be misleading to the reader to allow him to suppose, as some who have written on the Spiritual Exercises do leave their readers to suppose, that there was anything in these five points peculiar to Ignatius, except the skilful way in which he used the picture they draw in outline to produce the psychological result he desired. Generations before his birth this picture of hell had been fully developed from phrases in the gospels and was assumed as realistic even by men whose souls were not, like his, totally absorbed in religion. There was nothing peculiar to Ignatius and his followers in the use of a realistic image of hell as a strong motive for accepting Christian faith.

Jonathan Edwards was elected President of Princeton University nearly two hundred years after the death of Ignatius. He preached in his church at Northampton, Massachusetts, a sermon entitled "Sinners in the Hands of an Angry God" from which the following paragraphs are taken.

"The God that holds you over the pit of hell, much as one holds a spider or some loathsome insect over the fire, abhors you and is dreadfully provoked; His wrath towards you burns like fire; He looks upon you as worthy of nothing else than to be cast into the fire; you are ten thousand times as abominable in His eyes as the most hateful and venomous serpent is in ours. . . . And yet it is nothing but His hand that holds you from falling into the fire; . . . yes, there is nothing else that is to be given as a reason why you do not this very moment drop down into hell.

"Oh sinner! consider the fearful danger you are in. It is a great furnace of wrath, a wide and bottomless pit, full of the fire of wrath that you are held over by the hand of that God whose wrath is as much incensed against you as against many of the damned in hell: you hang by a slender thread with the flames of divine wrath flashing about it and ready every moment to singe and burn it asunder, etc."

The psychological object of such a sermon was precisely the psychological object of the meditation about hell of the Spiritual Exercises—to sear upon the soul a hatred of sin by terror. Men believed firmly in a blazing eternal hell beneath their feet for centuries before Ignatius was born: in Catholic and Protestant churches alike it was preached for nearly three hundred years after his death.

The meditation upon hell of the fifth exercise of the first week of the Spiritual Exercises describes a view of the world in its relations to human life which was not only fundamental to the thinking of Ignatius but extremely active in his teaching and living. How many readers of this book have ever heard a sermon remotely resembling the sermon of Jonathan Edwards, or read a recent religious book from which citations could be made comparable to those he has just read? The fact that such teaching is little heard now is just the reason for making its importance in the life of Ignatius clear. To give the impression that this vision of the unseen world was in any sense peculiar to him is to give a false picture of his life, but to fail to emphasize the importance in determining his character and directing his work, of the details of his fundamental conception of the unseen world, is to give a very imperfect picture of his life. Ignatius rose above the fear of hell and of the devils who, he believed, were trying from birth to death to drag men into it and his life rested in the love of God sustained by frequent visions of Him. But the conception of the eternal battle of the universe remained in his mind and especially in the minds of his followers poignant and effective upon conduct.

That conception and the determining influence it ought to exert upon the life of all men of good will, is set forth in the second week of the Exercises with grandiose imaginative power.

The taker of the Exercises (first *point*) is to imagine a human king chosen by God whom all Christians honour and obey. Second, he is bidden to hear the king speaking to all his followers saying, "My will is to conquer all the land of the infidels. Therefore whoever wants to come with me must be content with the clothes I use, and eat and drink as I do, etc. Also he must work with me in the day and watch by night, etc., because he must share the work if he is to have part in the victory. Third, let him consider then what all good subects ought to answer to a king so generous and so liberal and therefore if any one should refuse the call of such a king how much he would deserve to be vituperated by all the world and thought an unworthy knight." "The second part of this exercise consists in applying this example of the temporal king to Christ." This is to be carefully done under three heads and the exercise is to be repeated twice a day. A note says that during the following weeks it is profitable to read sometimes the Imitation of Christ, the gospels and lives of the saints.

Practical directions, called additions, are put in here at the end of the first week; with which the exercises often ended. The first exercise should be taken at midnight (omitted for the aged or those showing nervous strain), the second on rising, the third before dinner, the fourth at vespers, the fifth before supper. The taker of the Exercises "must not think of pleasant and joyful things, like glory, the resurrection, etc., but of death and judgment." He is not to laugh or provoke laughter. If a penance of restriction in food or sleep is adopted, the health must not be injured. In regard to mortifications of the flesh by wearing hair cloth, scourging oneself, etc., the most suitable are those which give pain but do not cause infirmity. The postulant should not make his meditations in full clear light, but the doors and windows of his room must be closed except when he is praying, reading or eating.

The first three days of the second week, are given up to *contemplations* upon the life of Christ. The first day contains five exercises: a *contemplation* of the incarnation, then one on the nativity followed by two repetitions and the *application* of the *senses* to the incarnation and the nativity. This consists in "seeing with the imaginative contemplative or meditative vision the vast variety of men upon the earth, some white, others black, some laughing, others weeping, some being born, others dying, etc., then seeing that the three divine Persons regarding the earth full of men and beholding them all descending into hell, determined in their eternity that the Second Person should become man to save the human race, hearing what the human persons in this transaction say or might say and touching with the inner touch [e.g. kissing or embracing] the places where Joseph, Mary or the Infant trod or sat, smelling and tasting the infinite softness and sweetness of the Divinity, etc."

The second and third day contain less elaborately developed meditations on the early life of Christ when he was obedient to His parents in Nazareth and how He left them and was found teaching in the temple. This brings the taker of the exercises naturally and skilfully up to the peak or crisis of the whole experience through which he is being led, i.e., to his *election* or *choice* of the *state* of *life*. A preamble to the consideration of *states* of life points out that Christ obedient to His parents in Nazareth represents the ordinary Christian. When He left His foster father and His natural mother to give Himself to the pure service of His eternal Father, he is a model of evangelic perfection. Stripped of all technical terms the question now brought forward before the taker of the Exercises is whether it is not his duty to become a monk. He must decide this for himself for the director of the Exercises is strictly forbidden to talk with him about it.

He is introduced to this question by the vision of the "two banners; the one of Christ our great captain, the other of Lucifer the mortal enemy of our human nature." The first preamble is the history, how Christ calls all men under His banner and Lucifer under his. The second preamble is *composition, seeing the place*, "to imagine a vast plain around Jerusalem where the supreme captain general of the good is Christ: and another plain at Babylon where the chief of the enemy is Lucifer." The *prayer for a definite desire* is "to ask for knowledge and help against the wiles of the evil chief and for knowledge of the true life shown by the true captain and grace to imitate Him." Then follows the *meditation*, divided as usual into *points* (here omitted). One must "imagine how the chief of all the enemies sits in that great plain of Babylon as on a high throne of smoke and fire, horrible and dreadful to look upon. He calls together countless devils and scatters them, some to one city, others to another city, throughout all the world, leaving out no province, place nor state of life, nor any individual person. He makes a speech and orders them to use nets and chains to take men captive who are first to be tempted with greed for riches in order that they may get the vain honour of this world and so become swollen with pride and from these three steps can be led on to all the other vices." "On the other hand consider how Christ Our Lord places Himself in a great plain around Jerusalem; in a lowly place, beautiful and pleasing to behold. He makes a speech to all His servants and friends whom he sends out on this expedition, charging them to wish to help all by drawing them first to the highest spiritual poverty ('poor in spirit') and (if it should please His divine majesty and he should wish to choose them) not less to actual poverty. Secondly He charges them to draw men towards a desire to be reproached and despised; because from these two things comes humility. So that there are three steps of good; poverty instead of riches, contempt as opposed to worldly honour, and humility instead of pride." From these three steps men are to be led on to all the other virtues. The exercise is closed by three *colloquies*, with Our Lady, the Son and the Father.

This *meditation* is to be made at midnight, on rising, about the time of mass and at vespers. Before supper there must be made the *meditation* on the "Three Classes of Men in order to Join the Best." Imagine three men, each of whom has gained 10,000 ducats. They all want to save their souls and to be at peace with God by ridding themselves of the weight of their love for this money. The first man would like this, but does not take means to carry out his wish until death. The second wishes to get rid of love for the money, but to keep it, so that God should come to what he desires rather than that he should come to God. The third man wants to get rid of the love of the money in such a way that he is no more inclined to keep it than not to keep it, except as God shall teach him and it may be better for God's service. Meanwhile he wishes to be in the attitude of one who actually leaves all for God; so that what finally moves him to keep or leave the money, is the desire of being better able to serve God.

There follow topics for eight days taken from the life of Christ and it is explained that as many of these are to be used as are found necessary. The second week closes with the *elections* or *choices of life*. This is to be preceded by instruction about the three sorts of humility. The first or minimum necessary to salvation, is the willingness to obey the law of God and refuse to commit *mortal* sin for any price "even to save my life." The second and more perfect sort consists of an attitude of indifference toward riches or poverty, honour or dishonour, long or short life and the determination that "not for the whole world, nor to save my life would I commit *venial* sin." The third sort includes the first two and, in order to be actually more like Christ, goes on to choose poverty with Him.

The sorts of elections are next considered. "In the first place things that are matters of choice must be good, or at best indifferent in themselves and approved by our holy mother, the Hierarchical Church." Choices about such things may be either unchangeable, like getting mar-

ried or becoming a priest, or changeable, like accepting
or refusing a benefice or secular property. An unchangeable choice may have been made from bad motives. In
this case there is nothing to do but to repent and do one's
duty the best way possible.

The *three times* when a good choice may be made are
then considered. The first is under the call of God as
when St. Paul and St. Matthew decided to follow Christ.
The second is when the soul is receiving good and evil
suggestions and requires the discernment of spirits. The
third *time* of election is tranquil when the soul is not
agitated by various spirits (good or evil) and can use
its faculties freely and quietly. In this the man, considering the true end of life and desiring to reach it,
chooses as a means a kind of life within the Church in
order to be helped in the service of God and the salvation of his soul. There are two methods of making a
choice out of this tranquil mood of the soul. The first
method which applies only to changeable choices, has six
points: (1) to understand thoroughly the thing to be
accepted or rejected, (2) to keep firmly in mind that
the end of life is to praise God and save the soul, (3)
to beg Him for enlightenment, (4) to consider definitely
each and all of the advantages of either choice and weigh
them against each and all the disadvantages of it, (5)
finally to decide the matter according to the way the
reason inclines and pray God to accept and confirm the
decision. The second method suggests by its terms the
decision to enter a religious order. It consists of four
points: First, the man is to be sure that the love which
moves him to his choice comes from above. Second,
he is to imagine a man he has never seen whose highest
spiritual perfection he desires and consider what he would
say to him about such a choice. Third, he is to imagine
himself about to die and consider what he would then desire that he had chosen. Finally he is to imagine him-

self on the Day of Judgment and to act in the way in which he would then wish to have acted.

A note on "Reforming one's present life and state," suggests that much of this matter can be used to help people who do not wish to enter the higher life by leading them to examine carefully how they ought to choose to manage their household or spend their income, etc. But the *election* for which all these rules were made is, in the first and chief instance, the decision whether to enter a religious order or not. And Ignatius' deep knowledge of the human heart, his skilful though unscientific psychological analysis, appears most plainly in this part of his book. After having impressed upon the mind of the taker of the Exercises the awful consequences of sin to the world and to himself, he appeals to every chivalrous impulse in his soul by the vision of the two banners set in the midst of meditations on the earthly life of Christ. If he had no dormant chivalrous impulses in his soul Ignatius did not want him in the Company. This is followed by careful reasoning about the choices of life from a religious point of view which suggests inevitably, though without bringing any pressure to bear except logic and a strong current of emotion, that the perfect life is to be found in a religious order. And in which one better than in this Company of the Great Captain of our Salvation? Nevertheless it is to be noted that a considerable number of people who took the Exercises went into other religious orders.

The remaining two *weeks* fill less than one quarter of the pages of the exercises proper, and appear almost an anti-climax after the first two weeks. But probably the man who had passed through the strenuous emotions of the part leading up to the *election* found in them a needed rest for his soul. The third week has seven days of meditation on the passion of Christ developed under the forms with which the reader is already familiar. At the

end are inserted eight practical rules about eating during
the Exercises; for Ignatius neglects nothing large or small
which might affect his purpose. No fasting is enforced.
It is recommended to imagine at table that one is eating with Christ and the apostles and to guide eating,
drinking and talking by that thought.

The fourth *week* is a series of *meditations* on the resurrection of Christ and this closes the exercises proper. But
three unconnected exercises follow to be used by the
director as he sees fit. A Contemplation for Obtaining
Love, a long Meditation on the Mysteries of the Life of
Our Lord; and Instruction in Three Ways of Praying.

The book closes with various series of rules; for the
distribution of alms; and three sets of rules which concern distinguishing among the moods of the soul those
which come from God or the craft of the devil: what St.
Paul calls "discerning of spirits." Ignatius laid great
stress on this, to defend his followers against being cheated
by the wiles of the enemy. To him the scene of the two
banners was no mere oratorical allegory. It was a sober
representation of fact. This world was the scene of a
constant struggle between Christ and his followers, visible
or invisible, and Satan and his innumerable ministers of
evil. That fight was to him the fundamental fact about
human life and the Company of Jesus was in that deadly
fight with every last ounce of energy of every single one
of its members. He believed as St. Paul wrote that his
Company "wrestled not against flesh and blood but against
spiritual wickedness in high places" and he thought the
skill and craft of the great enemy of mankind rendered
him dangerous only to timid and untrained fighters. For
example, in the twelfth rule for discerning spirits Ignatius
writes "the enemy acts like a woman in being weak in
force and strong only in malice. For, as it is the nature
of a woman when she quarrels with a man to lose courage
and flee when the man faces her boldly, but, on the other

hand, if the man loses courage and begins to flee, the vengeance, the wrath and the fierceness of the woman are greatly increased and become boundless; so the devil weakens, loses courage and flees when he is boldly faced. But if the taker of the Exercises begins to be afraid and to lose courage before temptation, there is no beast on the face of the globe so fierce as the enemy of human nature."

The book closes with eighteen "Rules for Thinking truly and as we ought in the Militant Church" and these few pages are very important for understanding the attitude and character of Ignatius. They have no special connection with the Exercises and the reader who sees them for the first time at once suspects that they were the last to be written.

Anyone brought up as a Protestant, who has read no Roman Catholic devotional books, must make a strong effort of the imagination to reach a sympathetic appreciation of the attitude Ignatius describes in them. These rules are manifestly directed against heresy which is not mentioned in the Spiritual Exercises. He does not attack it directly. Elsewhere he advised his preachers not to do that. But in these rules he stresses point by point the positive side of the main controversies with the heretics. He first exalts ready and prompt obedience to the Church, laying aside every personal judgment. He then enjoins the praise of a number of things: confession to a priest and taking the eucharist at least once a year; the frequent hearing of mass and fixed hours for prayer; virginity as a higher state than matrimony; monastic vows as leading to evangelical perfection; veneration of relics of the saints, pilgrimages, indulgences and candles lighted in churches; public fasts, penances, images in the churches, the scholastic theologians, Aquinas, the Master of the Sentences, etc., as more modern and better able to teach for our times what is necessary for salvation than the patristic fathers like Jerome, Augustine, et. al.; to praise finally all the precepts of the Church.

Ignatius then lays down the thirteenth rule that "to arrive at the truth in all things we ought always be ready to believe that what I see as white is black if the Church so defines it." That this expressed in general his conscientious attitude not only toward the inspired Church, but also toward all lawful authority is evident from the tenth rule "We ought to be more ready to approve and praise than to find fault with the enactments and customs of our superiors, because, even though sometimes they may not be worthy of praise, still to speak against them before the common people . . . may irritate them against their superiors *whether temporal* or spiritual. . . . But just as it does harm to talk to the common people of the evil of their superiors who are absent, so it is profitable to talk of their evil ways privately to those very superiors who are able to amend them."

Then follow five rules about teaching and preaching. "Although it is very true that no one can be saved unless he is predestinated" we ought not to speak much about predestination lest people be led into error. Likewise we must be careful lest by over emphasis on faith people become negligent in good works. We ought not to speak with such emphasis of grace as to suggest the poisonous teaching which destroys free will. Although pure love is the highest motive for God's service we ought to praise the fear of God, because it is a great help to rising out of mortal sin.

These are the orthodox statements on the points chiefly in dispute with the heretics.

CHAPTER XIX

HIS VIEW OF THE UNIVERSE

Ignatius Loyola's view of the world as the scene of a continuous active combat between God and Satan was rooted in his early experience. He tells in his Confessions how early he learned to recognize the diversity of the spirits which moved him. When he discovered the trick of the devil in giving him pleasure and consolation by the beautiful figure like a serpent, he always drove it away, with a contemptuous flourish of his pilgrim staff. (See page 44.)

One more struggle he had; not against the craft but against the terror of the infernal adversaries. Four or five years later, when he was at the University of Alcalá, he was charitably given lodging, in a somewhat ruinous part of a house which was popularly thought to be infested with nocturnal evil spirits. There Ignatius was smitten by a sudden terror which he reasoned was idle and, commending himself to God, he began in his soul and by words, to challenge the demons, that if God gave them any power over him, they should use it. He said he would willingly suffer whatever God let them do and they were not able to do anything more.[1] That firmness of soul and that ready faith and confidence in God not only freed him then from all fear of the devil but made him always afterwards immune to such terrors of the night.

For Ignatius plainly rose out of all fright before the unseen world, saw in the activity of the infernal host only a challenge to chivalrous knights errant of Christ, feared

[1] Pol. I, 34, compare Ribad. ed. 1572, p. 197.

the craft not the power of its leader and bade his followers
be bold and treat him like a vixenish woman. He said
the only danger was in cowardice for he believed with his
beloved friend, Francis Xavier, that "showing a timid
heart before the devil is strongly to be guarded against."[2]
All fear of the devil and what he might do to him had disappeared from the soul of Ignatius long before he founded
the Company.

His younger contemporary, the mystic St. Theresa,
reached the same result of fearlessness by a different way.
Ignatius never saw devils, at least he does not tell us of
seeing any. St. Theresa saw them so often that familiarity
bred contempt. For instance she writes: "I was once
in an oratory when Satan in an abominable shape appeared on my left hand. . . . A huge flame seemed to
issue out of his body. He spoke in a fearful way, and
said to me that, though I had escaped out of his hands,
he would yet lay hold of me again." At another time,
"I saw close beside me a frightful little negro gnashing
his teeth." On another occasion, "I saw a great multitude of evil spirits round about me. One day when I was
in prayer I saw a devil close by in a great rage tearing
to pieces some paper he held in his hands." She found
a remedy against these hideous visitors. "I know by
frequent experience that there is nothing which puts
devils to flight like holy water." When she thought the
evil spirits would have suffocated her one night and "the
sisters threw much holy water about, I saw a great troop
of them rush away as if tumbling over a precipice."
Nothing in the least resembling these diabolic visions is
to be found in the Confessions of Ignatius. Theresa herself came to treat them as of little importance for she
wrote: "These cursed spirits have tormented me so often
and I am now so little afraid of them, that I should weary

[2] Pol. I, 460.

both you and myself if I were to speak of these things
in detail."[3]

Many of the early comrades of Ignatius were unable
to reach this serene contempt of danger from devils. In
reading the Chronicle of their activities condensed from
their own accounts of it, one is impressed by the frequent cases of troublesome, dangerous or successful interference by the devil with their labours. In Sicily, where
many were possessed by devils, the Rector of the College
at Messina pointed out that it was not to be wondered
at, because Messina was in a valley called by the name
of the devil and not very far "from a certain open mouth
into hell; as some of the saints of great authority had
asserted."[4] This idea about volcanic actions was not
singular to the rector of Messina. For, when the heathen
inhabitants near a volcanic isle whose recent eruption
had killed fish in the sea and animals on land, asked the
missionary, St. Francis Xavier, what it was, he replied
that: "It was hell from which the souls of those who had
worshipped idols were being thrown out."[5]

The soldiers of the Company sometimes waged battles
with the devil over the beds of the dying. When a novice
of eighteen years was close to death and the demons
attacked him, he clung tightly to the crucifix, and when
they tried to tempt him away from the faith he told his
father superior about it. The superior warned him not
to dispute but to refer any devils who wished to dispute,
to him. The lad did this and sent the demons to Father
Cornelius that he might give them reasons for the faith
that was in him. "So those who by disobedience fell
from heaven were conquered by obedience."[6]

When one of the leading citizens of Salamanca was
in the last throes of life "and many nobles and monks
of other orders stood round his bed, and they kept silent,

[3] Autobiography XXXI, 2, 3, 4, 9 XXIV 5, etc. [4] Pol. II, 543. [5] Pol. I, 205.
[6] Pol. II, 230.

either from shyness or by the orders of others present, Father Torres of the Company did his best to arm the dying man against the temptations of the devil and, filled with a flame of love, exhorted him, now crying in his ear, to suggest weapons to use against the devil, and again consoling and encouraging him. To the astonishment of those present he kept this up for five hours without stopping, so that after many days he could hardly recover his former voice from hoarseness."[7] Father Niger at Ferrara "from the beginning of Sunday night spent twelve whole hours in passing into the other world or in agony and fought so bravely that the spectacle stirred the great admiration of *ours*. It was seen that he disputed with the devil and stood manfully to the combat. But the end was sweet and tranquil and his face after the soul had left the body more devout and beautiful than in life."[8]

Violent assaults of devils upon men in full health and strength are reported. As for example the cases of two citizens of Lisbon who were being instructed in the Christian life by *ours*. A man holding a high position in the administration of justice "rose one day before light, according to his custom, and went down without a candle to a certain little room. When he had settled himself in the usual place to pray, he received such a blow on the head that, to some extent he lost consciousness and thought he had received a great wound on the head for blood flowed from his mouth and injured gums. But he began to call on the name of Jesus and recognized that he suffered that from the devil and casting aside fear he did not omit his prayer."[9] The other man was on his knees with hands uplifted for prayer, when a most vile looking blackamoor appeared to him who seized his hands and with mocking words dragged him through the little room, threw him down a steep staircase and then kicked him and trampled on him. But two boys clad in white stood by him, encouraged him until dawn and consoled him. The next day when he was scourging himself at night and was finishing the penance, he perceived, as it were, a weight on his back and before his eyes a shade, black and thick. He was compelled to fall on his face. Then the shade, twisting the scourge out of the hands of the man, scourged him most cruelly. When he had borne this patiently, the same boys of the previous day consoled him until he fell asleep in that very place." [10]

This experience of being beaten by devils evidently seemed to many of the early members of the Company the honourable mark of a good fighter for God, because they told how it happened to Ignatius himself about the time when he was elected general.

Ribadeneira writes, "One night when Ignatius was sleeping, the devil, as it is believed, tried to suffocate him. He tried to strangle him, grasping his throat as if by a hand so strongly that Ignatius could not by any effort invoke the holy name of Jesus. But when he strung the nerves of his soul and body to the utmost, repelling force by force, he broke out at last with a most sweet voice and called out Jesus; by which voice the attempt of the devil was repulsed. From this struggle Ignatius (as we afterwards saw and noticed) was somewhat hoarse and without voice. I noticed that he was hoarse and I heard this if I am not mistaken in the year 1541." [11] Ribadeneira heard this incident when he was fourteen and recorded it forty-five years later. He recorded also another tale of an attack of devils on Ignatius. "I have heard from John Paul who was for a long time the attendant of Ignatius, a similar story. John was sleeping in a little room next to Ignatius and a certain stormy night he was wakened from sleep and seemed to hear the sound

[10] Pol. II, 685.   [11] Rib. 609. Not in first life. Compare de actis, Scripta, I, 345.

of blows and a noise as if of strong men beating Ignatius and the groans and sighs of Ignatius. He immediately ran to Ignatius and found him sitting up in bed with the covering pressed to his breast in his arms as if erect and unconquered and ready to receive blows. John said to him 'What is this, Father? What do I hear? What do I see?' Ignatius answered 'What have you heard?' When he told, 'Go back,' said Ignatius, 'and go to sleep.' John went back to his room and a little while afterwards heard Ignatius being severely beaten. He ran to him and found him unmoved but as if panting from a great fight and struggle of soul. He was ordered a second time to go back to bed and sleep and not to get up again."[12]

It is noticeable that even so long afterwards, Ignatius is not quoted as authority for these two stories. Nor did Ribadeneira put them into his first life of the founder. He says in regard to one tale "it is believed," "I heard" (manifestly not from Ignatius) and "I noticed that he was hoarse." In regard to the second story he records, thirty years after Ignatius' death, that John Paul told him that, in his youth, he woke out of sleep hearing blows in the next room, ran in to find Ignatius sitting up as if ready to fight the devil and was told to go back to sleep. (19)

No experience with devils in the least like these two is alluded to in any of the writings or sayings of Loyola, although he wrote a good deal about discerning of spirits. If he had gone through such an experience, or thought he had, it would have been extremely natural for him to warn his followers by telling them about it and not have left them to infer it. The argument often used by his biographers when they find it necessary to account for the silence of Ignatius in regard to some supernatural incident, is that his humility kept him from speaking of it. The argument in general is a very poor one. In the

[12] Rib. Second life, Bk. V, End of Cap. 9.

first place Ignatius was not shy in telling his experiences
to those who might profit by them. Secondly, Ribadeneira
gives us the following brief record of a conversation on
this very point. "Ignatius was accustomed to talk very
freely about his affairs and showed the greatest security
against the sin of vain-glory. When I said to him that
anyone who did not know him might suspect in him at
times vainglory or boasting, he said to me there was no
sin he was so little afraid of as that."[13]

Ignatius believed in devils but was not in the least
afraid of them. Many of his followers were. Such psychological experiences as those related were honestly recorded
and accepted without question on their face value. It
is conceivable that they might have been unconsciously
distorted in the record; they may conceivably be only
nervous reactions or contagious moods, they may conceivably be what those who recorded or believed in them
thought they were, terrifying demonstrations of the power
of immortal malignant beings. Take any explanation you
choose and it still remains true that such experiences come
only to people who live in a mental atmosphere where
there is a good deal of fear of devils.

The most illuminating instance of this fear and the
contrasted courage of Ignatius, is to be found in the
strange story told by Oliver Manareus, Rector of the
College at Loreto, in a solemn deposition made, in the
cold blood of mature age, years after the events described. "Asked if he had seen something of these spec-
tres, he said they greatly vexed the college in many ways.
The devil appeared to a Belgian novice in the form of
a black man clothed in green and tried to tempt him to
give up his intention to enter the Company. When the
lad resisted and made the sign of the cross, the demon
said: 'You won't listen to good advice' and blew into his
face stinking smoke which infected the room and the

[13] Dicta et facta, Scripta, I, 395.

hall in front of it for two days with a fetid smell plainly perceived by the deponent and many others. To another novice from Sardinia, the demon appeared in the form of the Apostle Paul advising him to lay aside Cicero and read the Epistles. The lad said nothing to his spiritual director but, trusting in himself, found great delight in reading Paul: the more so because he was acting against holy obedience."

When some of the brethren were praying the devil beat upon the stool where they kneeled or purred like a cat over their heads. Once when a young Englishman about twenty-three years old was eating supper the demon hit him so hard in the right side that he fell over backward pale and contorted. The demon leaped upon the bed of others in the form of a puppy which frightened them very much. But Manareus and three or four of the older brethren took great pains to suppress talk about the situation lest the fact that the house was haunted by demons should be noised abroad. The rector formed the habit of walking up and down in the hall for some hours on stormy nights in order to be able to help at once any young brethren attacked by the devil, and all the younger brethren were instructed, if the devil appeared to order him in the name of God to go to him. So it happened more than once that the devil came and beat on his door in the dead of night. He was ill for many nights with fever which made him sleepless; but one night he got a little sleep. The demon then beat on the door and the rector, thinking it to be one of the brethren told him to come in, but the knocking was repeated again and again. At last the rector guessed that it must be the demon and called out, "Open in the name of the Lord." Then the demon threw open the doors and windows with a great crash and din as if they were smashed. . . . "When the rector was a little better he heard once in the middle of the night a great noise like an earthquake in a remote part of the house. He got up and walked around and lo! the noise came towards him. At first he was terror-stricken but recovering his self control and arming himself with the sign of the cross, he turned toward the refectory where the noise and movement seemed to be. The noise grew louder and louder and finally there appeared a huge black dog with horrible burning eyes coming straight at him. Again he armed himself with the sign of the cross and stood firm. Then the dog, swerving toward the right side, three times, if he remembers rightly, barked with a very powerful bark, but one that sounded muffled as if it came out of some sort of vase, and let him go. No one ever saw the dog again.

"When sprinkling holy water, the ritual for exorcism and prayers could not stop the evil, the rector wrote to Father Ignatius who advised the rites of the Church. The rector let him know that he had used them in every possible way, but that the evil grew worse and he was afraid the thing might become known outside the house and so cause their adversaries to scatter abroad many evil reports.

"The blessed man then wrote other letters exhorting the brethren to patience and trust in God, saything that he would pray for them and adding he was confident that, by the goodness of God, they would in a short time be set free from their troubles. The rector called together all the brethren, read the letters to them and ordered them to have good hopes from the prayers and merits of such a father as Ignatius. His faith and hope were not in vain for, when the letters had been read, that evil was totally removed by God and the devils could never do anything more against the dwellers in the college for they were never seen or heard of again." [14] (20)

The modern reader, whether Catholic or Protestant, will suspect in this story certain elements which the man of the sixteenth or seventeenth century, whether Cath-

[14] Acta Sanct. 598 July. VII.

olic or Protestant, would not have suspected in it: the reactions in mass psychology of highly irritated nervous
systems, the panic of contagious cowardice, perhaps the
malignant pranks of an hysterical boy; certainly the half
recollected delirium of a frightened and fever stricken
man. But to forget all this and put oneself back in the
sixteenth century, still leaves us two things to wonder
at: the long reign over the hearts of university educated
men of idle fears, suspending their reason, weakening
their wills, obscuring their faith; and the power over the
hearts of his followers of Ignatius, who dissipated at once
the whole dark atmosphere of spiritual weakness by the
written word of his trust in God. This is indeed in any
sense you choose to take it "to have power to cast out
unclean spirits."

If Ignatius was not in the least afraid of devils, his
followers believed that devils were very much afraid of
him and therefore hated him with a very special hatred.

As they had experiences of devils localized in haunted
buildings, so they had frequent experiences of devils
dwelling in human bodies: the demoniacs. In these cases
they assumed that the haunting devil spoke in the ravings
of the man or woman who was "possessed." Among such
utterances they found the clearest proof of the fear and
hatred of Ignatius among the hosts of hell.

During the solemn ecclesiastical procedure leading
towards canonization begun forty years after Ignatius'
death, his aged friend Ribadeneira was asked what he
thought about the character of Ignatius. He gave as one
reason for thinking him a saint: "the great hatred which
the devil always had for Ignatius which he constantly expressed in persecutions. If the brethren were together
without Ignatius and all was quiet, when he came among
them some storm and tempest was always aroused by the
devil because he hated Ignatius." (It is noticeable that
Ignatius never makes the smallest allusion to anything

of the sort). Lainez told him that at Padua a poor soldier possessed of the devil—a man who had never seen Ignatius—described him perfectly, saying he was the greatest enemy that he (the devil in the man) had. When a certain demoniac was told that Ignatius was coming to drive out his devil he uttered screams, crying: "Ignatius is my greatest enemy." Another demon who possessed a man in Sicily said the same thing in the presence of the viceroy and the provincial of the Company. Ribadeneira adds: "This seems to me excellent testimony. For, though the devil is not to be believed when he speaks of himself, he is trustworthy in what God forces him to say for the glory of His saints."[15]

After the death of Ignatius, his followers believed that his pictures or relics had the same power to control and anger demons that his name had possessed while he was alive. We say his name because it is noteworthy that there is no testimony from the primary sources that Ignatius was present when these scenes of the confessions of devils took place. Three instances of this power of the picture or bones of Ignatius taken from the Acta Sanctorum, the official biography of Loyola published in 1731, will serve as examples. The first is dated at Siena five years after his death. "An honest and simple girl who was waiting maid to a noble lady was somewhat haunted by demons, who appeared to her in various shapes and beat her with astonishing cruelty. For twelve years she was involved in that calamity. When however she began to carry about with her a picture of the blessed Father, the impure spirits, though they appeared to her and ordered her to throw away the picture, never dared to touch her. The girl even mocked them, daring them to strike her but, so long as she had the picture, they never dared to do it. When however, being curious to test absolutely whether this fear of the demons came from the picture of

[15] Scripta, II, p. 150.

the blessed Father, she laid it aside, the demons at once attacked her and beat her so severely that they left her half dead. After that she kept the picture with her and the devils could only pound the walls and furniture of her room." [16]

Another is dated thirty-six years later. "A priest in Rome about to recite the ritual for exorcism took in his hands a reliquary which contained the relics of many saints and also of Ignatius (who was not yet made a saint). The devil called out that he was afraid of the relics of blessed Father Ignatius now in heaven, still unrecognized on earth, but soon to be consecrated a saint. The priest hung the reliquary around the neck of the woman. Whereupon the devil in her howled and cried aloud that the relics of Father Ignatius burnt him and departed from the woman." [17]

The third example of these stories was printed thirty years after the date of the second. In Poland, "a demon entered into a noble lady who like all her family was a heretic. The heretics frequently consulted together about freeing her from this enemy, but, as none of them dared to try it, they asked the Rector of the College of the Company to help her. One of the most urgent in their request was so insanely tenacious of Calvinism that he often said he would sooner be converted into a dog or a pig than a papist. Arrived at the house, the rector performs the rites of the Church for exorcism and secretly touches the woman with relics of Ignatius: whereupon she trembles and the devil calls out that he is tormented by the relics of Ignatius. The rector, desiring to cure not only the possessed but also the heretics, orders them to offer the Institutes of Calvin to the devil. He accepts them, to their great surprise, says they are wonderfully grateful and pleasant and warmly kisses them (by the lips of the woman of course). But when the rector offers him the

<hr>

[16] Acta Sanct. p. 803 B.   [17] Act. Sanct. p. 803 E.

same volume (after slyly slipping into it a picture of
Ignatius) as soon as it is held out, the demon draws back
howling in fury. Compelled to confess what he was afraid
of in it, 'You ask that,' he said, 'When you have put in
it a picture of Saint Ignatius?'   The devil is finally cast
out of the lady who rejects Calvinism and returns to the
Church."[18]

In regard to all this dealing with the devil three things
ought to be noticed by those who wish to get a true picture
of Ignatius. First that the farther we get away from him
the more frequent and the more crass do these tales of
physical diabolic action become. The devil plays an extremely minor role in the Confessions. Secondly, in these
three typical specimens of diabolic activity after Ignatius'
death, an attentive eye can observe elements that do not
appear in earlier testimony about his power over the unseen world: i.e. the strange curiosity of the terribly afflicted girl, completing, positively as well as negatively,
the logical proof that it was the picture of Ignatius which
made the devils stop beating her; or the clearness with
which the devil singles out the relics of Ignatius as more
effective than those of many other saints even though the
Church had not yet officially pronounced him a saint; or
the usefulness in debate of the story how the devil kissed
Calvin's Institutes (nicknamed the Bible of the Heretics).
The contrast between incidents like these and the trust in
God conquering the terrors of the night [19] or the contempt
which drives an unmasked Satan away as if he were a
troublesome dog,[20] seems to the writer to show fairly
enough the difference between the figure of Ignatius as it
appears in the earliest sources and the edifying or polemic
Jesuit Lives of the seventeenth and eighteenth centuries.   (21)

The third point to be noticed about any of these ideas

---

[18] Acta Sanct, p. 820, b.   [19] Ribadeneira, Bk. V, Cap. 9, Second Life. Pol.
I, 34. [20] Confessions, 55

concerning the unseen universe or any of these stories of the activity of devils is this. There is nothing in them, the crass as well as the more spiritual, which can in any particular sense be called Jesuit. The same ideas were held, similar stories were generally adopted as true during centuries before Loyola was born, during his lifetime and for generations after his death by Jesuit and non-Jesuit, Protestant and Catholic alike without very much distinction.

Demoniac possession, in which men were tormented and devils spoke by their mouth, is a prominent thing in the gospel life of Christ; who gave His apostles power to cast out devils. By the end of the fourth century the Church had a regular order of exorcists among the minor clergy, who received from the hands of the bishop a book with forms for driving out devils which they were told to commit to memory.[21] The mediæval chronicles abound in stories of the activity of the devil in the physical life of man.

Among Protestants who were contemporaries of Ignatius demoniac possession began gradually to disappear. But two hundred years after Ignatius the great Protestant preacher, John Wesley, reports in his journal cases he considers evident examples of it.[22] A missionary writes from Nova Scotia about a visit to a demoniac who had to be restrained from assaulting him by the strength of four men. The missionary fell on his knees in prayer, whereupon the frenzy subsided and the man began to praise Christ. Wesley writes, "It is well that Satan is constrained to show himself plainly in the case of these poor demoniacs."[23] He tells how he himself went to see a woman who "was in a way nobody could understand." He sang a verse or two of a hymn beside her bed and kneeled down to pray. "I had just begun when I felt as if I had

---

[21] Dictionary Christian Antiquities. Exorcist. [22] Journal, III, 300, 346-348. [23] Journal, I, 401.

been plunged into cold water and immediately there was such a roar that my voice was quite drowned though I spoke as loud as I usually do to three or four thousand people. However I prayed on. Then she was reared up in the bed, her whole body moving at once without bending one joint or limb just as if it were one piece of stone. Immediately afterward it was writhed into all kinds of postures, the same horrid yell continuing still. But we left her not until she was rejoicing and praising God." [24]

In the present day these phenomena so common for so many generations have entirely ceased. [25] A psychologist has recently written "We are able to produce and cure demoniacal possession in our laboratories." I do not know whether this claim is sound or not, but it seems to be evident that these phenomena do not now spontaneously occur among people, whether Catholic or Protestant, who do not expect and fear that they may occur.

One special form of the belief in the power of Satan or his evil angels to interfere directly in the bodily life of man was not weakened among Protestants when they seceded from the Roman Catholic Church. That was the belief in witchcraft or the power of human beings to sell their souls to the devil and to receive in return certain infernal pleasures, in the worship of Satan and certain malignant physical power over their fellows. This was a belief whose acceptance was for generations almost as universal as its rejection is now. Witchcraft was in most countries a crime at civil law punishable by death, and, under those laws, there perished in all European countries uncounted thousands of victims. The cowardly superstition crossed the Atlantic and stained the records of our colonial life with innocent blood. Its influence lasted until the nineteenth century. Witches died by

---

[24] Journal, III, 63, 1743. [25] Not long ago they were described as occurring in a certain district of China.

law in Switzerland, Spain, and Prussian Poland at the end of the eighteenth century. The cruelty and injustice which grew out of this belief may be judged from an instance in a work written by a Lutheran pastor, Anton Pratorius, who believed that there were witches but pleaded for mercy and common sense in the administration of the law against them. In 1597 women who were tortured and burnt in a neighbouring village denounced four women of his parish as witches. One of these hanged herself in prison, two died under the torture to make them confess, and the fourth was put to the torture. But when Pratorius heard of it, he ran to the castle and beat on the door of the torture room until they opened and he was able to stop it, but the woman died shortly after.[26]

The truly diabolic circle of malice or fear, torture, confession and false accusation to escape otherwise endless agony, fresh arrests, new torture, confession and false accusation, brought victims by the scores to the stake and the scaffold, and the accursed process went on during generations.

Luther who died ten years before Loyola not only accepted the basal beliefs on which this devastating superstition rested, but he also endorsed the terrible laws which grew out of those beliefs. From the pulpit he demanded the death of witches.[27] At the end of one sermon he cried, "We know some of these witches. If they do not repent we will order them into the hands of the public torturer. . . . Take care or you will be found out and come to the torture bench."[28]

Every protest against these laws and in many countries there were brave protesters, was answered among the Catholics by the authority of the Church, among the Protestant by the Bible; because in Exodus it says, "Thou shalt not suffer a sorceress to live."[29] Calvin commented

[26] Paulus, 187. [27] Weimar ed. XVI, 551. [28] Weimer, XXIX, 520. [29] Ex. XXII, 18.

in the puplit on this text as follows: "It is not to be doubted that this law retains its force today among Christians and therefore certain impure and profane men, despisers of the Word of God, should be driven out because they think it ridiculous to wish to exterminate this sort of witches and diviners—as if God speaking by his prophets could be deceived in prohibiting every kind of divination and magic." [30]

The same cruel law reaped a harvest of death in England during the seventeenth century; though a smaller one because the English law prohibited the use of torture. When the English statute against witchcraft was repealed in 1736, the reality of witchcraft was still maintained by many pious persons on the ground of the authority of the book of Exodus. John Wesley wrote in 1768, "It is true that the English in general and most of the men of learning in Europe have given up all accounts of witches and apparitions as mere old wives' fables. I am sorry for it." . . . "Infidels have hooted witchcraft out of the world." . . . "They well know (whether Christians know it or not) that the giving up of witchcraft is in effect giving up the Bible."[31]

Luther had been brought up in surroundings where fear of witches was rampant. He believed his own mother had suffered from the diabolic spells of a neighbour which made her children "nearly scream themselves to death."[32] Loyola also had been born and brought up in a region where belief in the power of witches was widespread.[33] Its strength may be sufficiently measured by the fact that the following story is told with full belief by Sandoval, one of the historiographers of the Emperor Charles V and bishop of Pamplona; where Ignatius was wounded: "The witch took her unguent and went up to the window of a very high tower and in the presence of a large crowd

[30] Opera, XXX, 631. [31] Wesley's Journal, V, 265, 375. [32] Tischreden, Weimar ed. III, 2982 (6). [33] Hansen, 402 n.

anointed herself with the unguent. That finished, she said in a loud voice, 'Are you there?' to which another voice answered, 'Yes, I am here.' Then the woman began to crawl down the wall head downward on her hands and feet like a lizard. Halfway down the wall she launched into the air in the sight of all and flew off, and was afterwards found three miles away." [35] Ignatius had been brought up a few miles from Pamplona where such a story could be related with full belief, in the serious historical work of a learned bishop. During his life both in Italy and Spain, a procession of witches was being sent to the stake. For example, in the diocese of Como, for a dozen years about a thousand were accused each year and about a hundred burnt, while in the Val Camonica the priests, calling for espiscopal visitation, said 5000 out of a population of 50,-000 were witches. One ex-inquisitor of Sicily gave thanks to God that in the last 150 years the inquisitors had burnt at least 30,000 witches. This superstition of witchcraft would have been scorned by both Cicero and Paul. Yet it flourished in those ages of the Renascence which appealed to the intellectual influence of both and for generations continued to paralyze the thinking and harden the hearts of men holding all varieties of Christian belief.

But in spite of the predisposing influences of a youth spent among the superstitious Basques, Ignatius resisted this contagion of opinion and example. His constant vision of life as a great combat between God and His angels and the devil and his ministers would have made it easy for him to become active as a witch hater, but his writings and his familiar talk reported by his intimates are entirely free from traces of that fear of witches, which in his own generation and in many succeeding generations, produced such terrible results of cruelty and injustice.

[34] Cited Hansen, 503.

CHAPTER XX

THE MYSTIC

Ignatius himself has told us that he had many wonderful visions of unseen things. Only one of these was a vision of evil; an often repeated figure in whose beauty he took much pleasure until he discovered accidentally that it came from the devil. Whereupon he drove it away, and, though for a long while it came back, he always banished it with contempt. For he seems to have had a certain amount of control over these visions and other extraordinary inner religious experiences. When he began a long course of study to make himself better able to help men, he found that his inner spiritual experiences prevented him from studying the Latin grammar. He decided they had become temptations and laid them aside. During the three years and a half he studied in Barcelona and in Alcalá and the seven years he studied in Paris, he apparently had no visions. It may be conjectured that this means he could put himself into the mood in which visions came to him and, when he kept himself out of that mood or attitude of soul, they did not come. Later in life he told Camara he could "find" God whenever he needed Him; [1] by which he probably meant feeling himself in direct communication with God from which visions or other spiritual illuminations would arise. This does not mean that he could have visions whenever he wanted. But more than ten years without them—a lack of spiritual delight of which he does not complain—would seem to indicate that

[1] Confessions, p. 55, 69, 85, 97.

303

his iron will could stop or prevent them when he thought
duty required it.

His first vision was not at all voluntary but a delightful
surprise. Lying awake one night soon after he had definitely decided not to go back to his old life but to imitate
the saints, he suddenly saw Our Lady with the Holy Child,
one of the many visions which wrought an especial effect
on him. For, though he had led the carelessly licentious
life of a young Spanish noble of the day, he never after
this vision felt the least desire for carnal indulgence.[2] His
next vision after the thing like a beautiful serpent, which
was a trick of the devil, was a guiding vision. He had
for a long time eaten no meat and one morning when he
got up "he saw, as if he saw it with his bodily eyes, meat
ready to eat," and concluded that God meant he should
eat meat. His confessor suspected this might be a tempting vision sent by the devil, but Ignatius could not doubt
that it was a sign from God.

Not long after he had five visions of the Trinity, the
creation, transubstantiation, the humanity of Christ, and
the whole body of theology and these five, with his first vision, give us specimens of the three sorts of visions
which came to him during the rest of his life. The
first sort is a distinct vision which needs no explanation,
like the Virgin Mary appearing to him at night in Loyola.
This was rare in his experience. In only one instance did
he hear any words as Paul during his converting vision
heard a voice "speaking in the Hebrew tongue." [3] Ignatius evidently needed no words to explain his visions because, some time after the only vision in which he heard
words, he had forgotten precisely what the words were.[4]

The second sort of vision which came to him might be
called symbolic visions. These were by far the most common, in his experience. He saw, for example, the Holy
Trinity like three keys of an organ. These symbolic

[2] Confessions, p. 42.   [3] Acts, XXVI, 14.   [4] Confessions, p. 95.

visions whose meaning he immediately recognized, usually took some form of light. How God created the world was shown him by "a white thing from which came rays out of which God made light," white rays coming down from above showed him Christ in the bread and wine. He saw the humanity of Christ "like a white body not very big and not very small." He saw Christ "as a large round gold thing," etc.[5] He frequently says he saw these visions with "the inner eyes," and as he had many of them in public it is evident that they were not visible to others. Sometimes a vision lasted a long time, for example during the walk from the Mount of Olives to the monastery in Jerusalem he saw Christ all the way over the head of his companions.[6] The same vision was often repeated up to as many as forty times.[7]

But although these visions were seen by the inner eye, there always seemed to be something about them external to his personality; for he could distinguish perfectly between them and his own thoughts or imaginations. When he was on his way back to Spain from Jerusalem, Spanish soldiers in an Italian town, after partly stripping him to search him as a spy, were leading him to their captain through three long streets, and he had a "representation of Christ being led through the streets of Jerusalem"; but he adds: "It was not a vision like the others," for these visions did not suspend his reason nor weaken his will power. He was able to decide by reason that a vision must be evil and for long years to suspend all visions when he judged that for a time they interfered with the holy purpose of his life.

He records a third class of spiritual experiences which are called "visions" for want of a better title. They were distinct inner enlightenments giving certainty of understanding of intellectual matters by a direct gift of God without any reasoning. The most important of these is

[5] Confessions, 62.   [6] Confessions, p. 65.   [7] Confessions, p. 54.

described as "a great illumination without seeing any vision." He says it taught him so much about "things of faith and learning and gave him such a great clearness of understanding, that all the divine help and all he has learned during thirty years since, have not profited him so much."[8] He had this experience before he had made any studies in theology and it may serve not only as an example of the similar less extensive illuminations which came to him, but also as a measure of how immutable his theological ideas were.

The Confessions of Ignatius give us a brief sketch of his memories of his inner life up to about the age of forty-seven. From that time on we have only letters and the scattered reminiscences of some of his intimate followers; except for one very remarkable document. This is a diary of his spiritual experiences for nearly a year written between the ages of fifty-six and fifty-nine.

It consists of two parts. In the second part, very little of which has been printed, there are brief notes of his religious experiences and sensations during three hundred and eleven days. The first part, printed in full,[9] gives an account of his soul's experience for forty days when he was seeking the guidance of God on a point in the Constitutions—whether the houses of the Company should own any income-bearing property or practise complete poverty. The diary is preceded by a document in which are set down sixteen distinct numbered reasons for poverty with eight reasons in favour of having an income and he notes that he frequently thought over these during the experiences of the first fifteen days of the diary. After having carefully reasoned the matter pro and con, he entered upon a series of masses from which he expected divine direction. His account of his experiences is confused and difficult to understand, as might be expected from such a hasty record of a highly mystical experience made by a man not facile

[8] Confessions, p. 55.   [9] Appendix XVIII, De la Torre.

in the use of words. He evidently succeeds in "finding" (his phrase is "to end with") the Virgin, the Holy Ghost, the Son, the Father and the Holy Trinity, as distinct spiritual existences from each of which he seeks aid and guidance.

The first seven days when he seeks the aid of Our Lady, his experiences are comparatively tranquil and his mind is steadily inclined toward the choice of poverty. On the seventh day he spends two periods of an hour and a half each in going over the reasons and making his choice or decision, which is for poverty. He wishes to have this decision presented to the Father by the Mother and the Son as mediators. He repeats his study of the reasons for and against poverty and on the tenth day it seems to him that he "sees or feels the Holy Spirit in a clarity, dense or in the colour of a flaming fire." That day he comes to feel that the matter is finished except for services of thanks and worship to the Father and the Holy Trinity. He does not offer these the next day, and the day after he feels he has failed and needs the intercession of the Mother and the Son to restore him to the earlier grace. The next day he "feels" (perceives) that the Son is very propitious to intercede with the Father "seeing Him in a way which cannot be written nor the other things explained." The twenty-sixth day he has "supernaturally" an "intellectual vision of the Holy Trinity with Jesus in the midst," and five days later "he feels (or perceives) in a lucid clarity an essence which draws me wholly to His love" (the Holy Trinity). A few days later he feels (perceives) and sees "not obscurely but in lucidity and great lucidity, the same being, or Divine Essence, in a spherical figure a little larger than the sun appears to be and from that Essence the Father seemed to proceed or derive." This was "the being of the Holy Trinity without distinction of the other persons." A little later he sees the spherical vision and "the Father, Son and

Holy Ghost derived from the Divine Essence without going outside of it." At night he saw the same thing; "not so large, clear or distinct but like a large ray of light."

During these forty days he records one hundred and twenty-nine times that he was moved to tears, ranging from "an inclination to tears" to "most intense," "very abundant," "many and very intense," "I covered myself with tears." He also mentions repeatedly that he could not articulate for a while. Most of this weeping came in connection with the mass he said every day. These weepings are mingled with intervals of "grace, suave, full of devotion warm, and very sweet." These religious exercises did not absorb all his time. He tells four times what happened when he went into the city, a thing he never did except for some necessary business. He was not fasting, for he speaks of things happening before or after dinner, and he resists an "impulse not to eat." Apparently he reaches his decision by the sixteenth day and feels nothing more need be done except to offer services of thanks. But he makes up his mind to seek a confirmation of the decision from the Holy Trinity, notwithstanding the fact that he already has it from the Father, the Son, and the Holy Ghost. He does not obtain this and he says he becomes "provoked with the Holy Trinity." His account of this is entirely free from any remote suggestion of irreverence and he speaks the next day of his intense love for the Trinity. He concludes it was "an evil mood which made him doubt and be indignant with the Holy Trinity." Nevertheless he finds himself in an attitude where he needs "to be reconciled with the Holy Trinity" and seeks the intercession of Jesus "to obtain his pardon from the Holy Trinity." This reconciliation is brought about by the disappearance from his soul of every sentiment "repugnant to it" (i.e. The Holy Trinity) bringing him "a tranquillity and

repose of soul" in which "he could not see or feel any of
the former discord or disgust."

The confirmation of the Holy Trinity is finally given to
him by Jesus.

The present writer frankly confesses that he does not
know what this mystic spiritual experience in connection
with the Holy Trinity means. To be "indignant" with
the Holy Trinity, to feel "discord" or "disgust" with the
Holy Trinity and then to be "reconciled" with the Holy
Trinity, suggest to him states of thought or feeling which
he cannot even remotely imagine. He attempts, in spite
of diffidence, to describe briefly Ignatius' account of it,
because, even imperfectly understood, it makes so plain
the mystic character of the man who, his intimates tell
us, always weighed with the utmost care all the reasons
for every action and, in all practical affairs, showed such
shrewd common sense knowledge of the average human
heart. It is necessary to make plain this union of qualities, one might almost say of characters, in him, to show
how extraordinary he was.

Ignatius was subject to these remarkable religious experiences during thirty-five years after his conversion, except during the eleven years of his student life. Nevertheless no one was more aware than he was of the danger
that beset them. He saw that danger in a double form:
truly pious people might be deceived by the craft of the
devil as he was himself deceived for a time by the vision
of the beautiful thing like a serpent; or deliberate hypocrites might feign their experiences to deceive others. His
knowledge of the human heart also evidently told him
(though he had never studied in the modern fashion the
extraordinary physical results of hysteria) that there might
be a combination of these two dangers in the case of people
whose heart was not firmly fixed on God but who were
deceived by the devil, or their own emotions, into thinking themselves more religious than they really were.

Very soon after his conversion he began to consider the
first danger and to study "discerning the spirits." To the
Spiritual Exercises he appended twenty rules to guide the
giver of them in teaching the taker how to discern spirits
and he wrote, or approved, seven years before his death,
a long discussion of some revelations he deemed false. A
few examples will show his ideas about judging visions and
extraordinary religious experiences.[10]

William Postello was admitted to probation. He was
a pious man of good character. He thought he had the
spirit of prophecy and said and wrote things "neither true
nor edifying." Ignatius assigned three fathers to judge
the case. They decided that although Postello's "will was
good, nevertheless his spirit and prophecies were manifest
illusions of the devil and nothing but human phantasies
without any base whatever and fitted to deceive the curious
and to work great harm and scandal in the Church of
God."[11] Postello refused to accept this judgment of those
he had sworn to obey and was dismissed.

Ribadeneira records that he had heard Father Reginald,
a Dominican monk, tell Ignatius about a holy woman, in
a cœnobium under his spiritual care in Bologna, who fell
frequently into states where she lay as if dead even when
touched by flame. But she always heard and obeyed the
voice of her mother superior. She had marks of nails on
her hands and wounds like those of the crown of thorns on
her head. Father Reginald had often seen them. He
added that he himself did not dare either to approve or
disapprove of them and asked the opinion of Ignatius.
The latter replied "of all these things you have told, the
sign most free from any doubt is the prompt obedience."
When they were alone Ribadeneira asked Ignatius what
he thought. He replied, "God may fill souls with His
grace and sometimes it may appear in bodily signs. The
devil because he has not power over the soul often de-

10 Letts. XII, 632.   11 Scripta, I, 709, Pol. 1, 149, May 10th, 1543.

ceives people by bodily signs, and he confirmed this opinion by examples." "The woman came to a very bad end
and all the flame ended in smoke."[12]

Ribadeneira also heard conversations of Ignatius with
the rector of Coimbra about a certain woman of Cordova in Spain, whose holiness he praised excessively.
Ignatius told the rector his attitude was foolish and unworthy of a member of the Company. Some years later
this woman regarded in Spain "almost like a virgin fallen
from heaven was caught as a plain hypocrite who for
years had deceived people by fraud."[13]

It is a distortion of the figure of Ignatius to regard an
experience with visions and illuminations as peculiar to
him or even extremely exceptional. It is true that few
people have left so detailed a record of such a continued
series of visions as he wrote, but the lives of the mediæval
saints are filled with visions. For example Raymond
Lull, a wealthy Catalan who had led a dissipated life had
in 1266, as he tells us, a vision of Christ on the cross
five times. As a consequence he gave his life to the cause
of Mohammedan missions and was finally stoned to death
in North Africa at the age of eighty.

In the eighteenth century occurred the well known case
of the conversion by a vision of James Gardiner. The
distinguished preacher, Dr. Philip Doddridge, wrote down
the story "the very evening I heard it from his own
mouth." Gardiner was then thirty-three, successful in
his profession (he rose to the rank of Colonel) but averse
to religion and with a reputation for debauchery. He
was in his room reading to pass the time before a sinful
rendezvous at midnight when "he saw an unusual blaze
of light fall on the book which he at first thought came
from some accident to the candle. But, lifting up his
eyes, he apprehended to his extreme amazement that there
was before him, as it were suspended in the air, a visible

---

[12] Ribadeneira, 620, not in first Life.   [13] Rib. 623, not in first Life.

representation of the Lord Jesus Christ on the cross surrounded on all sides by a glory and a voice to this effect,
'Oh, Sinner!   Did I suffer this for thee and are these
the returns?'   But whether this was an audible voice or
only a strong impression on his mind equally striking,
he did not seem very confident."   The change in his life
caused by this vision was immediate and permanent.   For
twenty-five years, until he fell trying to rally the defeated
royal army at Prestonpans, he was the model of a Christian soldier.[14]

Visions are still seen as a part of religious experiences
which produce marked effects on life. Here is the authen-
tic account of such an experience very recently recorded. A
young American minister who had neither peace nor zeal
in his heart entered a little village church in Cumberland
and joined a congregation of seventeen people. The leader
of the service spoke of some aspect of the cross "and
while he brooded on the idea, in a reverie of mind there
came to him very palpably and with the most poignant
realism, albeit with no suddenness or dramatic intensity,
a vision of the crucified. . . . A wave of strong emotion
seemed to lift his soul and bear it to the foot of the cross.
There he made his surrender to the divine Will."   Asked
some time afterward about his sensations, he said: "I
remember one sensation very distinctly; it was a vibrant
feeling up and down the spine as if a strong current of
life had suddenly been poured into me. . . ."   This vision
was followed by "the happiness which came to him from
his unbroken sense of the divine companionship."   This
sense of the divine companionship has been expressed
since in a career of great success in helping young men
to gain faith and express it by their works.[15]

Visions were especially common among the contemporaries of Ignatius.   Savonarola (executed 1498) has
described his and they came frequently to St. Theresa,

[14] Doddridge.   [15] Begbie, 24-26.

born six years before the conversion of St. Ignatius. Her greater facility in the use of language enables her to give in her autobiography a much more detailed account than the description of his visions by Ignatius. For example: "On one of the feasts of St. Paul when I was at mass there stood before me the most sacred humanity of Christ as paintings represent Him after the resurrection. . . . This vision I never saw with my bodily eyes, nor indeed any other vision, but only with the eyes of the soul. . . . If I were to spend many years in devising how to picture to myself anything so beautiful I could never be able . . . the whiteness and brilliancy alone are inconceivable. . . . It is like most pellucid water running in a bed of crystal reflecting the rays of the sun, compared with most muddy water on a cloudy day, flowing on the surface of the earth. Not that there is anything like the sun present here, nor is the light like that of the sun; this light seems to be natural; and, in comparison with it, every other light is something artificial. . . . In short, it is such that no man however gifted can ever in the whole course of his life arrive at any imagination of what it is."[16] "On one occasion when I was holding in my hand the cross of my rosary Christ took it from me into His own hand. He returned it; but it was then four large stones incomparably more precious than diamonds. . . . He said to me that, for the future that cross would appear so to me always; and so it did. . . . I never saw the wood of which it was made but only the precious stones. They were seen, however, by no one else—only by myself."[17]

During the lifetime of Ignatius visions sometimes appeared to men not especially predisposed before or after them to religion. When that artistic ruffian Benvenuto Cellini, a younger contemporary of Ignatius, was arrested on the charge of stealing gold from the pope, he had in

---

[16] Autobiography of St. Theresa XXVIII 4. 7. 8 Lewis. [17] Ib. XXIX 8.

his dark cell a magnificent dream vision of the sun, "like a ball of molten gold forming itself first into a crucifix and then into a Madonna and Child."[18] Ignatius, if he had heard of this vision and known Cellini's entire lack of repentance for the murders and vices of his life, would have pronounced it a delusion of Satan. However that may be, there is no reason to doubt that Cellini had this vision. His memory of it was so distinct that he made drawings and a wax model in order to reproduce it in gold or silver.

What modern psychologists can show us under the heading of visualization or hallucination in regard to such experiences as these is not, after all, of much importance for our purpose of trying to convey to the reader a clear understanding of the personality of Ignatius. The facts are that he and others before, during and since his day, have had these experiences; which, to some of them, became extremely vital elements to inspire conduct and form character.

It is not to be supposed that Ignatius failed to realize that there were other temperaments besides the mystic temperament. It is notable that the Spiritual Exercises do not suggest or expect such exalted states of feeling as those which led to his visions and illuminations. A single paragraph from the Chronicle of the secretary of Ignatius, Polanco, makes plain that he and his comrades did not expect all men to follow the same path toward holiness.

"Brother Dominic, in other respects a very excellent man, who proved that he had a high opinion of the Company, was sometimes in the habit of making a little fun of our contemplations and confessed to one of *ours* that for his part he did not know how to think of God unless he had the gospel before him and since God was invisible He immediately withdrew from his eyes. He added that

[18] Autobiography Bk. I XXII.

he could not understand what those could think about who remained on their knees two hours before the altar in prayer and said that he could not do it. Father Gutierrez and Father Antony explained to him, but he said he could not understand these things at all. So that it was easy to see how great a difference there is between speculative and mystical theology and because the good father Dominic had been very well trained in the first and, as it seemed, little trained in the latter, therefore he was in the habit of talking in this way about prayer and contemplation."[19]

The diary of Ignatius brings out very prominently one feature of his religious experiences which he and his followers, adopting a common opinion of the time, regarded as a gift of God: "the gift of tears." That age was more tolerant of excessive displays of emotion than this and that tolerance was more marked among Latin than among northern nations. The facility and frequency with which another contemporary of Ignatius, Catherine de Médicis, Queen Dowager of France, and the kings, queens and princes who were her children, joined in family weeping is remarkable. The reason for regarding tears as desirable in private devotion is evident. They were an assurance to the worshipper that the contrition or adoration he offered to God in prayer was sincere and deep. Ignatius therefore welcomed bursts of tears during prayer. He told Camara that when he "did not weep three times during mass he thought himself lacking in divine comfort."[20]

In this again we see the singular mixture of capacities in Ignatius. This intensely emotional nature could control his tears absolutely by his will and use his reason about them perfectly. At one time he wept so much that the doctor told him to stop or lose his eyes. He told Lainez "that ordinarily he wept six or seven times a day."[21]

[19] Pol. V, 419.   [20] Scripta, I, 244, Memoriale.   [21] Scripta, I, p. 127.

Ignatius always insisted on obedience to the doctor. He mastered his tears to such an extent that he could prevent or permit them at will and "found as much consolation as before in prayer and worship."[22]

One of the members of the Company was troubled by the fact that he had not the "gift of tears." Ignatius ordered a letter to be written to him full of pious common sense. "So far as the gift of tears is concerned, it is not necessary nor good and convenient for all. Our Father Ignatius will pray God to grant it to you so far as you need it for your work, which is to help souls, your own and your neighbors. What you quote about 'the hard heart,' my dear Father, is true, but the heart desirous as yours is to serve God and help your neighbours cannot be called hard and, since you have in your will and the higher parts of your soul, compassion for the miseries of your neighbours and want to help them and do all in your power to carry out your desire, no other tears and no other tenderness of heart are necessary. . . . So do not be troubled by the lack of external tears, but keep on showing your good will in deeds and that is enough for your own growth toward perfection, for helping your neighbours and for the service of God."[23]

[22] Rib. fol. 172—Scripta, I, 249.   [23] Letts. V, 714.

CHAPTER XXI

THE SUPERNATURAL IN THE LIFE OF IGNATIUS

The life of Ignatius as we read it in the Confessions and the early recorded recollections of his friends, is, in comparison with the lives of some of the saints, lacking in miracles. It seemed so to his intimate friends. In the first Life of Loyola begun thirteen years after his death by orders of Francisco Borgia, the General of the Company,[1] the last chapter is entitled "Concerning the Miracles wrought by Him." It is devoted to answering this question posed by the writer—"Why is not the sanctity of Ignatius more attested by miracles, and, like the life of many saints, approved by signs and marked by the doing of mighty works?" The writer then goes on to show that to such virtue as his, illustrated by such service of God, miracles are not necessary. There are better proofs of holiness than miracles, and he cites the words of Christ: "in the last day they shall say: 'Lord, Lord, have we not in Thy name cast out devils and done many mighty works,' and I will profess unto them 'I never knew ye, depart from me, ye that work iniquity.' "[2] He adds, "I am, however, far from thinking that miracles seem to be lacking to render illustrious the name of Ignatius," and he "brings his narrative to a close" by a short list of things in the life of Ignatius "which could not have happened without a miraculous element."

The miracles in this list are divisible into three classes. First, personal experiences, a long fast in his youth without marked loss of strength, an eight days' trance when

[1] End of preface.   [2] Matt. VII, 22.

317

he lay insensible, his visions. Secondly, works of healing, Father Simon saved from dangerous illness, Father Jay making a journey on foot and suddenly attacked by a great pain in the stomach was cured at once by calling on the name of Ignatius; after Ignatius' death Bobadilla was freed from a dangerous fever and the Rector of the College of Padua "from the terror of urgent pestilence" solely by the memory of Ignatius. Thirdly, prophesyings: "He told me just before I became ill for the second time, that I would have a third attack, and it happened"; when Nadal was sailing in the winter for Spain, Ignatius foretold an easy voyage; he foretold that Lainez would succeed him as general of the Company; when Baroelis was given up by the doctors he foretold "to me" his recovery.

The solemn and revised testimony of this first biographer of Ignatius was given in the process of beatification in 1595 at the age of sixty-eight. When he was asked about the miracles in his Life of the friend of his youth, he says "The miracles were the most certain part of the work," and gives nine, all found in both editions of his Latin Life.[3] Four of these have already been mentioned.[4] a fifth is the healing of the demoniac Matthew. (22) Another was the vision with audible words from God which fixed Ignatius upon the name of the Company of Jesus; another was Ignatius' calm assurance that a troublesome question about property given to the Company at Venice would be settled in their favour, as it shortly was. The two others were the sudden assurance given to Ignatius, who was at a distance from their sick beds, that two beloved members of the Company had died. One of these came in a vision of the dead man entering heaven.[5]

Instances of the certainty of death occurring at a distance are often recorded. For example, Henry M. Stan-

[3] Scripta, II, 150. [4] See p. 1. [5] Scripta, II, p. 150, Deposition of Ribadeneira.

ley writes in his autobiography that, during our Civil War, when he was a prisoner in St. Louis, he fell asleep and was in a dream transported to Wales and the bedroom of his Aunt Mary listening to her parting words. "I put forth my hand and felt the clasp of the long thin hand of the sick woman. I heard a murmur of farewell and immediately I awoke. . . . The next day, the 17th of April, 1862, my aunt died in Wales." [6]

The healing of the sick by the prayers of a fellow-believer would not necessarily constitute a miracle according to the definition and practice of the Church. People for whom no one thought of making claim to the honour of sainthood supported by miracles, might have what was known as the "gift of healing" given of God like the "gift of tears." Polanco tells of Father Michael of the Company "who had received from God the gift of healing." "I was suffering with a very troublesome fever which ordinarily lasted eighteen hours a day and Michael told me that he had wrought healings in Barcelona and elsewhere by certain prayers. I asked him what words he used and where he fixed his hope of healing. When I found that there was nothing but good in his forms of prayer and that he put his hope of healing in God, I asked him if he would heal me and he readily agreed to do so. I was not willing, however, to use his help until I had consulted Father Ignatius. But when Ignatius, who then had very few people to aid him in his labours, said he would be glad to have me seek the help of Michael, I sent for him and confessed my hope that God would heal me by the gift of healing granted to him. According to his custom he wrote out sacred words, saying three times the *Our Father* and the *Hail Mary* before the consecrated wafer, and hung the scroll on which he had written around my neck. Immediately I felt a refreshing coolness from head to foot and I was freed from the

[6] H. M. Stanley, Autobiography, p. 217.

raging fever. Nevertheless when the thing was over I persuaded Michael that he could use that gift of God without those words and the rolling up of a scroll of written prayers and hanging it around the neck, but simply by blessing and the imposition of hands. And so at Tivoli that same year and in Spain he often tried it and freed many from serious diseases merely by the laying on of hands or benediction." In Spain "his fame was so great that the sick came from two or three leagues around to get his blessing."[7]

The point is that there was nothing in this transaction or in the driving out of a devil by a priest using the regular ritual of exorcism, which Ignatius or his friends regarded as technically miraculous. Healing and exorcism might be only special forms of ordinary answers to the prayers of faith. Their attitude towards them was not essentially different from that taken by many Protestants in our own day toward answers to prayers. Here for instance is an instance from a widely circulated Protestant book printed in 1882. "A lady lay apparently at the point of death. Physicians who had attended her pronounced death within a few days inevitable." . . . The mother of the lady went to a daily prayer meeting held at noon to ask for the prayers of the meeting. There were so many requests for special prayers that hers could not be presented and she was promised it should be read the next day. "The next day she watched at home. A few minutes before noon she saw her daughter sink back as if dead, but she did not lose faith. Noon came and prayers were offered in the meeting. These prayers the Lord graciously answered, for, at a few minutes after noon, while prayer was being made, the daughter rallied and the mother poured forth thanksgivings to God."[8]

Among the direct interventions of God in their behalf which the members of the Company of Jesus noted with

[7] Pol. I, 270; IV, 43.   [8] Prime.

satisfaction, but which Ignatius did not relate or refer to, were what might be called punitive providences used by God to chastise opponents of the Company. For example Polanco relates that at Perugia there were "four citizens who were thought to make no secret of their opposition to the Company and they paid most heavy penalties for their fault. One died suddenly, a second lost his wife and fell into extreme poverty, another lost his eyesight by ophthalmia, and the last convicted of a terrible crime is said to have been condemned to the galleys."[9]

After the death of Ignatius some of his followers and admirers involved him retrospectively in this sort of judgment which seems to have been forbidden by Christ when he said: "Say ye of those upon whom the tower in Siloam fell that they were sinners above all others in Jerusalem. I tell you nay, for except ye repent ye shall all likewise perish." In his second life of Ignatius Ribadeneira, who afterwards wrote a pamphlet about God's punishments upon those who seceded from the Company, related this story,[10] without telling where it came from. A certain rich young man seeing Ignatius miserably dressed and barefoot said, laughing at him, "May I be burnt if that fellow is not worthy of being burnt." A few days later, setting off some fireworks on the tower of his house, he was consumed in a conflagration.[11] In pointing out that Ignatius seems to have differed from his followers in this tendency to hold a preliminary Day of Judgment on his fellowmen who opposed him, it is not the intention of the writer to suggest that the Jesuits differed from other people in their belief in punitive providences. In the savage controversies over religion of the sixteenth and seventeenth centuries, it was the commonest thing for people on both sides to see the especial wrath of God in every misfortune which befell their adversaries.

[9] e. g. Pol. IV, 153, Compare Pol. V, 281, etc.   [10] Scripta, I, 318, note 15.
[11] Rib. 2nd Life, 643.

Some forty years after the death of Ignatius the congregation of the Company voted to seek his canonization.[12] In 1622 the question came before a consistory of cardinals for the Pope's final decision.[13] Cardinal del Monte summed up the case for the sainthood of Ignatius.[14] In the last section of his plea he relates sixteen miracles. Ten of these were healings wrought after death by his relics or vows to him. The six miracles wrought during life include none of the nine Ribadaneira deposed to during the process for beatification. (23) They are the resuscitation of a man who had hanged himself "whom all thought dead," a man suddenly healed of an illness of many years' standing, the healing of the scorched hand of a cook, the freeing of a man from most grave temptations by which the devil had during two years beset him, the freeing of the College of Loreto from devils, and the supernatural shining of the countenance of Ignatius.

There is one very plain indication that the advisers of the Pope in the final action of the process of canonization did not think that the miracles examined during that process had what a writer in the Acta Sanctorum calls "the signs which mark those *great miracles* of the Apostles, also called prodigies." [15] It is noticeable that of the unanimous advisory opinions recorded in favour of the sainthood of Saint Ignatius by twenty-eight cardinals and nine other prelates, fifteen mention his miracles as more or less influential reasons for their decision and twenty-two do not mention them, but give as reasons for their judgment the holiness of his character and the great work he did for God. To read their speeches is to see that a much larger majority would have agreed with the opinion of a cardinal that Ignatius was not to be excluded from among the miracle workers, but that he believed the greatest miracle of all had been Ignatius himself.

[12] Acta Sanct. 614 E. [13] For process of canonization see Hinschius, IV, 252, Note 7. [14] Acta Sanct. 622 E. [15] Acta Sanct. 600, note 943.

Precisely the opposite tendency is observable in the speeches of the same twenty-eight cardinals in the case of Francis Xavier, the great missionary who was made a saint by the same bull of canonization. In the case of Xavier nineteen of the twenty-eight cardinals mention his miracles as reasons for their judgment while in voting on the case of Ignatius seventeen of them do not mention his miracles.

The case for Xavier was full of "those great miracles also called prodigies."[16]   Three of them accepted by the bull of canonization may be cited as examples.

A.   He saved his shipmates on a becalmed vessel from the danger of thirst by ordering all casks and other vessels filled with sea water and turning it into fresh water.[17]

B.   The bull cites three cases of his raising the dead. The first is the following.   "When he was preaching to the infidels in a church on the promontory of Comorin he could produce no effect because of the hardness of their hearts, so he offered prayer, ordered a tomb to be opened in which a man had been buried the day before and made the people understand that, by the will of God, the dead man would live again in order to prove the truth of the Christian faith.   Then the winding sheet in which the corpse was wrapped being cut open and prayer again offered to God, he ordered the dead to live, who, immediately and to the stupefaction of all, arose living. Because of this notable miracle all who were present and later many others, believed in God."[18]

C.   While he was allaying a tempest at sea by putting into the water the crucifix he wore around his neck, the force of the hurricane swept it from his hands, but, when he had come to land and was continuing his journey along the seashore, a crab suddenly emerged from the waves

<hr>

[16] Act. Sanct. 600.   [17] Mon. Xav. II, 712, Bull of Canonization.   [18] Mon. Xav. II, 712, 713, 710.   Bull of Canonization.

and stopped at his feet, holding up in his claws the lost crucifix." [19]

Miracles established by a regular process of canonization are not rested simply on the authority of the Church in matters of faith. A regular legal process is held, witnesses make affidavits and there is an advocate whose duty it is to invalidate this testimony if he fairly can. This fact gives history the right to review the official record of the testimony which the court has deemed sufficient to prove the miracles.

In regard to the miracles of Xavier two official investigations were held in India. The first was begun by order of the King of Portugal to his viceroy in 1556, four years after the death of Xavier. The commission sat in four places and collected the depositions of sixty-five witnesses. No one of these mention the three great miracles or prodigies (A, B and C) related above; nor does any contemporary document written by those who knew Xavier.

Seven witnesses say they have heard that (in the place where the miracle of raising the dead is placed by the bull of canonization) a boy who had fallen into a well and been drowned was brought to life by Xavier. One witness deposed that being on a ship with Xavier and an important functionary of state, the latter asked the missionary about this reported resurrection of a boy drowned in a well, and that Xavier told him the boy was not dead but alive.[20] Another deposed that he had been told by a teacher in the College of Goa about asking the same question of Xavier and getting the same answer. Both of these witnesses, however, in spite of the explicit denial by Xavier himself of what is to them only a matter of hearsay, evidently continue to believe the reports. To the "prodigy" of opening a tomb and raising a dead man as a proof that his preaching was true, none of these sixty-five witnesses makes any illusion.

[19] Mon. Xav. II, 713, Bull of Canonization.   [20] Mon. Xav. II, 228.

Not only is there no early evidence for this prodigy of opening a tomb and raising the dead but there is, from three separate sources, strong presumptive evidence that it did not occur.

In the process is included an affidavit from Joannes a Cruce, "one of the chief men of the province," where the bull says this opening of the tomb and resurrection took place. He not only does not mention it when asked if Xavier had performed any miracles, but responds to the question only in these words: "He accomplished great miracles in separating those who called themselves Christians from their sins and vices so that after having taken the name of Christ they should not be thrust down into hell."[21] That this miracle of opening the tomb and raising the dead to prove the truth of the Gospel could have taken place without Joannes a Cruce hearing of it is impossible, that knowing of it he would have made such a reply to a question whether Xavier had performed any miracles, is unbelievable.

The second presumptive witness against the correctness of this assertion that Xavier, in order to prove his preaching true, opened a tomb and raised a dead man, is Father Teixeira of the Company, author of a life of Xavier. In this life he puts medical evidence that the body of Xavier was in a way not natural, preserved many months from corruption, and classifies under five heads the results of inquiry into his miracles: 1—The spirit of prophecy foretelling future events; 2—During his many voyages he found ports for puzzled pilots; 3—A supernatural insight into consciences; 4—A great power to drive out demons; 5—Visions and revelations.[22] It is evident that Father Teixeira had no antecedent prejudice against the idea that God might work miracles through his living saints. When, thirty years after Xavier's death, Ribadeneira published in Spain a Spanish Life of Ignatius in

[21] Mon. Xav. II. 359.   [22] Mon. Xav. II. 912.

which he told of Xavier's miracles, it was sent to Teixeira with a request for comment and criticism. He wrote a letter saying that he had been thirty-three years in India and had some knowledge of the matters whereof he wrote. The most significant paragraph refers to the raising of the dead,—"As to what you say about God raising the dead by Father Francis, although his merit and sanctity was so great that Our Lord could have done it through him by His infinite goodness and power, nevertheless, after due inquiry, no certainty whatever has been arrived at in regard to it; only that it is commonly said that Our Lord did it through him. It is true that in regard to that matter it is said that God raised a dead man by him on Cape Comorin but, when one tries to get at the bottom of this, no one can be found who has seen it. Father Amrrique, who has been more than forty years there, tells me that he has made the most solemn inquiry into the matter and that he never could find anything which could be affirmed with certainty. This is not said because there was not virtue and sanctity in that blessed Father, but because in a matter of such importance certainty seems necessary; or at least evident probability. Because, as your Reverence well says in the prologue of your book on the life of our Father Ignatius, 'If every lie in any matter is unworthy of a Christian man, much more is it unworthy in the lives of the saints.' God does not need the help of our lies."[23]

Father Alexander Valignano who forwarded this letter did not mince words in his criticism. He speaks twice of something related as a "pure imagination" which never really happened. What the book says about miracles he calls "a very great hyperbole which in my judgment should be totally stricken out, because, although it is true that a great many things are talked about, there is not to be found firmly established, either in India nor in Japan, a

[23] Mon. Xav. II, 805.

single certain miracle outside of what appears in the first part of the Historia Indica."[24] This is pretty strong and certainly unprejudiced testimony from men who had known and loved Xavier, that he did not open a tomb and call a dead man out of it.

A second investigation of the miracles of Xavier was made by orders of the pope in 1616 and 1617, sixty-five years after Xavier's death. It was held in four places and collected the affidavits of 138 witnesses. All three of the "great miracles or prodigies" under discussion are referred to by some of these witnesses. In regard to the resurrection wrought after the opening of a tomb as a proof of the truth of Xavier's preaching, there are two hearsay witnesses. One says he knows it from public fame (he was born twenty years after Xavier died). The other man says he heard it from many old men of the neighborhood.[25] A third witness, a native otherwise unknown, says he saw it. This thread of testimony in itself slender, would seem to break completely under the force of the negative evidence given by Joannes a Cruce and Fathers Teixeira and Valignano. To the mind of a historian it is impossible to weigh seriously against their competent and unprejudiced testimony, these depositions made by very inferior witnesses more than sixty years after the event. Certainly no one would question this conclusion if the events concerned were ordinary and not miraculous events.

It is noteworthy that as you get away from the earliest sources, which deny the resurrections of Xavier,[26] the number of resurrections from the dead attributed to him steadily increases. In 1620 John Berckmans writes from Rome: "I myself have heard Father Vitelleschi assert with all certitude before eighteen cardinals that the blessed Francis Xavier had raised twenty-three or twenty-four

---

[24] Scripta, I, 743. [25] Mon. Xav. II, 628. [26] Xavier himself, Father Teixeira, Father Valignano.

from the dead, and, in the case of seventeen of these, there was such clear and irrefutable testimony that no shadow of a doubt could rest upon them."[27]   Later the number of his resurrections from the dead, including those by his relics, rose to fifty-six.[28]

We come now to the "great miracle or prodigy" of the salt water made fresh.   In the second process four witnesses depose they have heard it; two "from witnesses worthy of belief," two from men who were on the ship. Two witnesses depose that they were in the ship when the miracle took place; one a Chinaman eighty-five years old, otherwise unknown, describes it in detail and another man, an Eurasian ninety-eight years old, otherwise unknown, says he also was present and describes it with some variation.[29]

A hundred and seventy-five years after the death of Xavier the Rector of the Jesuit College at Goa wrote to Rome that Father Bokoski, going to the island of Sanchoan to visit the tomb of St. Francis Xavier, passed through a canal sixty Chinese leagues long with both ends open to the sea.   On it there was a village inhabited by fifty gentile families.   The inhabitants told him the European priest had preached in their village.   His throat grew dry and he asked for a drink of water, but he was told there was nothing but salt water in the canal.   He asked for that and drank it.   "Since that very day the water of the canal for twenty leagues to the north of the village and twenty leagues to the south of it, has remained fresh, although the water for ten leagues from each end where the canal goes into the sea remains salt.   Father Bokoski drank the water and took two jugs with him to Canton, where everybody said it was as sweet as spring water.

[27] Mon. Xavier II, p. 806, Note.   [28] Astrain, I, 490.   [29] The learned Jesuit historian Sacchini writes of the "opinions of old men whose memory can be sensibly changed by so long a lapse of time."   Scripta I, 702.

This, my Father, is the miracle worthy of being known and published."[30]

There remains the miracle of the crab and the crucifix. There is only one witness to this who says he heard it from a certain Emanuel Joannes. He adds that it is public and notorious in India.

When the Jesuits were expelled from Portugal in 1760 a scholasticus of the Company made affidavit that he took from the chapel of their college in Coimbra a crucifix of wood and silver. On the back of the silver cross was inscribed that this was the crucifix which by "an extraordinary prodigy" the crab brought back to St. Francis Xavier. In Rome, six of his comrades in exile, members of the Company, signed with him an affidavit that this was the crucifix thus miraculously restored.[31] These two affidavits made on the coast of India in 1616 and in Rome in 1760 are the only testimony to the miracle of the crab and the crucifix.

There are miracles recorded in the Bible which many a modern Protestant believer in inerrant verbal inspiration could wish, if he frankly expressed his inmost feelings, were not there, the devils and the swine, the floating axe head,[32] death in the pot.[33] Nevertheless, acting on his general principle of the inerrant verbal inspiration of the scriptures, he accepts them without question or scruple. This ought to enable him to understand by the sympathetic imagination, the attitude of his Roman Catholic brother towards the grotesque prodigy of the crab and the crucifix, when it has been accepted in solemn consistory and confirmed by a papal bull.

The tendency to the increase of miracles with the lapse of time, so very marked in accounts of the life of Xavier, is also noticeable, though to a much slighter degree, in the accounts of the life of Ignatius. In the

[30] Mon. Xav. II, 785. [31] Mon. Xav. II, 728. (With a picture of the crucifix.)
[32] II K. VI 5. [33] II K. IV 38.

earliest sources of his life, the miraculous element (aside from visions, which are not necessarily "miracles") is not prominent. This is so evident that, as we have seen, Ribadeneira makes at the end of his two first Lives a long explanation of it.[34] At the age of eighty-two he wrote a third short popular Life and says to introduce it: "In the last chapter of my former life I treated briefly of miracles as if he had done none, or as if they were not necessary to prove his sainthood. I have decided now to set forth more fully, not all, but a part of the miracles God deigned to work by His servant. For, even in 1572, when I wrote his Life in Latin I knew some other miracles had been wrought by him. But I had not made myself so certain of them by investigation that I could persuade myself to publish them. Now they have been thoroughly established by proper witnesses in public investigations."[35] This different attitude of the friend of Ignatius at fifty-five and at eighty-two years of age, is a partial measure of the growth of the tendency to write of the Blessed Ignatius the wonder working saint rather than of Father Ignatius, the holy man. Before the middle of the seventeenth century that tendency was firmly established among the members of the Company. No such list of "great miracles or prodigies" as was cited of St. Francis Xavier has ever been assigned to St. Ignatius. But the century was not very old before more than one hundred and fifty attested miracles wrought by Ignatius or by his name, his picture or his relics were being cited. Most of them were miracles of healing and driving out of devils, though there were some of fires stopped, or men saved from storm at sea. There was one of a village saved from a pack of ravening wolves which descended on it from the hills.

This, of course, is not, in comparison with similar lists,

---

[34] He expressly says he does not imply that Ignatius wrought no miracles.
[35] Chap. XVIII cited Act. Sanct. 600 N. 944.

an extremely large catalogue of miracles. In 1387 Prince Peter of Luxemburg died. He had been created Bishop of Metz at fourteen years of age and a cardinal at sixteen, and he died before he was eighteen with the reputation of a saint. Two years later the celebrated Pierre d'Ailli advocated before the Pope the canonization of the young cardinal. He cited 2128 miracles, which lacks only 62 of making one every day for six years. Among them were 73 resurrections from the dead.[36]

For many of the miracles of Loyola the case from an examination of testimony on a purely historical basis is very much better than the exceedingly weak case made out in the printed documents for the "great miracles sometimes called prodigies" of Xavier. On the other hand for some of these miracles of Loyola cited in the seventeenth century the case is extremely weak.

An example of a weak case is the assertion that the Virgin Mary dictated the Spiritual Exercises to Ignatius. The first traceable origin of this is in a revelation to the Venerable Marina d'Escobar printed in 1615 in a life by Luis de la Puente. It was spread by a picture painted two years later by the order of the general of the Company, copies of which were found before long in almost all Jesuit houses. Father Astrain[37] shows that it is entirely unsupported by serious evidence.[38]

Some of these stories of later tradition suggest to the reader the hope, to say the least, that they came from pure legend. How possible it is that some of them might have been creations of legend is shown by the following opinion of one who knows the period well.

"Legend, whose testimony is always so insecure, was then (the 16th century) in Spain the most lying testimony ever seen in the world. . . . Under the shield of local tradition our histories, and above all our lives of

---

[36] Tschackert, 79. [37] 161 n. [38] Father Venturi dismisses it as unworthy of critical consideration.

saints, have been filled with the most improbable fables.
. . . That century was the century of false seals, false
chronicles, false prophecies, false visions . . . in short,
the source of a deluge of devout falsehoods which defend themselves with the shield of local tradition."[39]

Here is a specimen of what these local traditions did
to the memory of Ignatius. "One day in Manresa when
the pilgrim (Ignatius) was following the rocky road which
is called Sobreroca, doubtless coming back from the
church del Carmen, he heard the sharp cries of a little
girl bending over an old well, which is still to be seen.
A hen escaping from her care had just drowned itself and
a crowd of curious onlookers was laughing at the lamen-
tations of the poor little girl looking forward to paternal
punishment. The heart of Ignatius was touched. He
kneeled down and said a devout prayer: immediately the
water of the well rising to the margin brought back the
resuscitated hen which the saint, with a smile, gave back,
with his own hands, to the little girl." An inscription in
an oratory near the well records "Here Ignatius Loyola
wrought in 1522 his first miracle: the resurrection of a
drowned hen."[40]

The sickly sentimentality of the idea of Ignatius using
the God given power to break the awful bounds of life
and death for the resurrection of a hen in order to stop
the facile tears of a little girl afraid of being punished
by her father, is surely more fitted for what was classified
in the writer's youth as books for Sunday school libraries
infant class section, than for the inspiring biography of
a mighty warrior of God such as Ignatius was.

The following grotesque tale, recorded by an official
biographer of Ignatius in the middle of the eighteenth
century, was dated about 1615. The Lenten sermons at a
town in Burgundy were being preached by a member of

[39] Astrain, I, 159. [40] Clair Rib. 50.

a certain religious order. He was invited to dinner by Dr. Gillabodus, a man noted for his character and knowledge. "At table the guest was annoyed by hearing the holiness and merits of Ignatius exalted by his host and the unhappy man dared to say 'The miraculous power of the founder of the Jesuits reached its height in curing the toothache. He could not do more than that.' Such a remark made in profane envy by a man of such a respected profession and robe, gravely offended those at table with him and was received in melancholy silence. The thing happened near the middle of Lent and, that he might finish the series of sermons he had begun, God, for the sake of the people, deferred the punishment of the crime. But the day after Easter he was again invited by the same host and paid the penalty of his impious temerity, for when he held the cup in his hands to drink, suddenly he shuddered and cried aloud that his teeth were burst asunder and his mouth closing up. Then his jaws became fixed and he uttered no word, but terrified those looking on by a bellowing and dull roaring like a man in despair. After this he was rent and wrenched, raged and was shaken by such a powerful fury that five or six men could hardly hold him. Doctors were called, but in vain, for the disease, brought on by God, could not be driven out by man. Amid such agonies he lingered three days. He spoke eloquently to the people, warning them by his punishment to show due reverence to the blessed saints and thus made an end of living without giving by a single other word any sign of penitence or a good mind."[41]

In this horribly grotesque tale the punitive miracle seems to reach its climax and the reader exclaims with Virgil "Can such wrath dwell in celestial minds!"

[41] The chronicler hints by this last statement that he went to hell. Acta Sanctorum, 817.

It is probably true that the image of no great religious leader in history has been more distorted by his enemies than the image of Ignatius. But it is also true that few have had more need of the prayer: "Save me from my friends."

CHAPTER XXII

THE CHARACTER AND DEATH OF IGNATIUS

The life of Ignatius after his comrades assembled at Rome to found the Company was marked by no outward events. During eighteen years he left Rome or its suburbs only once, on a rapid mission to Naples and towards the end of his life he left the house or garden of the Company only on rare errands. Two things absorbed him; the relation of his soul to God and his work for his fellow men. His days bound together by an unbroken continuity of intercourse with God flowed along under the stars he loved in a majestic current, guided by his will to spend his strength in saving souls, until it passed quietly into the boundless sea of eternity. The pleasures and sorrows of ordinary men were not only absent from his life; long before his death they ceased to exist for him. It required no effort to abstain from them; he neither felt them nor thought about them. His will finally so far dominated all his natural reactions to the world around us that it made him far more than able to give up the pleasures of life. He became entirely indifferent to them. The desire for sleep, the appetite for food, bodily health or pain, ambition, the sense of beauty, his love of music, family affection, these were elements to be considered by the use of reason directing the training of habit, only in relation to the single purpose of glorifying God and saving the souls of his neighbours. This is what underlies his doctrine of indifference as set forth in the chapter on obedience: to bring the members of the Company through the road he had travelled in his own experience to the place where they wanted nothing whatever but to know the will of God; where they disliked nothing except what prevented them from doing the will of God. This is the origin and explanation of a trait in his final attitude which seems oriental and there is no need trying to trace, as has been attempted, direct oriental influence in his thinking and writing. (24)

No follower of Christ (leaving out those who became absorbed in saving their own souls and gave up trying to help their neighbours) ever led a life more completely one—more absolutely dominated by a single purpose; a purpose fed in its turn solely by the inner springs of religious experience. To analyse the character of Ignatius, who was to such an extraordinary degree an individual (in the sense of an indivisible entity) is to risk turning a great personality into a bundle of qualities, but the writer sees no other way of throwing light on the character of a man who led during the years of his full maturity so eventless a life.

The strength of his will finally destroyed all traits of his soul which were, or might become obstacles to its purpose and brought him to regard with calm confidence all external obstacles, however serious they might seem to other men. The chief source of this strength of will was his certain conviction that God had begun soon after his conversion to teach him as a boy is taught in school, had given him direct revelations of the mysteries of the faith, had led him to abandon his original plan of leading his comrades to Jerusalem, had revealed to him in a vision the name of the Company, had guided him in the details of writing the Constitutions and was now so close that he could "find Him" whenever needful.

This divine guidance did not seem to him anything peculiar to himself. On the contrary he said that anyone who abandoned his will to God might find a large measure of it. If he had ever heard of the idea which began to circulate more than two generations after his death that the Virgin Mary had dictated to him the Spiritual Exercises, he would have rejected it. What he did say was that God had taught him through his own experience how to write it. He thought God had helped him to decide rightly doubtful details of the Constitutions by the use of his reason, in hours when his soul had been freed by direct intercourse with God from all personal choice. When his friends wrote that the Spiritual Exercises were a gift of God, a teaching received from God—done by the great help of God—by the unction of the Holy Spirit, etc., they probably meant no more than Luther's pupil Mathesius meant when he wrote "This is one of the greatest miracles which our Lord has caused to be performed by Dr. Martin Luther that he gives us Germans a very beautiful version of the Bible in good intelligible German words." They would, like the modern Jesuit editor of the Spiritual Exercises, have rejected the suggestion that they wished to put the writings of Ignatius on the same plane of inspired authority with the scriptures.[1] Confident as he was in God's guidance, his confidence was of a sort which made him humbly and devoutly obedient to the Church and her supreme ruler. To one who knows him the suspicion of his early critics that he might be one of the *alumbrados* who felt that the voice of God in their soul set them above all other authority, is ridiculous. He refused all suggestions of union with other orders and thought the company most efficient when it worked apart from them, simply because it had its own work to do in its own way.[2]

Once when Lainez, in reply to a question from him about God's relation to the founders of other orders, said he believed the fundamental points of all their institutions were revealed to them of God and less important details left to their decision, Ignatius said "I think en-

[1] Mon. Ig. Series II, vol. 1, p. 38.   [2] Scripta, I, 439.

tirely as you do." [3] For his firm faith that God had guided and would always help him, never led Ignatius consciously or unconsciously to look on himself as a favorite of the Divine Ruler of the Universe.

That severe discipline which he held over himself until it became second nature and required no effort to maintain, was also applied to his subordinates. We have seen that the programme imposed on his colleges was less severe, and the treatment in other respects milder, than that which prevailed in a leading college of the University of Paris for years after his death. So it must be remembered that the severe discipline imposed on a Jesuit house by Loyola was, in at least two respects, less severe than that of many other monasteries which lived strictly by their rule: there were no ascetic practices, scourgings, extra fastings, etc., imposed, nor was there any rising for common nocturnal prayer. The bell that rang in a Jesuit house after seven hours' sleep was the first to break the silence of the night. [4]

But Ignatius' ideal was that of a strictly policed barracks with all free time suspended; for the warfare in which they fought was continuous. No one might leave the house or receive or send letters without the permission of his superior. [5] Every month everybody wrote all faults he had noted in any others to the head of the house. [6] If he noted any serious faults in the head of the house he told them to Ignatius, who never revealed the name of his informant. There was not much time for recreation in the house or college of Rome under the immediate supervision of Ignatius. But he believed in the recreation which ought to be given to the body. "If those at Modena," he writes, "had taken into account some proper bodily exercise, perhaps so many good young men would

[3] Rib. 530, second Life.　[4] Scripta I, 483.　[5] Letts. XII, 619.
[6] Scripta I, 484. This was also done at the College of Montaigu at Paris. Godet.

not have died."[7]   He seems, however, to have thought
that walking in the garden of some friend of the Company
once a week or "oftener if it can be done without missing
graver occupations" was proper bodily exercise.[8]

At Rome there was a suburban vineyard belonging to
the Company, where the scholars went twice a week for
recreation.[9]   At first in addition to "strolling and pleasant
talk" he seems to have allowed two games, "the *lusus
trudiculorum* in which, either on a table or on the ground,
globes are driven by a mallet through an iron circle," [10]
or "the game of round flat pieces of wood which are driven
in long courses upon tables under certain regulations."
This last was undoubtedly the ancestor of squails. Ignatius
had seen it played in Paris and there was evidently an
out of door form of it. He called it *piastrelle* and, outside
of singing and strolling about, it came to be the only
pastime permitted in the vineyard.[11]   Not long before his
death he sent word to a college where they were playing
at ball and at marbles, that he preferred to have nothing
played in any college except *piastrelle* in the open air
"which gave exercise to the arms and to almost the whole
body."[12]   Voluntary or impromptu sports were not welcomed; for Ignatius had no confidence in any life for the
Company which did not go by rule. Once young "Ribadeneira, Father Olave and others, got to throwing around
an orange and the man who muffed it must recite the
Angelic Salutation." Ignatius heard of it and gave them
a penance that others should not follow their example and
bring in some new game.[13]

The minute discipline extended even to table manners.[14]
This, together with his extreme care for cleanliness came
in the last analysis from the fact that Ignatius was a
Basque noble who had lived up to thirty among Spaniards

[7] Letts. IX, 121.   [8] Letts. VI, 312.   [9] Pol. IV, 13.   [10] Is this an ancestor of
croquet?   [11] Scripta, I, 240, 502.   [12] Letts. IX, 43, 120, VIII, 31.   [13] Scripta, I,
502.   [14] I, 487.

of high social rank. How necessary such training was is shown by the elementary character of some of the rules. They seem to have been imposed only by the force of public opinion, which held that certain things were "indecorous" or "rustic"; for example, it was thought "boorish" to eat with the mouth always open or to make a noise when drinking. But it may be assumed that Ignatius' shrewd common sense was at the bottom of this also. For no detail was too minute for his attention if it armed his Company better for the fight with sin. After his death when Jesuits began to play such influential parts in worldly society as tutors or confessors to young princes and nobles, it was no small advantage to the cause that, when dining in noble houses, they did not shock the tastes of their hosts. If some of the more ascetic orders characterized his care for such things as trivial or even as wicked worldliness, he replied that nothing was trivial or worldly which helped in teaching religion to men. He learned this practical lesson quite early in his service of God, when he returned to his old neatness about the care of his nails and hair at the time he found pupils in some families of social position at Manresa.[15]

So severe and minute a discipline as that of Loyola might be expected to produce occasionally hysterical outbreaks which probably astonished those concerned in them. An example of one of these has been preserved.

A short time before the death of Ignatius, four lay coadjutors got into a lark in the kitchen and threw water over each other. Ignatius imposed this penance: once every week for some time they were to eat at a table apart; Matteo in the same kitchen vessel from which he had thrown the water. "When the dinner is half over dirty water shall be thrown in his face and clean water in the faces of the others because the water they threw was not dirty. After dinner each must kiss the feet of the others.

[15] Astrain, 36 cited. Confessions, 48, 54.

Every Sunday they must eat in the stable with the mules, with the water thrown in their faces again." The two ringleaders were given a very severe admonition by Father Ignatius who told them they could "have his permission if they wished to leave the Company, just because of that foolish conduct, for he did not know what he could hope to make out of two persons ten and twelve years in it who could act so little to edification."[16]

Such cases, however, seem to have been rare, and the days in the model establishment of the Company which Ignatius formed at Rome, must have flowed on usually in a calm monotony of prayer and effort to grow better and do more in the service of man.

It is a great mistake to suppose, as some have, that Ignatius with all his virtues was an unlovable and unloved man. There is abundant testimony that, though stern, he was not harsh. Affection mingled with the reverence in which he was held. The whole Company felt as soldiers sometimes feel toward a just officer whose severity is plainly for the good of the service and whose discipline does not conceal his care of them and his sympathy for them. No one suspected Ignatius of personal ambition. Even if he had not twice tried to resign as general, no one would ever have questioned his entire devotion to the Company for which he was working himself to the verge of exhaustion. The simple sincerity of the man is his most outstanding trait and the end showed it strong in death.

This sincerity which led him to trample under foot every natural taste in the service of what he believed, is so apparent to anyone who studies his life, that it is difficult to understand how the opposite opinion could have found credence, even among those who disbelieve strongly in the truth, the institution, the ideal to which he was devoted. It may be fanciful, but the writer sus-

[16] Scripta, I, 577.

pects that a large share in producing this particular misunderstanding may be attributed to Jesuit art of the
seventeenth and eighteenth centuries. In some of the
series of engravings illustrating the life of Ignatius made
then and widely circulated, he is misrepresented with a
sickly sweetness of smile, an exaggerated elegance of at-
titudinizing gesture in accord with the taste of the age
when they were made, but utterly out of accord with the
character and life of him they try to portray. The pious
intentions of these artists do not change the fact that they
have produced caricatures. They show us an overcare-
fully posed figure in sacred tableaux vivants and not the
man Ignatius was. This attempt of the art of the eighteenth century to make the early heroes of the Jesuits
figures of elegance is very evident also in literature. A
modern writer thus admirably characterizes it.[17] "Father
Poussines, in an age (1666) when the simplicity and negligence of the style of the letters of the saint (Xavier)
would not have been found sufficiently pleasing, thought
himself obliged, for the honour of the saint and the welfare of souls, to translate him into Latin which was elegant.
God reward his holy intentions in heaven, but it is plain
that the honour of the saint and the welfare of souls demand today very different procedure."[18] Elsewhere he
protests against the evident effort to turn the hasty letters
of a hard-working missionary into the style of an address
before the French Academy.

The tenderness of Ignatius to the sick and his unre-
mitting care for the health of all his subordinates, made
evident to them that the severity of his discipline was quite
compatible with deep affection for them. This affectionate
care appears from the very beginning of his life at Rome
when there was very little money. The steward was required to report to him twice a day what the brother in
charge of the infirmary needed for his patients and the

[17] Father Cros, I, XLVI.   [18] Cros. XVLI.

money for that was the first thing taken out of the a.
on which the house lived. If money was wanting, lc
were drawn to see which of three blankets, those o.
Ignatius, of the financial agent, and of the steward, should
be pawned or sold.[19] Years later the doctor induced him
to rest and he was always very scrupulous about obeying
the doctor's orders, and seeing that everybody else did. So
he handed over his duties in the house to Nadal, but he still
kept for himself the oversight of the care of the sick.[20]
This oversight was a real oversight and not merely listening to reports. When young Ribadeneira had been bled
Ignatius sent some one three times during the night to
see that the bandages had not slipped or were not too
tight.[21] Whenever there was serious illness he was apt to
drop into the sickroom at night. Once when medicine
was to be taken at midnight, Ignatius coming in found
no one by the bed and learned from the sick man that
no medicine had been given. He ordered the careless
nurse to leave the house at once. The probationer went
out the doors but lingered in the vestibule because he
had not been ordered to leave that. When the righteous
wrath of Ignatius cooled, he forgave the offender who
became Rector of the Roman College.[22] When Father
Otelo was in danger of breaking down from nervous over-
strain, Ignatius had him sleep in the same room with him
and eat at his table, forbade him to offer prayers or to
study, took him out into the country and in three weeks
restored him to usefulness.[23]

It is exceedingly common for Ignatius in his letters to
advise the man to whom he is writing to look after his
health, or to ask him to watch over the health of some
one else. To one brother, who wished to abstain from
wine as a mortification to the flesh, he repeated the advice
of Paul to Timothy, replacing the "little" of the Apostle's

[19] Scripta, I, 363. [20] Scripta, 170, Memoriale. [21] Rib. Life, folio 192.
[22] Scripta, I, 167, Mem. [23] Scripta, I, 452.

ʒr to Timothy by the phrase "properly diluting it." [24]
ʒ kept a sharp eye on the novices, and, when he noticed
ʌat any one of them looked weak or pale, he ordered
him to sleep longer and omit some of the tasks of his fellows.[25] One of his novices remembered long after how
Ignatius had come to see him when he was unwell and
consoled him like a loving father. Once he brought a little box of sweets, saying, "Here, Oliver, is something sent
me by the wife of the Viceroy of Sicily. Eat it,"
and then with a smile, "It is by the doctor's orders." [26]
His care of the sick was so evident, so continuous, so manifestly the outcome of tender sympathy, in a man stern
to himself and stern to others, that it must have become
known through the entire company until all its members
came to believe "no mother has such care for her sons as
our blessed Father has for his sons—especially the weak
and sick." This was a right conclusion, for Ignatius said
many times to one of his intimates that "it was an admirable providence of God which had sent him so much
illness in order that he might learn to feel the anguish
of others." [27]

His especial concern for novices young in years or
young in the Christian life as it was set before the as-
pirants for the Company, was very noticeable. For the
discipline of Ignatius was no iron-clad system, applied
without discrimination to all. He tempered the wind to
the shorn lamb,[28] and he expected his subordinates to do
the same. For example, when a wall to the garden was
being built, Ignatius sent word to the minister of the
house that all inmates were to work on it for a certain
time every day, carrying stones, moving dirt, etc. Among
the novices was a certain young noble who was terribly
mortified by this, because the wall was along the street
and he could be seen working by his acquaintances. One

[24] Pol. III, 175. [25] Scripta, I, 258, Memoriale. [26] Scripta, 508. [27] Scripta, I, 368. [28] Scripta, I, 416, 420. Rib. Dicta et Facta.

day when Ignatius was watching the work, he saw by the face and manner of the young noble that he was very much tempted by the situation. "So our Father said quietly to the minister, 'Don't you see that young man is very much tempted? Why did you order him to do this work?' The minister answered, 'Because your orders were to call everybody to it without exception.' Then our Father said, 'Because I give such an order do you think that you, being minister of the house, are forbidden to use discretion?' And he called the novice and ordered him not to work because it was not a duty for him."[29]

When we remember the terrible humiliations to his pride as a noble Ignatius had inflicted on himself in the early days after his conversion, we see in this and similar incidents that experience had taught him not to destroy intelligence and sympathy and depend mechanically upon iron-clad discipline to train the souls of men. There was only one thing which he would never tolerate either in young or old, and that was persistent disobedience which struck at the very root of his ideal for the Company.

He was able thus to fit the rule to the man by his great knowledge of human nature about which his intimates are unanimous. They even said that Father Ignatius had to talk only once with a man to know him "from head to foot."[30] He was not of course infallible in his judgments of men: witness his mistakes in appointments noted on pages 233 and 261. Certainly he spared no pains to win the confidence and love of his young men that he might help their souls. A novice wished to withdraw from the house and would not say why. Ignatius suspected the reason was an unnecessary scruple over something in the past life of the youth, so he told the young man of the evil things he, Ignatius, had done before his own conversion. Thus encouraged the young man told why he thought himself unworthy to enter the com-

[29] Scripta, I, Rib. 410.   [30] Scripta, I, 253.

pany and Ignatius showed him it was "a very small thing before the mercy of God."[31]

This tact in handling novices and his patient kindness toward them show most plainly in the case of Nadal. Ignatius had tried to win him at Paris and failed. When some years later he applied at Rome for admission to the Company, Ignatius said "with this man we shall have trouble, because he is strongly inclined to melancholy as you can see by looking at his eyes. It is to be feared that, if God does not call him to the Company he may sink into melancholy and lose his mind entirely." We can trace from Nadal's diary the handling of this ticklish situation. "I was afflicted by melancholy and weak health. . . . Ignatius showed me the greatest kindness, often inviting me to eat at table with him. He came frequently to my room and often took me for a walk in the vineyard. . . . Fearing my melancholy he ordered a room to be found for me looking out on a pleasant garden." Ignatius ordered him to dig in the garden. In consequence Nadal began to have a good appetite. Fearing this was sinful he consulted Ignatius. "The Father asked 'Why do you want to eat?' I answered 'To live in order to do penance for my sins and to serve God.' 'Well,' he said placidly, smiling a little, 'All right. Eat, then,' and when I heard this every scruple was taken away.

"He told me not to fast and when I hesitated—saying others would be scandalized—he said if anyone was scandalized he would put him out. He even arranged for the Pope's Vicar to order me not to fast in Lent. He never would give me a penance and when I asked for one he said, 'Your penance is to free your mind from care.' "[32] Nadal's health was established and he became a very efficient member of the Company.

A few open sinners were sent away without mercy, but among the many he dismissed from the novitiate or

[31] Scripta, I, 193, Memoriale.　　[32] Nadal, Chronicon M. H. S. J. 16-23.

the lower ranks of the company because he decided they were not fitted for its service, those were rare who did not leave at peace with him and friendly to the institution. Among the training exercises was a pilgrimage and Ignatius' favourite method of dismissal was to order the man on pilgrimage with the quiet understanding that he was not to come back. He several times wrote that men were to be dismissed in such a way as to spare them any feeling of public disgrace.

To help him gain and keep the affection of his novices Ignatius used continuously one device of which many readers will probably disapprove; which is just the reason why it should be frankly told; though it does not seem to the writer very important. He seldom gave directly orders which a postulant for the Company might dislike, but always through a subordinate, who never revealed that the disagreeable orders came from Ignatius. On the contrary all orders which were pleasing to the men, Ignatius gave himself.[33] For instance, a certain Dr. Loarte, a Spaniard of noble family, a learned theologian and a distinguished preacher much given to prayer, came to Rome to join the Company. Ignatius believed that men of high position, great learning and marked ability, should be most strictly disciplined because, when well trained, they could be so extremely useful. He therefore ordered the minister of the house to give Loarte a very severe course of training in humiliation and self-mortification. He carried out so well these orders that the learned Doctor often "cried like a child," and then Ignatius was wont to treat him kindly and console him. The much tried Doctor had no idea that his severe discipline came from Ignatius and when he was asked by the minister himself what he thought of the two replied, "Father Ignatius is a fountain of oil and your Reverence a fountain of vinegar."[34]

Ignatius was so much master of his conduct and even

[33] Scripta, I, 196, Memoriale.   [34] Scripta, I, 299, Mem. ib. 482.

of his feelings that it is hard to be sure that he had among
his disciples those whom he especially loved; because he
undoubtedly felt it his duty to love all members of the
Company.   There are indications, however, besides the
letter already quoted, that his heart went out in especial
tenderness across the sea to Xavier.   It has already
been pointed out that the early fathers of the Company
were afraid of family affection as a possible obstacle to
that more perfect life to which they felt themselves called
and that they cited the sayings of Christ in support of
this fear.   They were also evidently afraid, in spite of their
affectionate language each toward the other, of a too
specialized personal affection for any brother; which might
perhaps step between them and that love for all the Company which was the perfected ideal.   This may possibly
throw some light on a feature of the conduct of Ignatius
during the last years of his life for which his puzzled intimates conjectured another explanation.   He often praised
his subordinates when they did well and unless it was
needful to reprehend them, always treated them with
consideration.   To this rule there were three marked exceptions, and they were the men who stood closest to him
in his daily work,—Nadal, the minister of the house, whom
he treated so harshly sometimes as to bring tears to his
eyes, Polanco, the secretary, who "for nine years was his
hands and feet," and to whom he "scarcely said a good
word," Lainez, whom he had picked for his successor,
but who got the same treatment.   Once when he was discussing something of importance with Lainez and the
latter insisted a little too much on his opinion, Ignatius
broke in, "All right, take the Company and govern it
yourself," in such a tone that poor Lainez did not say
another word.[35]   Lainez told Ribadeneira that during the
last year of the life of Ignatius he was sometimes so dis-
tressed by the harsh treatment of our Father that he used

[35] Scripta, I, 202, Mem.

to pray to God to let him know what he had done against the Company "that this saint treats me in this way."[36]

At his orders Polanco wrote once a very harsh letter to Lainez and poor Polanco begs Lainez to remember that he is only the pen of Father Ignatius. The letter recites certain things Lainez has done which Ignatius considers contrary to obedience of the judgment.[37] But it was not his policy to repress in fact the expression of their judgment by trusted subordinates and the things he recites hardly seem to merit this stinging rebuke. Father Ignatius "has ordered me to write to tell your Reverence to attend to his office, because if he fills that as he ought he will do no small task, and not to tire himself by expressing his opinion about what concerns the General, because he does not need advice from your Reverence except when he asks it and less now than before your Reverence took his present office; because in the administration of it your Reverence has not gained with him much credit in matters of government."[38] He came to treat all the first fathers in this peremptory fashion.[39] But they loved him none the less and after his death concluded that he thought this harshness good for their character: milk for babes but strong meat for men.[40] It seems that Ignatius hardly would have made such a mistake in a matter of human nature. Doubtless there was in it an element of the ragged nerves of a man nearly worn out by long years of intense emotion and incessant overwork who felt instinctively he could let himself go a little with those who knew him intimately. But perhaps there was more than this. We have seen in the case of the weak brother Simon Rodriguez (page 236) that deep down in his heart there was (half hidden perhaps from himself) a soft spot for his old comrades. This harshness of his later years towards

[36] Scripta, I, 455, De Ratione Gubernandi. [37] See page 227. [38] Letts. IV, 498. [39] Scripta, I, 202—Mem. 455. [40] Scripta, I, 203, 455.

men in whom he had perfect confidence may have been self defense against a heart that feared its own tenderness because his will was bent to keep faithful, even in the affections, to a superhuman ideal that would not give up to his old comrades what God wished given to all the Company.

So he was, toward the end of his life, harsh in words toward his old friends. But, though he was not graceful in his use of language, his sincerity sometimes found beautiful healing phrases, as when his nephew, Father Araoz, was hurt by something in a former letter and Ignatius wrote: "I say only this—if I doubted your fidelity I know no man in whom I could trust—of this no more." [41]

It is the fashion nowadays to ask about every man, Had he a sense of humour? and to rank him low in the scale when the answer is No. A sense of humour is a pleasant thing and we ordinary men become even more uninteresting when we lack it. But many great men have not possessed it. A volume entitled the Wit of the Apostle Paul would be without leaves and no one has yet attempted to collect the humorous sayings of Augustine. So, in spite of the prevailing fashion, it would not be an absolute condemnation of him if Ignatius Loyola had been without a sense of humour. But as a matter of fact, we may judge that he had a sense of humour from the traces of it which have survived in spite of the attitude of the men from whom we have our knowledge of him.

Long before his death Ignatius was regarded not only with love but with reverence. His disciples thought of him while still alive in the character given by the Church after his death, a saint—an intercessor with God for human sins—a mediator of divine grace and power to men, whose relics would be able to work miracles for those who had faith. For instance, when Ignatius had an aching tooth pulled, Nadal secretly tried to keep the tooth, but

[41] Letts. VII, 273.

Ignatius, noticing this, ordered him to throw it away, "which he did so seriously that he was never able to find it again no matter how hard he looked for it."[42] What would have happened to the tooth may be inferred from the following paragraph from a "Chronicle of the Company on the Lower Rhine," at the end of the year 1553, shortly before the death of Ignatius. "Among these troubles Father Kessel and his associates were comforted in the course of that same year by a robe brought from Rome which Ignatius, wearing it, had blessed by long contact. Bernard Oliver, coming from Italy in the month of November, rendered the college happy by this great gift, and the joy which this present gave can not be told in words. Everybody wished to venerate this relic of Ignatius with a pious kiss and take it in his hands to examine it carefully. In order to satisfy the wishes of the brethren Father Kessel permitted that there should fall to the lot of each one a fragment of a small piece of cloth torn from one of the sleeves. . . . The robe is now kept in the altar of the blessed Father, wrapped in red silk and enclosed in a silver box, the gift of a noble lady." [43]

Companions who took such an attitude might easily come to feel that humour was out of place in the talk of a man whose relics they were already beginning to treat with veneration. They were apt not to see it, to forget it is as unimportant or even perhaps to delete it from the record as unedifying. Of course such an attitude was not required by anything in the teaching of the Church. Sir Thomas More, who died as a martyr the year Ignatius finished his studies at Paris, was famed for a humour which did not desert him even as he was laying his head on the block, and St. Philip Neri, canonized by the same papal bull which definitely placed his friend Ignatius among the saints, was noted for his wit.

[42] Nadal, Acta Quaedam, Scripta, I, 472. [43] Reiffenberg, Bk. II, XXXIII, p. 45.

But after all such an attitude was natural enough to men who thought themselves always at death grips with the devil for their own souls and the souls of their neighbours. We know at least one instance to confirm this probable conjecture.

Not long after his election as general, Ignatius wrote to a friend of the Company in Spain "M. Doime, say to my brother, the Friar Barbaran, that, as he says all of *ours* in Spain from Perpignan to Seville ought to be burnt, I say and desire that he and all his friends and acquaintances, not only those between Perpignan and Seville but throughout the whole world, should be set on fire of the Holy Ghost. So that all of them, arriving at great perfection, may be much marked in the glory of His Divine Majesty. Also say to him that our affairs are now being discussed before the Governor of Rome and the Vicar of His Holiness who are about to give sentence in the case and if he has anything against *ours*, that I invite him to make deposition and prove it before those judges, because I should be more content if I owe anything to the law to pay it myself, so that I alone should suffer and all those who are to be found between Perpignan and Seville should not have to be burnt." Twenty-five years after this was written in Spanish, Ribadeneira printed in his first Life of Ignatius a Latin translation which makes this letter merely solemn and rhetorical and leaves out every trace of its gentle irony.[44]

So far as we can judge from the specimens we have of it, the humour of Ignatius was like some dry, pale, very delicately flavoured wine which does not keep well nor bear transportation. For example when one of his lieutenants reported from Bologna that he had closed the door of the house there against a certain priest Ignatius wrote "You did well to bar the door against him and if

[44] Letts. I, 408, Rib. First Life.

you barred it with one bolt do it with two."[45]   To Dr.
Loarte, who by his orders had been put through such
a trying test as a novice, Ignatius wrote soon after he
had been sent to Genoa, "We have not heard from you
here except from Gonzales who met you on the journey
and we would gladly know in what condition the ham-
pers you wanted sent arrived.   Pay for the trifling care
we took over that matter by writing to your friends
here of your journey, your health and your progress in
the use of Italian."   And then Ignatius adds slyly, "I do
not believe you suffered too much from the sun because
you had when you went away a quite sufficient provision
of cappelli"—literally "hats," but a slang phrase meaning a hard rebuke.[46]

It was in the same tone that he said to distinguished
visitors to the house "If your Excellency wishes to do
penance stay to dinner with us."[47]

A novice who was offended when Ignatius said to him
once, "If you do not wish to be obedient you are not fit
to be a member of the Company," insisted on leaving because our Father had said he was not fit for the Company.   When after arguments which lasted a good part
of the night, the lad was brought to a better frame of
mind, Ignatius asked him to name his own penance (a
thing he often did with penitents).   The lad replied,
"Whatever you think best."   "Very well," said Ignatius,
"Your penance is not to be tempted any more.   I'll do
penance for you every time I have one of my pains in
the stomach." [48]

Camara, in his Boswellian notes, records this, marking
it simply as a proof of Ignatius' great love for his brethren.
"He took the greatest pleasure in hearing all the details of
the life of the brethren and made me read letters, espe-

---

[45] Letts. II, 488.   [46] Letts. IX, 633.   Crusca, VIII, dare un cappello—objugare
o increpare.   [47] Scripta, I, 246, Memoriale.   [48] Scripta, I, 295.

cially from India, two or three times and wanted to know what they ate, how they slept, etc., and once he broke out, 'Oh, I should like to know how many fleas bite my fathers at night.' "[49]

The author of the first printed Life of Ignatius devotes most of the last book ⋅of it to discussing under fourteen heads his characteristics. The suggestion that he should add a chapter on his humour would probably have seemed to him almost profane. His other contemporary biographer who worked with him for many years, has recorded only one joke which is in the same tone of pleasant irony. A member of the Company was going on a short journey with two laymen and they all came to say good-bye to Ignatius. He remarked as they left, "Be sure you make saints of both of them."[50] These anecdotes, which have been preserved not for the wit but for something else in them, seem like small fragments; but they were hardly the only ones which might have been recorded and they indicate that through the talk of Ignatius there ran sometimes a vein of delicate humour,—almost shy as if he were a little afraid of it himself.

Although his intimates seem to have failed to see or to have forgotten, the humour of Ignatius, their memories of him were not stern. We know that Nadal, one of the faithful ones closest to him at the end of his life, was sometimes moved to tears by the "terrible rebukes" of his beloved master, but he wrote: "Everybody in the room of Ignatius was always most joyful and smiling."[51] For, pleasureless as the life of Ignatius seems to most of us, to him, in spite of the monotony of heavy labour broken by recurrent weariness and pain, it was filled with joy. The only self denial which now cost him effort was his duty to obey the doctors who warned him that he must restrict the happy tears, the nervous exaltation, of his intercourse with God in prayer. But this was not what

[49] Scripta, I, 196, Mem.   [50] Pol. I, 290.   [51] Scripta, I, 202, 454, 471.

George Eliot aptly called "other-worldliness"—the sense
that it was a good bargain to trade earthly joys for
heavenly. After all the master motive of his life was
not hope of the next world; it was what he could do in this.
We have this conversation from Lainez himself. Ignatius
said, "Tell me, Lainez, what would you do if God said
to you 'If you wish to die on the instant I will set you
free from the prison of the body and give you eternal
glory. . . .'" And if you knew that by staying longer
in this world you could render more service to God, which
would you choose?" Lainez answered, " 'For my part,
my Father, I confess I would choose to go immediately to
the enjoyment of God and I would assure my salvation
which is a thing of too great importance to be given up.'
'Well,' answered Father Ignatius, 'certainly I would not
make such a choice. If I thought I could render the
smallest service to Our Lord, I would pray Him to leave
me in this world so long as my task was not finished.' "[52]

This inner joyfulness in communion with God, this sense
of contentment in God's service, which made all burdens
light to him, showed in his face. Oliver Manareus, whom
Ignatius made a rector of the Roman College, told the
judge in one of the processes for canonization that he remembered how the face of Ignatius had a certain joy and
good will almost divine, so lighted up was it by heavenly
brilliance.[53] Thirty years after the death of Ignatius,
Alexander Petronius, one of his physicians, "at the urgent
request of the reverend fathers of the Company of Jesus"
took oath before a notary to an affidavit to the following
effect. He was ill and his friend Ignatius came to see him.
The servants admitted the well known visitor who went
straight to the room of the doctor, who was sleeping.
So, treading softly, Ignatius withdrew from the room.
"The doctor awaking called out suddenly to his wife:

---

[52] Father Clair's trans. of Rib. Life, pg. 410. [53] Act. Sanct. 597 b.

'Felicitas, what is this new splendor which fills my room with so great a light?' She responded in all simplicity that the windows were closed and that Ignatius had been there. By which visitation the deponent was wonderfully rejoiced and soon after got entirely well, and from that day looked up to Father Ignatius more and more as a being higher than a mere mortal man."[54] It is, of course, entirely in accord with what has happened in similar cases, that this glowing face of Ignatius should not remain entirely in the shape of a tender memory but finally take a form usable as evidence in a court of canon law; an affidavit that the light of Ignatius' countenance once continued to light a room like a lamp for a man who did not know Ignatius had been there. But perhaps some readers may think it more illuminating for the character of Ignatius to know simply that his friends recollected that his face often shone with joy because his heart was radiant with the love of God and man.

Some years before his death, his friends thought him ready for heaven and he had many warnings that he might not be long for earth. His correspondence shows that in fifteen years he was ill fifteen times; frequently many weeks in bed, often in a condition to cause anxiety.[55] But his friends and the doctors had seen him rally so often from pain and weakness when some sudden difficulty arose in which he was needed, that, as often in the case of men of feeble health and great will power, they came to look rather calmly on his periods of illness. When therefore, he was intermittently ill for the first six months of his sixty-sixth year, the doctors were not discouraged. There were many sick in the house and Ignatius had told the house doctor to devote himself to them. But Dr. Petronius, who was a sort of visiting physician, came every day to see him. On the 31st of July, 1556, at eight in the evening, Ignatius, after sending out the nurse, told Polanco

[54] Act. Sanct. 597 E.   [55] Boehmer has collected the allusions. 270.

that death was near and bade him let the Pope know and
"humbly beg the benediction of His Holiness upon him and
Lainez, who was gravely ill; (25) and if God took them
to heaven they would pray there for His Holiness as they
did every day here,' I replied 'The doctors do not think
there is danger in the illness of your Reverence and I hope
God will keep you many years for His service here. Do
you feel so very badly?' He said to me, 'I am in such a
state that there is nothing left for me except to die.' " Polanco continued to express hope and asked if it would not
do to go to the Pope the next day, because he wanted that
night to finish letters for the courier to Spain via Genoa,
who left in the morning. "He said to me, 'I should like
it better today than tomorrow, the sooner the better. I
should like it, but do what you think best. I leave it freely
in your hands.' " Polanco a little later asked Dr. Petronius if he thought Ignatius was in danger and whether
he had better tell the Pope he was. The doctor examined him and said he could see no sign of immediate
danger, but he would come tomorrow and speak definitely.
That evening Polanco and Father Madrid supped with
Ignatius, who ate with what was, for him, a good appetite,
and Polanco went back to his writing. The nurse of
Ignatius said he was restless during the night and called
him frequently, but about midnight lay quiet, occasionally
murmuring "O! God!" The nurse then went down to the
kitchen to cook two eggs which the doctor had ordered,
leaving Father Madrid to watch. When he came back
in a few minutes Ignatius was dying. Polanco started at
once for the Vatican. The nurse went to find one of the
fathers to give extreme unction, but when he returned to
say he could not find him, Ignatius was dead.[56]

So died the creator of the Company of Jesus. Few
great religious leaders of his own or for many succeeding

[56] Pol. VI, 37. Polanco's letter written 6 days later. Examination of the
nurse. Act. Sanct. pages 520-523.

generations would willingly have turned his back on the world thus in silence, with no last solemn exhortation to his followers.   But Ignatius had already taught his disciples all he had learned from God.   Twice already he had tried to put the burden of leadership from his enfeebled shoulders.   Death had long seemed to him all in the day's work for God and its approach a joyful thing. Among people prone to make of every deathbed a scene as dramatic as possible, where friends watched a spectacular entry into heaven, he chose to say farewell to life quietly.   This seems like the ruling passion—strong in death—the last expression of that simplicity, that humility, that sincerity, that self-forgetfulness of his life which prompts this question: "Who of all those who have confessed themselves followers of Christ, has been more faithful than Ignatius Loyola to the ideal which seemed to him true?"

NOTES

(1) There is a story widely accepted in the seventeenth century that Ignatius' mother went to the stable to give birth to her expected son in order that he might begin life as Christ did. The story seems to have had its origin in a picture painted for a Jesuit house in Antwerp some fifty years after Loyola's death. It is rejected by the best modern biographers as lacking any foundation in the testimony of those who might know the facts. It is worthy of notice only because it is a good example of the rapid growth of legend about Ignatius Loyola as soon as the men who knew him had died or grown old. Page 16.

(2) The idea that Ignatius' words divide his youth into two parts appears in Henao, whose work was approved in 1687. His earliest source is 1599. It is therefore a product of the uncritical, edifying and apologetic writing on Ignatius, of the seventeenth century. Fito in Boletin 17, p. 506, quotes in a note the opening sentence of the Confessions of Ignatius from the Latin version, "Ad annum usque vigesimum sextum fuit mundi vanitatibus deditus (mox) praecipue vero armorum exercitio delectabatur magno et inani desiderio ductus honoris comparandi," and translates it into Spanish with this sense: "Disillusioned about the hopes and vanities of the court and of its strife and tourneys, he gave his affections more to the professional exercise of arms or in following the military career extremely desirous of gaining honor and fame." The distorting gloss in the words *court-tourney, professional-military career,* is too evident to need demonstration. Astrain, p. 6, n., says this may appear "a somewhat gratuitous" explication of the text, but is inclined to accept it. Boehmer says "the unprejudiced reader" will neglect this gloss. Susta says this attempt "to divide his youth before conversion into two periods, one wild and careless, the other given to serious study of the profession of arms, can never be brought into accord with the first two sentences of the Confessions." p. 93-94. This last remark seems plainly true. Page 18.

(3) A note on the margin we do not know from whom, says, "It had 300 pages in quarto all written." This book, in whose recollection Ignatius took such evident pleasure, is lost. It was doubtless lost when he dictated this account of it. None of his friends know anything of it except what he told them. Page 32.

(4) Three hundred years earlier the sainted King Louis IX of France had similar sentiments toward Jews who called in question the virginity of Mary the mother of Christ. He told Joinville that once a conference between Jews and clergymen was assembled at the monastery of Cluny. There was at the monastery a poor crippled chevalier who was being lodged and fed by the abbot. He asked one of the Jews if he believed in the virgin birth. When the Jew confessed his disbelief, the chevalier swung one of his crutches and knocked him down. "I tell you," added the pious King, "that no one unless

359

he is a very learned clerk ought to enter into dispute with them. A layman when he hears Christian doctrine evil spoken of should defend it only with the sword, plunging it to the hilt in the infidel's body." Page 35.

(5) It seems strange that Ignatius did not here recall or allude to the vision of Peter which removed his scruples about eating meat that was "unclean." Ignatius was well read in the scriptures. Quotations are to be found in his letters from all the books of the New Testament except Titus and Jude, but they are mainly in his more formal letters like that on Obedience, etc. In his ordinary letters they are rare. He does not naturally quote. We know that for years he read a chapter of the Imitation of Christ every day and together with the New Testament, it lay always on the table in his room. So far as the writer has noted in the entire range of the writings of Ignatius there is no formal quotation from the Imitation. And, although some may have been overlooked, they must be infrequent. Page 42.

(6) One partial exception to this observation should be noted here. In 1546 Father Franciscus Strada preached in a Spanish city. "When they thought the sermon was finished, Strada asked for a crucifix and, when he showed it to the people, adding some words to arouse compassion, so great an outburst of weeping arose from the whole audience, both men and women, that, for a quarter of an hour, as if there were in all only one will and feeling, the whole church was filled with sighs and groans and laments, so that those who were present said they had never seen anything like it and it seemed as if the souls of many wished to leave their bodies because of this anguish." Pol. I, 193.

(7) Astrain and Venturi disagree with Boehmer about this highly improbable trait of kneeling at the feet of Ignatius. Astrain refers in a footnote to Ribadeneira for "this curious episode." Venturi relegates the whole matter to a short footnote and calls "gratuitous" Boehmer's judgment that the image of the principal of the largest college at the University of Paris kneeling in tears at the feet of a student who had disobeyed orders, is the fabrication of college gossip years later. But neither of these authors tell the story. Now that it is told plainly the reader can judge for himself how probable the weeping and kneeling of Dr. Gouvea is. Page 87.

(8) Fouqueray's comment on this is astonishing. Without giving any grounds he accuses de Thou of bad faith because he says, "Lainez se repandit en injures contre les Protestants," and then admits that Lainez did just that by adding: "The truth is the orator had cited the Holy Scripture, branding in advance the heretics by the name of snakes, foxes, wolves in sheep's clothing, to warn us against their lies." As if epithets were any less injurious because they had been used in Scripture! Fouqueray is ignorant of the ms. cited by Bouillé. The ms. of Lainez' speech he prints in his appendix is just such a redaction as a man who felt he had been a little too vehement in form, would make. Page 92.

The writer's judgment on this episode is sustained by Rocquain, p. 21. "Lainez s'y était signalé (at Poissy) par les emportements de son orthodoxie, qualifiant des noms les plus injurieux Théodore de Bèze et ses compagnons."

(9) It seems that both Astrain (page 79) and Venturi (page 69) have been unconsciously affected in their account of the content of this vow by the idea of the triple monastic vow. They say it was a vow of poverty, chastity, pilgrimage to Jerusalem. Ignatius was not asking these pious students to found an order nor was he looking forward to founding an order. Venturi and Boehmer agree in this, Astrain dissents; but there is abundance of direct proof to show that he is mistaken. This vow of Montmartre was not modeled

after the monastic vow and it was not triple. None of the early witnesses, neither Lefèvre, nor Lainez, mention a vow of chastity; neither does Riba-deneira (edition of 1572) nor Polanco, the first biographers, who must have talked with many of those present. Of course if they were to become priests it was implied. Page 94.

(10) I cannot find in either Astrain p. 97 or Venturi 294 any citation from a primary source to support their assumption that the five capitoli were formu-lated in writing by Ignatius. It seems preferable therefore to adopt the attitude of Boehmer p. 248 which assumes nothing. He says, "After the formula was successfully reduced to writing, etc." Whoever wrote it the capitoli must have been approved by the poor pilgrim priests and Ignatius must have been entirely in accord with them. Page 136.

(11) Many members of the older monastic orders had for centuries been appointed to bishoprics and several members of the Company were urged to accept ecclesiastical dignities. Ignatius was extremely opposed to it and thought it a great menace to the Company. When the Emperor Ferdinand wanted to make Jay a bishop, Ignatius had a private interview with the Pope to beg him not to command it. He gave five reasons why it should not be done. The Pope listened graciously but was not convinced. Ignatius left no stone unturned, visiting almost all the cardinals to get their influence in preventing the appointment. When the Emperor, whom the Pope did not like to refuse, wrote to bid his ambassador not to press the matter any more, the Roman house said masses and sang the Te Deum Laudamus (Letts. I 45-460). Later Ignatius made every effort to prevent Borgia from being appointed a cardinal by the irresistible command of the Pope (Pol. II, 425). Page 155.

(12) It is possible that Father Borgia may have read More's Utopia. "They the Utopians do not so much as know dice or any such foolish or mischievous game. They have however two sorts of games. . . . The other game resembles a battle between the virtues and the vices in which the enmity in the vices among themselves and their agreement against virtue is not unpleasantly represented; together with the special oppositions between the particular virtues and vices; as also the methods by which vice openly assaults or secretly undermines virtue; and virtue on the other hand resists it. Book II, Section 4. Page 190.

(13) This attitude was reciprocated. A Franciscan writer of the early eighteenth century claims that the real reason for the extraordinary success of the Company was that Ignatius had gained his perfection and holiness from the third order of Franciscans whose habit he had worn and whose vow he had taken. (Act. Sanct. p. 427, E.) The official life of Ignatius com-ments on this extraordinary statement truly enough, but with rather amusing scorn, "I am sorry for the credulity of these good men who are caught by so crass an error and pay attention to a pure unadulterated fable." Page 196.

(14) John Ricasoli, a noble Florentine fifteen years old had never been out of Florence except to neighbouring villas. He wished to join the Company of Jesus in whose college he was a student. Knowing that he could not obtain the consent of his father and mother, he left the city and made his way to Rome, in spite of the fact that the Duke, moved by the complaints of the mother, sent mounted messengers on the roads towards Genoa and Rome to find him and bring him back. At the request of Ignatius the Pope had appointed three cardinals to hear such cases and they decided that the boy's vocation was of God and he must be allowed to become a novice of the Company (Pol. IV, 18, 164, 167, 168, 169). His uncle the bishop of Cortona on his return from an

embassy to England said merely "His mother has other sons" (Pol. IV, 18, 164, 167, 168, 169). Page 205.

(15) The name Jesuits was also not in very high repute in some places. There was a small order of Jesuates which had been founded in the 14th century. It had become a lay order whose most conspicuous work was distilling liquors for medical use. Hence they were nicknamed, in some parts of Italy, by an irreverent pun "Fathers of the water of life" (Acqua Vitae) (Acta Sanct. July Vol. VII, p. 259). The name had also been used at Louvain by a knot of priests and beguines whose secret morals were not on the high level of their professions of Christian zeal. Page 206.

(16) The charge was brought against the later Jesuits of teaching that the end justifies any means. This book is not concerned with the Jesuits after the death of Ignatius. As far as Ignatius is concerned I agree with Mr. Sedgwick that there is nothing whatever in his words or actions to suggest that he ever taught or held any such doctrine. Page 230.

(17) Eight years after the death of Ignatius, General Lainez defined three classes of educational establishments requiring respectively foundations for a staff of twenty, fifty and seventy members of the Company. Before the end of the sixteenth century General Acquaviva raised the minimum of each of the lower grades of colleges to fifty and eighty and refused to take charge of any university with a staff of less than one hundred and twenty (Hughes 59).

(18) Polanco and Ribadeneira give a different version of this incident which they transfer to Barcelona. They say that Ignatius began to read this book, "but finding that it chilled his devotion to God and sensibly diminished the ardour of his devotion, he put the book from him and never wanted to read any of the works of that author." (Rib. f. 29, first ed. Pol. I, 33.) Venturi accepts this version of the incident but evidently only because he has overlooked the other, for he calls the Memoriale "a precious supplement to the Confessions" and Camara "truly worthy by the Confessions and the Memoriale to hold the first place among the primary sources of our knowledge of Ignatius." (Venturi II, XVII, XVIII.) Page 251.

(19) The same experience was attributed to St. Francis Xavier. After St. Francis' death the vicar of the church of St. Thomas at Meliapour wrote that Father Francis had spent three or four months in his house. Father Francis was accustomed to go out nearly every night to pray and flagellate himself at the shrine of St. Thomas. "I said to him one day: 'Father Francis, don't go to that place, it is a nest of devils. They will beat you.' He laughed but nevertheless he took with him a young native who lived with him" and the boy slept near the door of the shrine, while his master prayed. "One night the lad was wakened to hear the cry many times repeated, 'Our Lady will you not help me?' And he heard the sound of blows without knowing who struck them." The next morning Father Francis did not come to morning prayers and the vicar found him in bed because he was not feeling very well. When the vicar heard the story of the lad he repeated it to Father Francis, adding "Didn't I tell you not to go at night to St. Thomas' shrine." He smiled. He was ill two days without saying anything to the vicar about this experience "only when we got up from the table I said to him, by way of a joke, repeating his own words 'My Lady, will you not help me' and he blushed and smiled and by his very silence supported my conjecture as to what had happened." The great similarity of this story and the one told by the disciples of Ignatius about their master is evident. (Cros. II, etc., pg. 308, Comp. Mon. Xav. II, 800.) Both might have been flagellating themselves and unwilling to talk

about it. Page 290.

(20) Increase Mather gives an account of somewhat similar things occurring in the house of William Morse at Newberry in 1679. A similar story of long continued disturbances in the house of a Mr. Mompesson is vouched for by the Reverend Joseph Glanville a chaplain of Charles II. who wrote frequently in defense of the reality of witchcraft. His chief writings on this subject were collected in "Sadducismus Triumphatus or A Full and Plain Evidence Concerning Witches and Apparitions." (4th Edition, London, 1726.) Page 293.

(21) He has already expressed the opinion that the true Ignatius has been found again by some of his modern biographers both Catholic and Protestant, notably by Astrain, Venturi, and Boehmer. Page 297.

(22) This incident is dated 1541. It first appears in the second life by Ribadeneira published in 1586, and he says: "I knew the boy before and after the devil was driven out of him." Sometimes when his fits took him eight or ten men could hardly hold him down. Although he was an ignorant lad and knew only his own language, yet during his fits he spoke correctly in various languages. At first his face swelled. When the priest marked it with the sign of the cross, the tumor went to some other part of the body whence it could again be driven elsewhere by the sign of the cross. When the boy, "Whom I several times saw," was told that Ignatius was away but would soon come back and cure him, the devil in him called out "Don't talk to me of Ignatius for I consider him my greatest enemy." "When Ignatius got back and heard from us what had happened, he sent for the lad and talked with him entirely alone. What he said or did I never found out, but the lad was freed from the tyranny of the demon. He became a Camaldulensian Eremite by the name of Father Basil." (Not in 1st life. Rib. 585.) Page 318.

(23) This seems somewhat puzzling for, in regard to five of the six miracles cited to the Pope, any historian would say that the testimony to the facts was far inferior to that accessible for the nine included in Ribadeneira's list, which was not used in the final plea for sainthood. Four of Ribadeneira's list came from the Confessions of Ignatius, two from Lainez, his close helper who wrote the first memorabilia of him, one from a patron of his youth and the other two are related of his own knowledge by Ribadeneiro who lived for years in the house with him. The ante mortem miracles pleaded before the Pope are not equally well vouched for by the intimates of Ignatius, with a single exception,—the freeing of the College of Loreto from demons told on page 291. Page 322.

(24) H. Hüller has attempted to show a Mussulman influence in the Spiritual Exercises. His method is the familiar one of asking leading questions about things that might have happened, without suggesting the smallest reason to believe they did happen, and subsequently assuming those suggested opinions as if the questions had been answered authoritatively in the affirmative, e. g. pages 42-76, 44-225-250-251. The whole hypothesis is superfluous and the book contains no direct contemporary evidence which even suggests that Ignatius "drew inspiration from the works of Islam and the practices of its religious orders." Page 336.

(25) It may be conjectured that one reason for this was precisely the fact that the Pope had shown himself unfriendly toward the Company. He was the old opponent of Ignatius, Cardinal Caraffa. Ignatius was smitten with dismay when he heard of his election. (Scripta, I, 198 Memoriale ib 389.) When the Pope broke with Spain he ordered the Governor of Rome to search publicly the house of the Company for arms. (Cited, Boehmer 294, note 3.)

To this insult he added injury for he suspended the allowance to the German College made by his predecessors and most of the cardinals cut off their subscriptions. (Pol. VI 15.) It came to the ears of the Company that he was threatening to investigate them and saying disagreeable things about their relation to Ignatius. (Nadal ctd. Boehmer 294. Ephemerides 1557.) It may be suspected that Ignatius wished to set an example of obedience and devotion to his followers—to make one last sacrifice of his pride and to teach his disciples that the blessing of the Vicar of Christ, whether he was a friendly patron of the Company or not, must always be sought by its members. Page 357.

LIST OF BOOKS CITED

The primary sources of the life of Loyola are discussed by Venturi, Vol. II, Chap. I. He has also printed new documents in his first and second volume and given a list of two hundred and thirty four titles of books cited. Astrain, Vol. I, has a Bibliographical Introduction and a list of eighty four works cited. Boehmer 308-340 has an excellent discussion of the primary sources. The following list of ninety-two works does not comprise all those consulted, but only those cited by the writer. Some of these have been difficult to procure. One was located after trying in vain fifteen institutions, by the sixteenth letter. To Mr. Young, the Reference Librarian of Princeton University, the writer's best thanks are due for his tireless efforts in finding books. He is grateful for the loan of books to the librarians of Boston College, The Catholic University of America, The Library of Congress, Cornell University, Harvard University, Princeton Theological Seminary, Union Theological Seminary, and Woodstock College.

R. Academia de la Historia. Boletin. Madrid.
Acta Sanctorum. Julii. Tomus VII. 1731. Edition 1868.
Albèri, Eugenio. Cited Relazioni.
    Le Relazioni degli Ambasciatori Veneti al Senato. Firenze 1839-63.
Altamira y Crevea, Rafael.
    Historia de España y de la civilización Española. Barcelona 1900.
Amadis de Gaul.
    Biblioteca de Autores Españoles. t. 40.
Astrain, P. Antonio.
    Historia de la Compañia de Jesús en la Asistencia de España. Tomo I, San Ignacio de Loyola. Madrid 1912.
Bailey, N. (Translator.)
    The Colloquies of Desiderius Erasmus. London 1900.
Bartoli, Daniele (1608-1685).
    Histoire de Saint Ignace de Loyola. Paris 1844.
Begbie, Harold.
    More Twice Born Men. New York 1923.
Bobadilla, Nicolaus Alphonsus de.
    Gesta et Scripta. M. H. S. J.
Boehmer, Heinrich.
    Studien zur Geschichte der Gesellschaft Jesu-Loyola. Bohn am Rhein 1914.
Boissonade, P.
    Histoire de la Réunion de la Navarre à la Castille. Paris 1893.

Boletin.
   See *Academia.*
Bordenave, Nicholas de
   Histoire de Béarn et Navarre. Société de l'Histoire de France. Paris
   1893.
Bouillé, René (Marquis de).
   Histoire des Ducs de Guise. Paris 1849.
Brown, P. Hume.
   George Buchanan. Edinburgh 1890.
Calvini, Joannis. Opera omnia. Corpus Reformatorum.
Father Gonzales de Camara. Cited as Memoriale.
   Scripta I, 153. Acta P. Ignatii, cited as Confessions, Scripta I, 31.
The Cambridge Modern History, Vol. II.
   The Reformation. New York and London 1904.
Clair, Father Charles. Cited Clair Rib.
   La Vie de Saint Ignace de Loyola d'après Pierre Ribadeneira. A para-
   phrase of the second Life of Ribadaneira, with additions and appendices.
Confessions. Often called the Autobiography of Loyola.
   Dictated to Gonzales de Camara, who took notes he afterward wrote out.
   Most of it is in Spanish, in which it was all dictated but, lacking a
   Spanish amanuensis, Camara dictated the last one-seventh of it into
   Italian. Scripta I, where it is entitled Acta P. Ignatii.
Consilium Delectorum Cardinalium.
   See Mansi.
Cros, Leonardo.
   A ms. monograph containing unprinted documents on the family of
   Ignatius cited by Venturi.
Cros, Father Marie, S. J.
   Saint François de Xavier, Sa Vie et Ses Lettres. Paris 1900.
Diary—Ephemerides.
   Loyola's account of his visions. Published in part in De la Torre, Consti-
   tutions, 349-363, App. XVIII.
Dictionary of Christian Antiquities.
   Smith and Cheetham. London 1880.
Dictionary of National Biography.
   Edited by Sidney Lee.
Doddridge, P.
   The Life of Colonel James Gardiner. London 1748.
Ehses, Stephanus.
   Concilii Tridentini Actorum, etc. Pars Prima.
Epistolæ Mixtæ, M. H. S. J.
Erasmus, Desiderius.
   Opera, 1703. 10 vols. in 11.
Fouqueray, Le Père Henri, S. J.
   Histoire de la Compagnie de Jésus en France. Paris 1910.
Fabri, Beati Petri, Monumenta.
   M. H. S. J. Madrid 1914.
Fabri. Memoriale.
   Pp. 489-696. Latin, Fabri Mon.
Froude, J. A.
   Life and Letters of Erasmus. New York 1896.

Füssly, P.
Wahrhafte beschrybung der reyss und fart, so Peter F. und Heinrich Zeigler beid burger zu Zurich . . . mit einander gaan Venedig . . . gethan, etc. Züricher, Taschenbuch V (1884).

Godet, Marcel.
Le Collège de Montaigu, Revue des Etudes Rabelaisiennes, VII. 285.

Guiffrey, Georges. Cronique du Roy Francoys premier de ce nom. Paris 1860.

Hansen, Joseph.
Zauberwahn, Inquisition und Hexenprocess im Mittelalter, etc. München and Leipzig 1900.

Henao, Gabriel de.
Averiguaciones de las Antiquedades de Cantabria, etc. Salamanca 1689.

Hinschius, Paul.
System des Katholischen Kirchenrechts. Berlin 1869-1895.

Hughes, The Reverend Thomas, S. J.
The Great Educators. "Loyola and the Educational System of the Jesuits." New York, Scribner's, 1892.

James, William.
Varieties of Religious Experience. 1911.

Jortin, John.
The Life of Erasmus. London 1808.

Lainez, Father J.
Epistola de S. Ignatio. Scripta I, 98.

Lainez.
Epistolae et Acta Lainii, Vols. VIII, M. H. S. J.

Lefranc, Abel.
La Jeunesse de Calvin. Paris 1888.

Le Collège de France.

Lenient, C.
La Satire en France au XVL e Siècle. Paris 1886.

Lewis, David.
The Life of St. Teresa of Jesus, written by Herself, translated from the Spanish. London 1904.

Longridge, W. H.
The Spiritual Exercises translated from the Spanish with a commentary, etc. London 1919.

Loyola, Ignatius.
The Spiritual Exercises M. H. S. J. Mon. Ig. Series Secunda.
Epistolae et Instructiones XII volumes. Cited as Letts.
Constitutiones, De la Torre.

Luther, Martin.
Werke. Weimar 61 vols. 1906-1921.

Mansi, J. D.
Sacrorum Conciliorum nova et amplissima Collectio. Paris, 1901-24.

Mather, Increase.
Remarkable Providences. Ed. George Offor. London 1890.

Monumenta Historica Societatis Jesu. The sources of the early history of the Company, printed by its care in about seventy volumes.

Müller, Herrmann.
Les Origines de la Compagnie de Jésus. Paris 1898.

Nadal, P. Hieronymi, Epistolae. M. H. S. J.

Natal, Acta Quaedam. P. N. Ignatii A. P. Natali. Scripta I, 471. Latin.

Pastor, Ludwig von.
    Geschichte der Päpste Seit dem Ausgang des Mittelalters. Freiburg im
        Breisgau. 1913.
Paulus, N.
    Hexenwahn und Hexenprocess vornehmlich im 16 t. Jahrhundert. Frei-
        burg in Breisgau, 1910.
Polanco, J. A. de. Cited Pol.
    Vita Ignatii Loiolae. et Rerum Societatis Jesu Historia. The Life of
        Ignatius occupies the first 70 pages of the first of six volumes. M. H. S. J.
Prime, S. Irenaeus, D. D.
    Prayer and Its Answer. New York 1882.
J. Quicherat.
    Histoire de Sainte-Barbe. Paris 1860.
Ranke, Leopold von.
    Deutsche Geschichte im Zeitalter der Reformation. Sämmtlichte Werke.
        Leipzig 1894.
Raynaldus, O.
    Annales Ecclesiastici ubi desinit C. Baronius, etc. Auctore O. Raynaldo,
        etc. Lucae 1747.
Relazioni. Cited Rel. See Alberi.
Frederici Reiffenbergi e Soc. Jesu Presbyteri Historia Societatis Jesu ad
    Rhenum Inferiorem. Cologne 1564.
Reumont, Alfred von.
    Geschichte der Stadt Rom. 3 vols. Berlin 1867.
Ribadeneira, Father Peter. Cited Rib. or Ribad.
    De actis patris nostri Ignatii. Scripta, I, 337.
    Dicta et facta S. Ignatii. Scripta, I, 393.
    Vita Ignatii Loiolae. Neapoli 1572.
    All citations from this edition marked f. (folio). If marked p. (page)
        from second enlarged Life; edition Lyons, 1593. All passages cited
        p. wanting in first Life.
    Patris Petri de Ribadeneira Confessiones, Epistolae, etc. M. H. S. J.
Rocquam, Félix.
    La France et Rome pendant les Guerres de Religion. Paris 1924.
Scripta.
    Monumenta Historica Societatis Jesu.
    Monumenta Ignatiana Series quarta. I.
    Scripta de Sancto Ignatio de Loyola. Madrid 1904. Contains the pri-
        mary sources mentioned in Chapter I under I, II and III, except II E.
Sedgwick, Henry Dwight.
    Ignatius Loyola. New York. Macmillan 1923.
Stewart, Edith A.
    The Life of St. Francis Xavier. Headley Brothers, 1917.
Theresa, Saint.
    Autobiography—see Lewis.
De Thou, Jacques Auguste.
    Histoire Universelle . A La Haye 1740.
De la Torre, Joannes, S. J.
    Constitutiones Societatis Jesu Latinæ et Hispanicæ. Madrid 1892.
Tschackert, Paul.
    Peter von Ailli. Gotha, 1877.

Tyerman, L.
  The Life and Times of the Reverend John Wesley. London 1890.
Villari, Pasquale.
  Life and Times of Girolamo Savonarola. Trans. Linda Villari. New
  York 1888.
Venturi, Father Pietro Tacchi.
  Storia della Compagnia de Gesù in Italia. Vols. I and II. Roma 1910
  and 1922.
Vives, J. L. Concerning the Relief of the Poor. Trans. M. Sherwood.
Vocabolario degli Academici della Crusca. Verona 1806.
Watrigant, Henrique S. J.
  La Genèse des Exercices de St. Ignace de Loyola. Amiens 1897.
Wesley, John.
  The Journal of the Rev. John Wesley, A.M. Ed. Nehemiah Curnock.
  8 vols.
Xavier, Father Francis.
  M. H. S. J. Monumenta Xaveriana, Vols. I and II.

INDEX

INDEX